THE POEMS
OF
HENRY VAN DYKE

THE POEMS
OF
HENRY VAN DYKE

A NEW AND REVISED EDITION
WITH MANY HITHERTO UNCOLLECTED

Fredonia Books
Amsterdam, The Netherlands

The Poems of Henry van Dyke

by
Henry van Dyke

ISBN: 1-4101-0574-1

Copyright © 2004 by Fredonia Books

Reprinted from the 1921 edition

Fredonia Books
Amsterdam, The Netherlands
http://www.fredoniabooks.com

All rights reserved, including the right to reproduce this book, or portions thereof, in any form.

In order to make original editions of historical works available to scholars at an economical price, this facsimile of the original edition of 1921 is reproduced from the best available copy and has been digitally enhanced to improve legibility, but the text remains unaltered to retain historical authenticity.

𝔇𝔢𝔡𝔦𝔠𝔞𝔱𝔢𝔡 𝔦𝔫 𝔉𝔯𝔦𝔢𝔫𝔡𝔰𝔥𝔦𝔭 𝔱𝔬

KATRINA TRASK
AND
JOHN HUSTON FINLEY

CONTENTS

SONGS OUT OF DOORS
EARLY VERSES

The After-Echo	3
Dulciora	4
Three Alpine Sonnets	6
Matins	9
The Parting and the Coming Guest	10
If All the Skies	12
Wings of a Dove	13
The Fall of the Leaves	14
A Snow-Song	16
Roslin and Hawthornden	17

SONGS OUT OF DOORS
LATER POEMS

When Tulips Bloom	21
The Whip-Poor-Will	24
The Lily of Yorrow	27
The Veery	29
The Song-Sparrow	31
The Maryland Yellow-Throat	33
A November Daisy	35
The Angler's Reveille	37
The Ruby-Crowned Kinglet	41

CONTENTS

School	45
Indian Summer	46
Spring in the North	47
Spring in the South	51
A Noon Song	53
Light Between the Trees	55
The Hermit Thrush	57
Turn o' the Tide	58
Sierra Madre	59
The Grand Canyon	61
The Heavenly Hills of Holland	67
Flood-Tide of Flowers	69
God of the Open Air	71

NARRATIVE POEMS

The Toiling of Felix	81
Vera	101
Another Chance	120
A Legend of Service	125
The White Bees	129
New Year's Eve	137
The Vain King	142
The Foolish Fir-Tree	147
"Gran' Boule"	151
Heroes of the "Titanic"	157
The Standard-Bearer	158
The Proud Lady	159

CONTENTS

LABOUR AND ROMANCE

A Mile with Me	165
The Three Best Things	166
Reliance	169
Doors of Daring	170
The Child in the Garden	171
Love's Reason	172
The Echo in the Heart	173
"Undine"	174
"Rencontre"	175
Love in a Look	177
My April Lady	178
A Lover's Envy	179
Fire-Fly City	180
The Gentle Traveller	182
Nepenthe	183
Day and Night	185
Hesper	186
Arrival	187
Departure	188
The Black Birds	189
Without Disguise	192
An Hour	193
"Rappelle-Toi"	194
Love's Nearness	196
Two Songs of Heine	197

CONTENTS

Eight Echoes from the Poems of Auguste Angellier . . 198
Rappel d'Amour 209
The River of Dreams 210

HEARTH AND ALTAR

A Home Song 217
"Little Boatie" 218
A Mother's Birthday 220
Transformation 222
Rendezvous 223
Gratitude 224
Peace 225
Santa Christina 226
The Bargain 229
To the Child Jesus 230
Bitter-Sweet 231
Hymn of Joy 232
Song of a Pilgrim-Soul 234
Ode to Peace 235
Three Prayers for Sleep and Waking 239
Portrait and Reality 242
The Wind of Sorrow 243
Hide and Seek 244
Autumn in the Garden 246
The Message 248
Dulcis Memoria 249

CONTENTS

The Window	251
Christmas Tears	253
Dorothea, 1888–1912	255

EPIGRAMS, GREETINGS, AND INSCRIPTIONS

For Katrina's Sun-Dial	259
For Katrina's Window	260
For the Friends at Hurstmont	261
The Sun-Dial at Morven	263
The Sun-Dial at Wells College	263
To Mark Twain	264
Stars and the Soul	266
To Julia Marlowe	268
To Joseph Jefferson	268
The Mocking-Bird	269
The Empty Quatrain	269
Pan Learns Music	270
The Shepherd of Nymphs	270
Echoes from the Greek Anthology	271
One World	274
Joy and Duty	274
The Prison and the Angel	275
The Way	275
Love and Light	276
Facta non Verba	276
Four Things	277

CONTENTS

The Great River	277
Inscription for a Tomb in England	278
The Talisman	279
Thorn and Rose	280
"The Signs"	281

PRO PATRIA

Patria	287
America	288
The Ancestral Dwellings	289
Hudson's Last Voyage	292
Sea-Gulls of Manhattan	299
A Ballad of Claremont Hill	301
Urbs Coronata	304
Mercy for Armenia	306
Sicily, December, 1908	308
"Come Back Again, Jeanne d'Arc"	309
National Monuments	311
The Monument of Francis Makemie	312
The Statue of Sherman by St. Gaudens	313
"America for Me"	314
The Builders	316
Spirit of the Everlasting Boy	330
Texas	337
Who Follow the Flag	352

CONTENTS

Stain not the Sky 362
Peace-Hymn of the Republic 364

THE RED FLOWER AND GOLDEN STARS

The Red Flower 369
A Scrap of Paper 371
Stand Fast 372
Lights Out 374
Remarks About Kings 376
Might and Right 377
The Price of Peace 377
Storm-Music 378
The Bells of Malines 381
Jeanne d'Arc Returns 384
The Name of France 385
America's Prosperity 387
The Glory of Ships 388
Mare Liberum 391
"Liberty Enlightening the World" . . . 393
The Oxford Thrushes 395
Homeward Bound 397
The Winds of War-News 399
Righteous Wrath 400
The Peaceful Warrior 401
From Glory Unto Glory 402

xiii

CONTENTS

Britain, France, America	404
The Red Cross	405
Easter Road	406
America's Welcome Home	408
The Surrender of the German Fleet	410
Golden Stars	412
In the Blue Heaven	417
A Shrine in the Pantheon	418

IN PRAISE OF POETS

Mother Earth	421
Milton	423
Wordsworth	425
Keats	426
Shelley	427
Robert Browning	428
Tennyson	429
"In Memoriam"	430
Victor Hugo	431
Longfellow	434
Thomas Bailey Aldrich	437
Edmund Clarence Stedman	439
To James Whitcomb Riley	441
Richard Watson Gilder	442
The Valley of Vain Verses	443

CONTENTS

MUSIC

Music	447
Master of Music	464
The Pipes o' Pan	466
To a Young Girl Singing	467
The Old Flute	468
The First Bird o' Spring	470

THE HOUSE OF RIMMON

A DRAMA IN FOUR ACTS

The House of Rimmon	473
Dramatis Personæ	474

APPENDIX

CARMINA FESTIVA

The Little-Neck Clam	551
A Fairy Tale	555
The Ballad of the Solemn Ass	558
A Ballad of Santa Claus	562
Ars Agricolaris	565
Angler's Fireside Song	570
How Spring Comes to Shasta Jim	571
A Bunch of Trout-Flies	574
Index of First Lines	577

SONGS OUT OF DOORS

EARLY VERSES

THE AFTER-ECHO

How long the echoes love to play
  Around the shore of silence, as a wave
  Retreating circles down the sand!
  One after one, with sweet delay,
The mellow sounds that cliff and island gave
  Have lingered in the crescent bay,
  Until, by lightest breezes fanned,
They float far off beyond the dying day
    And leave it still as death.
      But hark,—
    Another singing breath
  Comes from the edge of dark;
    A note as clear and slow
  As falls from some enchanted bell,
  Or spirit, passing from the world below,
    That whispers back, Farewell.

    So in the heart,
When, fading slowly down the past,
  Fond memories depart,
And each that leaves it seems the last;
Long after all the rest are flown,
Returns a solitary tone,—
The after-echo of departed years,—
And touches all the soul to tears.

1871.

DULCIORA

A TEAR that trembles for a little while
Upon the trembling eyelid, till the world
Wavers within its circle like a dream,
Holds more of meaning in its narrow orb
Than all the distant landscape that it blurs.

A smile that hovers round a mouth beloved,
Like the faint pulsing of the Northern Light,
And grows in silence to an amber dawn
Born in the sweetest depths of trustful eyes,
Is dearer to the soul than sun or star.

A joy that falls into the hollow heart
From some far-lifted height of love unseen,
Unknown, makes a more perfect melody
Than hidden brooks that murmur in the dusk
Or fall athwart the cliff with wavering gleam.

Ah, not for their own sake are earth and sky
And the fair ministries of Nature dear,
But as they set themselves unto the tune
That fills our life; as light mysterious
Flows from within and glorifies the world.

DULCIORA

For so a common wayside blossom, touched
With tender thought, assumes a grace more sweet
Than crowns the royal lily of the South;
And so a well-remembered perfume seems
The breath of one who breathes in Paradise.

1872.

THREE ALPINE SONNETS

I

THE GLACIER

At dawn in silence moves the mighty stream,
  The silver-crested waves no murmur make;
  But far away the avalanches wake
The rumbling echoes, dull as in a dream;
Their momentary thunders, dying, seem
  To fall into the stillness, flake by flake,
  And leave the hollow air with naught to break
The frozen spell of solitude supreme.

At noon unnumbered rills begin to spring
  Beneath the burning sun, and all the walls
Of all the ocean-blue crevasses ring
  With liquid lyrics of their waterfalls;
As if a poet's heart had felt the glow
Of sovereign love, and song began to flow.

Zermatt, 1872.

THREE ALPINE SONNETS

II

THE SNOW-FIELD

White Death had laid his pall upon the plain,
  And crowned the mountain-peaks like monarchs dead
  The vault of heaven was glaring overhead
With pitiless light that filled my eyes with pain;
And while I vainly longed, and looked in vain
  For sign or trace of life, my spirit said,
  "Shall any living thing that dares to tread
This royal lair of Death escape again?"

But even then I saw before my feet
  A line of pointed footprints in the snow:
  Some roving chamois, but an hour ago,
Had passed this way along his journey fleet,
And left a message from a friend unknown
To cheer my pilgrim-heart, no more alone.

Zermatt, 1872.

SONGS OUT OF DOORS

III

MOVING BELLS

I love the hour that comes, with dusky hair
    And dewy feet, along the Alpine dells,
    To lead the cattle forth. A thousand bells
Go chiming after her across the fair
And flowery uplands, while the rosy flare
    Of sunset on the snowy mountain dwells,
    And valleys darken, and the drowsy spells
Of peace are woven through the purple air.

Dear is the magic of this hour: she seems
    To walk before the dark by falling rills,
And lend a sweeter song to hidden streams;
    She opens all the doors of night, and fills
With moving bells the music of my dreams,
    That wander far among the sleeping hills.

Gstaad, August, 1909.

MATINS

Flowers rejoice when night is done
Lift their heads to greet the sun;
Sweetest looks and odours raise,
In a silent hymn of praise.

So my heart would turn away
From the darkness to the day;
Lying open in God's sight
Like a flower in the light.

THE PARTING AND THE COMING GUEST

Who watched the worn-out Winter die?
  Who, peering through the window-pane
  At nightfall, under sleet and rain
Saw the old graybeard totter by?
Who listened to his parting sigh,
  The sobbing of his feeble breath,
  His whispered colloquy with Death,
  And when his all of life was done
Stood near to bid a last good-bye?
  Of all his former friends not one
Saw the forsaken Winter die.

Who welcomed in the maiden Spring?
  Who heard her footfall, swift and light
  As fairy-dancing in the night?
Who guessed what happy dawn would bring
The flutter of her bluebird's wing,
The blossom of her mayflower-face
  To brighten every shady place?
  One morning, down the village street,
"Oh, here am I," we heard her sing,—
  And none had been awake to greet
The coming of the maiden Spring.

THE PARTING AND THE COMING GUEST

But look, her violet eyes are wet
  With bright, unfallen, dewy tears;
  And in her song my fancy hears
A note of sorrow trembling yet.
Perhaps, beyond the town, she met
  Old Winter as he limped away
  To die forlorn, and let him lay
  His weary head upon her knee,
  And kissed his forehead with regret
  For one so gray and lonely,—see,
Her eyes with tender tears are wet.

And so, by night, while we were all at rest,
I think the coming sped the parting guest.
1873.

IF ALL THE SKIES

If all the skies were sunshine,
  Our faces would be fain
To feel once more upon them
  The cooling plash of rain.

If all the world were music,
  Our hearts would often long
For one sweet strain of silence
  To break the endless song.

If life were always merry,
  Our souls would seek relief,
And rest from weary laughter
  In the quiet arms of grief.

WINGS OF A DOVE

I

At sunset, when the rosy light was dying
  Far down the pathway of the west,
I saw a lonely dove in silence flying,
    To be at rest.

Pilgrim of air, I cried, could I but borrow
  Thy wandering wings, thy freedom blest,
I'd fly away from every careful sorrow,
    And find my rest.

II

But when the filmy veil of dusk was falling,
  Home flew the dove to seek his nest,
Deep in the forest where his mate was calling
    To love and rest.

Peace, heart of mine! no longer sigh to wander
  Lose not thy life in barren quest.
There are no happy islands over yonder;
    Come home and rest.
1874.

THE FALL OF THE LEAVES

I

In warlike pomp, with banners flowing,
  The regiments of autumn stood:
I saw their gold and scarlet glowing
  From every hillside, every wood.

Above the sea the clouds were keeping
  Their secret leaguer, gray and still;
They sent their misty vanguard creeping
  With muffled step from hill to hill.

All day the sullen armies drifted
  Athwart the sky with slanting rain;
At sunset for a space they lifted,
  With dusk they settled down again.

II

At dark the winds began to blow
With mutterings distant, low;
  From sea and sky they called their strength
    Till with an angry, broken roar,
    Like billows on an unseen shore,
  Their fury burst at length.

THE FALL OF THE LEAVES

I heard through the night
   The rush and the clamour;
The pulse of the fight
   Like blows of Thor's hammer;
The pattering flight
Of the leaves, and the anguished
Moan of the forest vanquished.

At daybreak came a gusty song:
"Shout! the winds are strong.
The little people of the leaves are fled.
Shout! The Autumn is dead!"

III

The storm is ended! The impartial sun
Laughs down upon the battle lost and won,
And crowns the triumph of the cloudy host
In rolling lines retreating to the coast.

But we, fond lovers of the woodland shade,
And grateful friends of every fallen leaf,
Forget the glories of the cloud-parade,
And walk the ruined woods in quiet grief.

For ever so our thoughtful hearts repeat
On fields of triumph dirges of defeat;
And still we turn on gala-days to tread
Among the rustling memories of the dead.

1874.

A SNOW-SONG

Does the snow fall at sea?
  Yes, when the north winds blow
  When the wild clouds fly low,
  Out of each gloomy wing,
  Silently glimmering,
  Over the stormy sea
    Falleth the snow.

Does the snow hide the sea?
  Nay, on the tossing plains
  Never a flake remains;
  Drift never resteth there;
  Vanishing everywhere,
  Into the hungry sea
    Falleth the snow.

What means the snow at sea?
  Whirled in the veering blast,
  Thickly the flakes drive past;
  Each like a childish ghost
  Wavers, and then is lost;
  In the forgetful sea
    Fadeth the snow.

1875.

ROSLIN AND HAWTHORNDEN

FAIR Roslin Chapel, how divine
The art that reared thy costly shrine!
Thy carven columns must have grown
By magic, like a dream in stone.

Yet not within thy storied wall
Would I in adoration fall,
So gladly as within the glen
That leads to lovely Hawthornden.

A long-drawn aisle, with roof of green
And vine-clad pillars, while between,
The Esk runs murmuring on its way,
In living music night and day.

Within the temple of this wood
The martyrs of the covenant stood,
And rolled the psalm, and poured the prayer
From Nature's solemn altar-stair.

Edinburgh, 1877.

SONGS OUT OF DOORS
LATER POEMS

WHEN TULIPS BLOOM

I

When tulips bloom in Union Square,
And timid breaths of vernal air
  Go wandering down the dusty town,
Like children lost in Vanity Fair;

When every long, unlovely row
Of westward houses stands aglow,
  And leads the eyes to sunset skies
Beyond the hills where green trees grow

Then weary seems the street parade,
And weary books, and weary trade:
  I'm only wishing to go a-fishing;
For this the month of May was made.

II

I guess the pussy-willows now
Are creeping out on every bough
  Along the brook; and robins look
For early worms behind the plough.

SONGS OUT OF DOORS

The thistle-birds have changed their dun,
For yellow coats, to match the sun;
   And in the same array of flame
The Dandelion Show's begun.

The flocks of young anemones
Are dancing round the budding trees:
   Who can help wishing to go a-fishing
In days as full of joy as these?

III

I think the meadow-lark's clear sound
Leaks upward slowly from the ground,
   While on the wing the bluebirds ring
Their wedding-bells to woods around.

The flirting chewink calls his dear
Behind the bush; and very near,
   Where water flows, where green grass grows
Song-sparrows gently sing, "Good cheer."

And, best of all, through twilight's calm
The hermit-thrush repeats his psalm.
   How much I'm wishing to go a-fishing
In days so sweet with music's balm!

WHEN TULIPS BLOOM

IV

'Tis not a proud desire of mine;
I ask for nothing superfine;
　No heavy weight, no salmon great,
To break the record, or my line.

Only an idle little stream,
Whose amber waters softly gleam,
　Where I may wade through woodland shade
And cast the fly, and loaf, and dream:

Only a trout or two, to dart
From foaming pools, and try my art:
　'Tis all I'm wishing—old-fashioned fishing,
And just a day on Nature's heart.

1894.

THE WHIP-POOR-WILL

Do you remember, father,—
  It seems so long ago,—
The day we fished together
  Along the Pocono?
At dusk I waited for you,
  Beside the lumber-mill,
And there I heard a hidden bird
  That chanted, "whip-poor-will,"
  "*Whippoorwill! whippoorwill!*"
  Sad and shrill,—"*whippoorwill!*"

The place was all deserted;
  The mill-wheel hung at rest;
The lonely star of evening
  Was throbbing in the west;
The veil of night was falling;
  The winds were folded still;
And everywhere the trembling air
  Re-echoed "whip-poor-will!"
  "*Whippoorwill! whippoorwill!*"
  Sad and shrill,—"*whippoorwill!*"

You seemed so long in coming,
  I felt so much alone;
The wide, dark world was round me
  And life was all unknown;

THE WHIP-POOR-WILL

The hand of sorrow touched me,
  And made my senses thrill
With all the pain that haunts the strain
  Of mournful whip-poor-will.
    "Whippoorwill! whippoorwill!"
    Sad and shrill,—*"whippoorwill!"*

What knew I then of trouble?
  An idle little lad,
I had not learned the lessons
  That make men wise and sad.
I dreamed of grief and parting,
  And something seemed to fill
My heart with tears, while in my ears
  Resounded "whip-poor-will."
    "Whippoorwill! whippoorwill!"
    Sad and shrill,—*"whippoorwill!"*

'Twas but a cloud of sadness,
  That lightly passed away;
But I have learned the meaning
  Of sorrow, since that day.
For nevermore at twilight,
  Beside the silent mill,
I'll wait for you, in the falling dew,
  And hear the whip-poor-will.
    "Whippoorwill! whippoorwill!"
    Sad and shrill,—*"whippoorwill!"*

SONGS OUT OF DOORS

But if you still remember
   In that fair land of light,
The pains and fears that touch us
   Along this edge of night,
I think all earthly grieving,
   And all our mortal ill,
To you must seem like a sad boy's dream.
   Who hears the whip-poor-will.
   "Whippoorwill! whippoorwill!"
   A passing thrill,—*"whippoorwill!"*
1894.

THE LILY OF YORROW

Deep in the heart of the forest the lily of Yorrow is growing;
Blue is its cup as the sky, and with mystical odour o'erflowing;
Faintly it falls through the shadowy glades when the south wind is blowing.

Sweet are the primroses pale and the violets after a shower;
Sweet are the borders of pinks and the blossoming grapes on the bower;
Sweeter by far is the breath of that far-away woodland flower.

Searching and strange in its sweetness, it steals like a perfume enchanted
Under the arch of the forest, and all who perceive it are haunted,
Seeking and seeking for ever, till sight of the lily is granted.

Who can describe how it grows, with its chalice of lazuli leaning
Over a crystalline spring, where the ferns and the mosses are greening?
Who can imagine its beauty, or utter the depth of its meaning?

SONGS OUT OF DOORS

Calm of the journeying stars, and repose of the mountains olden,
Joy of the swift-running rivers, and glory of sunsets golden,
Secrets that cannot be told in the heart of the flower are holden.

Surely to see it is peace and the crown of a life-long endeavour;
Surely to pluck it is gladness,—but they who have found it can never
Tell of the gladness and peace: they are hid from our vision for ever.

'Twas but a moment ago that a comrade was walking near me:
Turning aside from the pathway he murmured a greeting to cheer me,—
Then he was lost in the shade, and I called but he did not hear me.

Why should I dream he is dead, and bewail him with passionate sorrow?
Surely I know there is gladness in finding the lily of Yorrow:
He has discovered it first, and perhaps I shall find it to-morrow.

1894.

THE VEERY

The moonbeams over Arno's vale in silver flood were
    pouring,
When first I heard the nightingale a long-lost love de-
    ploring.
So passionate, so full of pain, it sounded strange and
    eerie;
I longed to hear a simpler strain,—the wood-notes of
    the veery.

The laverock sings a bonny lay above the Scottish
    heather;
It sprinkles down from far away like light and love
    together;
He drops the golden notes to greet his brooding mate,
    his dearie;
I only know one song more sweet,—the vespers of the
    veery.

In English gardens, green and bright and full of fruity
    treasure,
I heard the blackbird with delight repeat his merry
    measure:
The ballad was a pleasant one, the tune was loud and
    cheery,
And yet, with every setting sun, I listened for the veery.

SONGS OUT OF DOORS

But far away, and far away, the tawny thrush is singing;
New England woods, at close of day, with that clear
    chant are ringing:
And when my light of life is low, and heart and flesh
    are weary,
I fain would hear, before I go, the wood-notes of the
    veery.

1895.

THE SONG-SPARROW

THERE is a bird I know so well,
  It seems as if he must have sung
  Beside my crib when I was young;
Before I knew the way to spell
  The name of even the smallest bird,
  His gentle-joyful song I heard.
Now see if you can tell, my dear,
What bird it is that, every year,
Sings "*Sweet—sweet—sweet—very merry cheer*."

He comes in March, when winds are strong
  And snow returns to hide the earth;
  But still he warms his heart with mirth,
And waits for May. He lingers long
  While flowers fade; and every day
  Repeats his small, contented lay;
As if to say, we need not fear
The season's change, if love is here
With "*Sweet—sweet—sweet—very merry cheer*."

He does not wear a Joseph's-coat
  Of many colours, smart and gay;
  His suit is Quaker brown and gray,
With darker patches at his throat.
  And yet of all the well-dressed throng

SONGS OUT OF DOORS

Not one can sing so brave a song.
It makes the pride of looks appear
A vain and foolish thing, to hear
His "*Sweet—sweet—sweet—very merry cheer.*"

A lofty place he does not love,
  But sits by choice, and well at ease,
  In hedges, and in little trees
That stretch their slender arms above
  The meadow-brook; and there he sings
  Till all the field with pleasure rings;
And so he tells in every ear,
That lowly homes to heaven are near
In "*Sweet—sweet—sweet—very merry cheer.*"

I like the tune, I like the words;
  They seem so true, so free from art,
  So friendly, and so full of heart,
That if but one of all the birds
  Could be my comrade everywhere,
  My little brother of the air,
I'd choose the song-sparrow, my dear,
Because he'd bless me, every year,
With "*Sweet—sweet—sweet—very merry cheer.*"

1895.

THE MARYLAND YELLOW-THROAT

When May bedecks the naked trees
With tassels and embroideries,
And many blue-eyed violets beam
Along the edges of the stream,
I hear a voice that seems to say,
Now near at hand, now far away,
  "*Witchery—witchery—witchery.*"

An incantation so serene,
So innocent, befits the scene:
There's magic in that small bird's note—
See, there he flits—the Yellow-throat;
A living sunbeam, tipped with wings,
A spark of light that shines and sings
  "*Witchery—witchery—witchery.*"

You prophet with a pleasant name,
If out of Mary-land you came,
You know the way that thither goes
Where Mary's lovely garden grows:
Fly swiftly back to her, I pray,
And try to call her down this way,
  "*Witchery—witchery—witchery!*"

SONGS OUT OF DOORS

Tell her to leave her cockle-shells,
And all her little silver bells
That blossom into melody,
And all her maids less fair than she.
She does not need these pretty things,
For everywhere she comes, she brings
 "Witchery—witchery—witchery!"

The woods are greening overhead,
And flowers adorn each mossy bed;
The waters babble as they run—
One thing is lacking, only one:
If Mary were but here to-day,
I would believe your charming lay,
 "Witchery—witchery—witchery!"

Along the shady road I look—
Who's coming now across the brook?
A woodland maid, all robed in white—
The leaves dance round her with delight
The stream laughs out beneath her feet-
Sing, merry bird, the charm's complete,
 "Witchery—witchery—witchery!"

1895.

A NOVEMBER DAISY

AFTERTHOUGHT of summer's bloom!
Late arrival at the feast,
Coming when the songs have ceased
And the merry guests departed,
Leaving but an empty room,
Silence, solitude, and gloom,—
Are you lonely, heavy-hearted;
You, the last of all your kind,
Nodding in the autumn wind;
Now that all your friends are flown,
Blooming late and all alone?

Nay, I wrong you, little flower,
Reading mournful mood of mine
In your looks, that give no sign
Of a spirit dark and cheerless!
You possess the heavenly power
That rejoices in the hour.
Glad, contented, free, and fearless,
Lift a sunny face to heaven
When a sunny day is given!
Make a summer of your own,
Blooming late and all alone!

SONGS OUT OF DOORS

Once the daisies gold and white
Sea-like through the meadow rolled:
Once my heart could hardly hold
All its pleasures. I remember,
In the flood of youth's delight
Separate joys were lost to sight.
That was summer! Now November
Sets the perfect flower apart;
Gives each blossom of the heart
Meaning, beauty, grace unknown,—
Blooming late and all alone.

November, 1899.

THE ANGLER'S REVEILLE

WHAT time the rose of dawn is laid across the lips of night,
And all the little watchman-stars have fallen asleep in light,
'Tis then a merry wind awakes, and runs from tree to tree,
And borrows words from all the birds to sound the reveille.

> This is the carol the Robin throws
>   Over the edge of the valley;
> Listen how boldly it flows,
>   Sally on sally:
> > *Tirra-lirra,*
> > *Early morn,*
> > *New born!*
> > *Day is near,*
> > *Clear, clear.*
> > *Down the river*
> > *All a-quiver,*
> > *Fish are breaking;*
> > *Time for waking,*
> > *Tup, tup, tup!*
> > *Do you hear?*
> > *All clear—*
> > *Wake up!*

37

SONGS OUT OF DOORS

The phantom flood of dreams has ebbed and vanished
  with the dark,
And like a dove the heart forsakes the prison of the ark;
Now forth she fares thro' friendly woods and diamond-
  fields of dew,
While every voice cries out "Rejoice!" as if the world
  were new.

    This is the ballad the Bluebird sings,
      Unto his mate replying,
    Shaking the tune from his wings
      While he is flying:
        Surely, surely, surely,
          Life is dear
          Even here.
          Blue above,
          You to love,
        Purely, purely, purely.

There's wild azalea on the hill, and iris down the dell,
And just one spray of lilac still abloom beside the well;
The columbine adorns the rocks, the laurel buds grow
  pink,
Along the stream white arums gleam, and violets bend
  to drink.

    This is the song of the Yellow-throat,
      Fluttering gaily beside you;

THE ANGLER'S REVEILLE

Hear how each voluble note
  Offers to guide you:
    Which way, sir?
    I say, sir,
    Let me teach you,
    I beseech you!
    Are you wishing
    Jolly fishing?
    This way, sir!
    I'll teach you.

Then come, my friend, forget your foes and leave your fears behind,
And wander forth to try your luck, with cheerful, quiet mind;
For be your fortune great or small, you take what God will give,
And all the day your heart will say, "'Tis luck enough to live."

  This is the song the Brown Thrush flings
    Out of his thicket of roses;
  Hark how it bubbles and rings,
    Mark how it closes:
      Luck, luck,
      What luck?
      Good enough for me,
      I'm alive, you see!

SONGS OUT OF DOORS

Sun shining,
No repining;
Never borrow
Idle sorrow;
Drop it!
Cover it up!
Hold your cup!
Joy will fill it,
Don't spill it,
Steady, be ready,
Good luck!

1899.

THE RUBY-CROWNED KINGLET

I

WHERE's your kingdom, little king?
  Where the land you call your own,
  Where your palace and your throne?
Fluttering lightly on the wing
  Through the blossom-world of May,
  Whither lies your royal way,
        Little king?

Far to northward lies a land
Where the trees together stand
Closely as the blades of wheat
When the summer is complete.
Rolling like an ocean wide
Over vale and mountainside,
Balsam, hemlock, spruce and pine,—
All those mighty trees are mine.
There's a river flowing free,—
All its waves belong to me.
There's a lake so clear and bright
Stars shine out of it all night;
Rowan-berries round it spread
Like a belt of coral red.
Never royal garden planned
Fair as my Canadian land!

SONGS OUT OF DOORS

There I build my summer nest,
There I reign and there I rest,
While from dawn to dark I sing,
Happy kingdom! Lucky king!

II

Back again, my little king!
  Is your happy kingdom lost
    To the rebel knave, Jack Frost?
Have you felt the snow-flakes sting?
  Houseless, homeless in October,
    Whither now? Your plight is sober
      Exiled king!

Far to southward lie the regions
Where my loyal flower-legions
Hold possession of the year,
Filling every month with cheer.
Christmas wakes the winter rose;
New Year daffodils unclose;
Yellow jasmine through the wood
Flows in February flood,
Dropping from the tallest trees
Golden streams that never freeze.
Thither now I take my flight
Down the pathway of the night,
Till I see the southern moon

THE RUBY-CROWNED KINGLET

*Glisten on the broad lagoon,
Where the cypress' dusky green,
And the dark magnolia's sheen,
Weave a shelter round my home.
There the snow-storms never come;
There the bannered mosses gray
Like a curtain gently sway,
Hanging low on every side
Round the covert where I bide,
Till the March azalea glows,
Royal red and heavenly rose,
Through the Carolina glade
Where my winter home is made.
There I hold my southern court,
Full of merriment and sport:
There I take my ease and sing,
Happy kingdom! Lucky king!*

III

Little boaster, vagrant king,
  Neither north nor south is yours,
  You've no kingdom that endures!
Wandering every fall and spring,
With your ruby crown so slender,
Are you only a Pretender,
          Landless king?

SONGS OUT OF DOORS

Never king by right divine
Ruled a richer realm than mine!
What are lands and golden crowns,
Armies, fortresses and towns,
Jewels, sceptres, robes and rings,—
What are these to song and wings?
Everywhere that I can fly,
There I own the earth and sky;
Everywhere that I can sing.
There I'm happy as a king.

1900.

SCHOOL

I PUT my heart to school
In the world where men grow wise:
"Go out," I said, "and learn the rule;
"Come back when you win a prize."

My heart came back again:
"Now where is the prize?" I cried.—
"The rule was false, and the prize was pain
"And the teacher's name was Pride."

I put my heart to school
In the woods where veeries sing
And brooks run clear and cool,
In the fields where wild flowers spring.

"And why do you stay so long
"My heart, and where do you roam?"
The answer came with a laugh and a song,-
"I find this school is home."

April, 1901.

INDIAN SUMMER

A SILKEN curtain veils the skies,
And half conceals from pensive eyes
  The bronzing tokens of the fall;
A calmness broods upon the hills,
And summer's parting dream distils
  A charm of silence over all.

The stacks of corn, in brown array,
Stand waiting through the tranquil day,
  Like tattered wigwams on the plain;
The tribes that find a shelter there
Are phantom peoples, forms of air,
  And ghosts of vanished joy and pain.

At evening when the crimson crest
Of sunset passes down the West,
  I hear the whispering host returning;
On far-off fields, by elm and oak,
I see the lights, I smell the smoke,—
  The Camp-fires of the Past are burning.

Tertius and Henry van Dyke
November, 1903.

SPRING IN THE NORTH

I

Ah, who will tell me, in these leaden days,
Why the sweet Spring delays,
And where she hides,—the dear desire
  Of every heart that longs
For bloom, and fragrance, and the ruby fire
Of maple-buds along the misty hills,
And that immortal call which fills
  The waiting wood with songs?
The snow-drops came so long ago,
  It seemed that Spring was near!
  But then returned the snow
With biting winds, and earth grew sere,
  And sullen clouds drooped low
To veil the sadness of a hope deferred:
Then rain, rain, rain, incessant rain
  Beat on the window-pane,
Through which I watched the solitary bird
That braved the tempest, buffeted and tossed
With rumpled feathers down the wind again.
  Oh, were the seeds all lost
When winter laid the wild flowers in their tomb?
  I searched the woods in vain
For blue hepaticas, and trilliums white,
And trailing arbutus, the Spring's delight,

SONGS OUT OF DOORS

Starring the withered leaves with rosy bloom.
  But every night the frost
To all my longing spoke a silent nay,
And told me Spring was far away.
Even the robins were too cold to sing,
Except a broken and discouraged note,—
Only the tuneful sparrow, on whose throat
Music has put her triple finger-print,
Lifted his head and sang my heart a hint,—
"Wait, wait, wait! oh, wait a while for Spring!

II

But now, Carina, what divine amends
For all delay! What sweetness treasured up,
  What wine of joy that blends
A hundred flavours in a single cup,
Is poured into this perfect day!
For look, sweet heart, here are the early flowers
  That lingered on their way,
Thronging in haste to kiss the feet of May,
Entangled with the bloom of later hours,—
Anemones and cinque-foils, violets blue
And white, and iris richly gleaming through
The grasses of the meadow, and a blaze
Of butter-cups and daisies in the field,
  Filling the air with praise,
As if a chime of golden bells had pealed!

SPRING IN THE NORTH

The frozen songs within the breast
Of silent birds that hid in leafless woods,
  Melt into rippling floods
  Of gladness unrepressed.
Now oriole and bluebird, thrush and lark,
Warbler and wren and vireo,
Mingle their melody; the living spark
Of Love has touched the fuel of desire,
And every heart leaps up in singing fire.
  It seems as if the land
Were breathing deep beneath the sun's caress,
  Trembling with tenderness,
  While all the woods expand,
In shimmering clouds of rose and gold and green
To veil a joy too sacred to be seen.

III

Come, put your hand in mine,
True love, long sought and found at last,
And lead me deep into the Spring divine
  That makes amends for all the wintry past.
For all the flowers and songs I feared to miss
    Arrive with you;
And in the lingering pressure of your kiss
    My dreams come true;
And in the promise of your generous eyes
    I read the mystic sign

SONGS OUT OF DOORS

Of joy more perfect made
Because so long delayed,
And bliss enhanced by rapture of surprise.
Ah, think not early love alone is strong;
He loveth best whose heart has learned to wait
Dear messenger of Spring that tarried long,
You're doubly dear because you come so late.

SPRING IN THE SOUTH

Now in the oak the sap of life is welling,
  Tho' to the bough the rusty leafage clings;
Now on the elm the misty buds are swelling;
  Every little pine-wood grows alive with wings;
Blue-jays are fluttering, yodeling and crying,
  Meadow-larks sailing low above the faded grass,
Red-birds whistling clear, silent robins flying,—
  Who has waked the birds up? What has come to pass?

Last year's cotton-plants, desolately bowing,
  Tremble in the March-wind, ragged and forlorn;
Red are the hillsides of the early ploughing,
  Gray are the lowlands, waiting for the corn.
Earth seems asleep, but she is only feigning;
  Deep in her bosom thrills a sweet unrest;
Look where the jasmine lavishly is raining
  Jove's golden shower into Danäe's breast!

Now on the plum-tree a snowy bloom is sifted,
  Now on the peach-tree, the glory of the rose,
Far o'er the hills a tender haze is drifted,
  Full to the brim the yellow river flows.
Dark cypress boughs with vivid jewels glisten,
  Greener than emeralds shining in the sun.
Whence comes the magic? Listen, sweetheart, listen!
  The mocking-bird is singing: Spring is begun.

SONGS OUT OF DOORS

Hark, in his song no tremor of misgiving!
    All of his heart he pours into his lay,—
"Love, love, love, and pure delight of living:
    Winter is forgotten: here's a happy day!"
Fair in your face I read the flowery presage,
    Snowy on your brow and rosy on your mouth
Sweet in your voice I hear the season's message,
    Love, love, love, and Spring in the South!

1904.

A NOON SONG

There are songs for the morning and songs for the night,
   For sunrise and sunset, the stars and the moon;
But who will give praise to the fulness of light,
   And sing us a song of the glory of noon?
      Oh, the high noon, the clear noon,
         The noon with golden crest;
         When the blue sky burns, and the great sun turns
         With his face to the way of the west!

How swiftly he rose in the dawn of his strength!
   How slowly he crept as the morning wore by!
Ah, steep was the climbing that led him at length
   To the height of his throne in the wide summer sky.
      Oh, the long toil, the slow toil,
         The toil that may not rest,
         Till the sun looks down from his journey's crown,
         To the wonderful way of the west!

Then a quietness falls over meadow and hill,
   The wings of the wind in the forest are furled,
The river runs softly, the birds are all still,
   The workers are resting all over the world.
      Oh, the good hour, the kind hour,
         The hour that calms the breast!
         Little inn half-way on the road of the day,
         Where it follows the turn to the west!

SONGS OUT OF DOORS

There's a plentiful feast in the maple-tree shade,
  The lilt of a song to an old-fashioned tune,
The talk of a friend, or the kiss of a maid,
  To sweeten the cup that we drink to the noon.
    Oh, the deep noon, the full noon,
      Of all the day the best!
    When the blue sky burns, and the great sun turns
      To his home by the way of the west!

1906.

LIGHT BETWEEN THE TREES

Long, long, long the trail
  Through the brooding forest-gloom,
Down the shadowy, lonely vale
  Into silence, like a room
    Where the light of life has fled,
  And the jealous curtains close
  Round the passionless repose
    Of the silent dead.

Plod, plod, plod away,
  Step by step in mouldering moss;
Thick branches bar the day
  Over languid streams that cross
    Softly, slowly, with a sound
  Like a smothered weeping,
  In their aimless creeping
    Through enchanted ground.

"Yield, yield, yield thy quest,"
  Whispers through the woodland deep
"Come to me and be at rest;
  I am slumber, I am sleep."
    Then the weary feet would fail,
  But the never-daunted will
  Urges "Forward, forward still!
    Press along the trail!"

SONGS OUT OF DOORS

Breast, breast, breast the slope
  See, the path is growing steep.
Hark! a little song of hope
  Where the stream begins to leap.
    Though the forest, far and wide,
Still shuts out the bending blue,
We shall finally win through,
  Cross the long divide.

On, on, on we tramp!
  Will the journey never end?
Over yonder lies the camp;
  Welcome waits us there, my friend
    Can we reach it ere the night?
Upward, upward, never fear!
Look, the summit must be near;
  See the line of light!

Red, red, red the shine
  Of the splendour in the west,
Glowing through the ranks of pine,
  Clear along the mountain-crest!
    Long, long, long the trail
Out of sorrow's lonely vale;
  But at last the traveller sees
  Light between the trees!

March, 1904.

THE HERMIT THRUSH

O WONDERFUL! How liquid clear
The molten gold of that ethereal tone,
Floating and falling through the wood alone,
A hermit-hymn poured out for God to hear!

O holy, holy, holy! Hyaline,
Long light, low light, glory of eventide!
Love far away, far up,—up,—love divine!
Little love, too, for ever, ever near,
Warm love, earth love, tender love of mine,
In the leafy dark where you hide,
You are mine,—mine,—mine!

Ah, my belovèd, do you feel with me
The hidden virtue of that melody,
The rapture and the purity of love,
The heavenly joy that can not find the word?
Then, while we wait again to hear the bird,
Come very near to me, and do not move,—
Now, hermit of the woodland, fill anew
The cool, green cup of air with harmony,
And we will drink the wine of love with you.

May, 1908.

TURN O' THE TIDE

The tide flows in to the harbour,—
 The bold tide, the gold tide, the flood o' the sunlit sea,—
And the little ships riding at anchor,
 Are swinging and slanting their prows to the ocean, panting
  To lift their wings to the wide wild air,
  And venture a voyage they know not where,—
 To fly away and be free!

The tide runs out of the harbour,—
 The low tide, the slow tide, the ebb o' the moonlit bay,—
And the little ships rocking at anchor,
 Are rounding and turning their bows to the landward, yearning
  To breathe the breath of the sun-warmed strand,
  To rest in the lee of the high hill land,—
 To hold their haven and stay!

My heart goes round with the vessels,—
 My wild heart, my child heart, in love with the sea and the land,—
And the turn o' the tide passes through it,
 In rising and falling with mystical currents, calling
  At morn, to range where the far waves foam,
  At night, to a harbour in love's true home,
 With the hearts that understand!

Seal Harbour, August 12, 1911.

SIERRA MADRE

O MOTHER mountains! billowing far to the snow-lands,
  Robed in aërial amethyst, silver, and blue,
Why do ye look so proudly down on the lowlands?
  What have their groves and gardens to do with you?

Theirs is the languorous charm of the orange and myrtle,
  Theirs are the fruitage and fragrance of Eden of old,—
Broad-boughed oaks in the meadows fair and fertile,
  Dark-leaved orchards gleaming with globes of gold.

You, in your solitude standing, lofty and lonely,
  Bear neither garden nor grove on your barren breasts;
Rough is the rock-loving growth of your canyons, and only
  Storm-battered pines and fir-trees cling to your crests.

Why are ye throned so high, and arrayed in splendour
  Richer than all the fields at your feet can claim?
What is your right, ye rugged peaks, to the tender
  Queenly promise and pride of the mother-name?

Answered the mountains, dim in the distance dreaming:
  "Ours are the forests that treasure the riches of rain;
Ours are the secret springs and the rivulets gleaming
  Silverly down through the manifold bloom of the plain.

SONGS OUT OF DOORS

"Vain were the toiling of men in the dust of the dry
    land,
  Vain were the ploughing and planting in waterless fields,
Save for the life-giving currents we send from the sky-
    land,
  Save for the fruit our embrace with the storm-cloud
    yields."

O mother mountains, Madre Sierra, I love you!
  Rightly you reign o'er the vale that your bounty
    fills,—
Kissed by the sun, or with big, bright stars above you,—
  I murmur your name and lift up mine eyes to the hills.

Pasadena, March, 1913.

THE GRAND CANYON

DAYBREAK

WHAT makes the lingering Night so cling to thee?
Thou vast, profound, primeval hiding-place
Of ancient secrets,—gray and ghostly gulf
Cleft in the green of this high forest land,
And crowded in the dark with giant forms!
Art thou a grave, a prison, or a shrine?

A stillness deeper than the dearth of sound
Broods over thee: a living silence breathes
Perpetual incense from thy dim abyss.
The morning-stars that sang above the bower
Of Eden, passing over thee, are dumb
With trembling bright amazement; and the Dawn
Steals through the glimmering pines with naked feet
Her hand upon her lips, to look on thee!
She peers into thy depths with silent prayer
For light, more light, to part thy purple veil.
O Earth, swift-rolling Earth, reveal, reveal,—
Turn to the East, and show upon thy breast
The mightiest marvel in the realm of Time!

SONGS OUT OF DOORS

'Tis done,—the morning miracle of light,—
The resurrection of the world of hues
That die with dark, and daily rise again
With every rising of the splendid Sun!

Be still, my heart! Now Nature holds her breath
To see the solar flood of radiance leap
Across the chasm, and crown the western rim
Of alabaster with a far-away
Rampart of pearl, and flowing down by walls
Of changeful opal, deepen into gold
Of topaz, rosy gold of tourmaline,
Crimson of garnet, green and gray of jade,
Purple of amethyst, and ruby red,
Beryl, and sard, and royal porphyry;
Until the cataract of colour breaks
Upon the blackness of the granite floor.

How far below! And all between is cleft
And carved into a hundred curving miles
Of unimagined architecture! Tombs,
Temples, and colonnades are neighboured there
By fortresses that Titans might defend,
And amphitheatres where Gods might strive.
Cathedrals, buttressed with unnumbered tiers
Of ruddy rock, lift to the sapphire sky
A single spire of marble pure as snow;
And huge aërial palaces arise

THE GRAND CANYON

Like mountains built of unconsuming flame.
Along the weathered walls, or standing deep
In riven valleys where no foot may tread,
Are lonely pillars, and tall monuments
Of perished æons and forgotten things.
My sight is baffled by the wide array
Of countless forms: my vision reels and swims
Above them, like a bird in whirling winds.
Yet no confusion fills the awful chasm;
But spacious order and a sense of peace
Brood over all. For every shape that looms
Majestic in the throng, is set apart
From all the others by its far-flung shade,
Blue, blue, as if a mountain-lake were there.

How still it is! Dear God, I hardly dare
To breathe, for fear the fathomless abyss
Will draw me down into eternal sleep.

What force has formed this masterpiece of awe?
What hands have wrought these wonders in the waste?
O river, gleaming in the narrow rift
Of gloom that cleaves the valley's nether deep,—
Fierce Colorado, prisoned by thy toil,
And blindly toiling still to reach the sea,—
Thy waters, gathered from the snows and springs
Amid the Utah hills, have carved this road
Of glory to the Californian Gulf.

SONGS OUT OF DOORS

But now, O sunken stream, thy splendour lost,
'Twixt iron walls thou rollest turbid waves,
Too far away to make their fury heard!

At sight of thee, thou sullen labouring slave
Of gravitation,—yellow torrent poured
From distant mountains by no will of thine,
Through thrice a hundred centuries of slow
Fallings and liftings of the crust of Earth, —
At sight of thee my spirit sinks and fails.
Art thou alone the Maker? Is the blind
Unconscious power that drew thee dumbly down
To cut this gash across the layered globe,
The sole creative cause of all I see?
Are force and matter all? The rest a dream?

Then is thy gorge a canyon of despair,
A prison for the soul of man, a grave
Of all his dearest daring hopes! The world
Wherein we live and move is meaningless,
No spirit here to answer to our own!
The stars without a guide: The chance-born Earth
Adrift in space, no Captain on the ship:
Nothing in all the universe to prove
Eternal wisdom and eternal love!
And man, the latest accident of Time,—
Who thinks he loves, and longs to understand,
Who vainly suffers, and in vain is brave,

THE GRAND CANYON

Who dupes his heart with immortality,—
Man is a living lie,—a bitter jest
Upon himself,—a conscious grain of sand
Lost in a desert of unconsciousness,
Thirsting for God and mocked by his own thirst.

Spirit of Beauty, mother of delight,
Thou fairest offspring of Omnipotence
Inhabiting this lofty lone abode,
Speak to my heart again and set me free
From all these doubts that darken earth and heaven
Who sent thee forth into the wilderness
To bless and comfort all who see thy face?
Who clad thee in this more than royal robe
Of rainbows? Who designed these jewelled thrones
For thee, and wrought these glittering palaces?
Who gave thee power upon the soul of man
To lift him up through wonder into joy?
God! let the radiant cliffs bear witness, God!
Let all the shining pillars signal, God!
He only, on the mystic loom of light,
Hath woven webs of loveliness to clothe
His most majestic works: and He alone
Hath delicately wrought the cactus-flower
To star the desert floor with rosy bloom.

SONGS OUT OF DOORS

O Beauty, handiwork of the Most High,
Where'er thou art He tells his Love to man,
And lo, the day breaks, and the shadows flee!

Now, far beyond all language and all art
In thy wild splendour, Canyon marvellous,
The secret of thy stillness lies unveiled
In wordless worship! This is holy ground;
Thou art no grave, no prison, but a shrine.
Garden of Temples filled with Silent Praise,
If God were blind thy Beauty could not be!

February 24–26, 1913.

THE HEAVENLY HILLS OF HOLLAND

The heavenly hills of Holland,—
  How wondrously they rise
Above the smooth green pastures
  Into the azure skies!
With blue and purple hollows,
  With peaks of dazzling snow,
Along the far horizon
  The clouds are marching slow.

No mortal foot has trodden
  The summits of that range,
Nor walked those mystic valleys
  Whose colours ever change;
Yet we possess their beauty,
  And visit them in dreams,
While ruddy gold of sunset
  From cliff and canyon gleams.

In days of cloudless weather
  They melt into the light;
When fog and mist surround us
  They're hidden from our sight;
But when returns a season
  Clear shining after rain,
While the northwest wind is blowing,
  We see the hills again.

SONGS OUT OF DOORS

The old Dutch painters loved them
    Their pictures show them fair,—
Old Hobbema and Ruysdael,
    Van Goyen and Vermeer.
Above the level landscape,
    Rich polders, long-armed mills,
Canals and ancient cities,—
    Float Holland's heavenly hills.

The Hague, November, 1916.

FLOOD-TIDE OF FLOWERS
IN HOLLAND

The laggard winter ebbed so slow
With freezing rain and melting snow,
It seemed as if the earth would stay
Forever where the tide was low,
In sodden green and watery gray.

But now from depths beyond our sight,
The tide is turning in the night,
And floods of colour long concealed
Come silent rising toward the light,
Through garden bare and empty field.

And first, along the sheltered nooks,
The crocus runs in little brooks
Of joyance, till by light made bold
They show the gladness of their looks
In shining pools of white and gold.

The tiny scilla, sapphire blue,
Is gently seeping in, to strew
The earth with heaven; and sudden rills
Of sunlit yellow, sweeping through,
Spread into lakes of daffodils.

SONGS OUT OF DOORS

The hyacinths, with fragrant heads,
Have overflowed their sandy beds,
And fill the earth with faint perfume,
The breath that Spring around her sheds
And now the tulips break in bloom!

A sea, a rainbow-tinted sea,
A splendour and a mystery,
Floods o'er the fields of faded gray:
The roads are full of folks in glee,
For lo,—to-day is Easter Day!

April, 1916.

ODE
GOD OF THE OPEN AIR

I

Thou who hast made thy dwelling fair
  With flowers below, above with starry lights
And set thine altars everywhere,—
    On mountain heights,
In woodlands dim with many a dream,
    In valleys bright with springs,
And on the curving capes of every stream:
Thou who hast taken to thyself the wings
    Of morning, to abide
Upon the secret places of the sea,
  And on far islands, where the tide
Visits the beauty of untrodden shores,
Waiting for worshippers to come to thee
    In thy great out-of-doors!
To thee I turn, to thee I make my prayer,
    God of the open air.

II

Seeking for thee, the heart of man
    Lonely and longing ran,
In that first, solitary hour,
    When the mysterious power

SONGS OUT OF DOORS

To know and love the wonder of the morn
Was breathed within him, and his soul was born;
    And thou didst meet thy child,
    Not in some hidden shrine,
But in the freedom of the garden wild,
    And take his hand in thine,—
There all day long in Paradise he walked,
And in the cool of evening with thee talked.

III

Lost, long ago, that garden bright and pure,
Lost, that calm day too perfect to endure,
And lost the child-like love that worshipped and was
    sure!
For men have dulled their eyes with sin,
And dimmed the light of heaven with doubt,
And built their temple walls to shut thee in,
And framed their iron creeds to shut thee out.
    But not for thee the closing of the door,
        O Spirit unconfined!
        Thy ways are free
        As is the wandering wind,
And thou hast wooed thy children, to restore
        Their fellowship with thee,
In peace of soul and simpleness of mind.

GOD OF THE OPEN AIR

IV

Joyful the heart that, when the flood rolled by,
Leaped up to see the rainbow in the sky;
And glad the pilgrim, in the lonely night,
For whom the hills of Haran, tier on tier,
Built up a secret stairway to the height
Where stars like angel eyes were shining clear.
From mountain-peaks, in many a land and age,
   Disciples of the Persian seer
Have hailed the rising sun and worshipped thee;
And wayworn followers of the Indian sage
Have found the peace of God beneath a spreading tree

V

But One, but One,—ah, Son most dear,
And perfect image of the Love Unseen,—
   Walked every day in pastures green,
And all his life the quiet waters by,
Reading their beauty with a tranquil eye.
To him the desert was a place prepared
     For weary hearts to rest;
   The hillside was a temple blest;
   The grassy vale a banquet-room
Where he could feed and comfort many a guest.
    With him the lily shared
The vital joy that breathes itself in bloom;

SONGS OUT OF DOORS

And every bird that sang beside the nest
Told of the love that broods o'er every living thing.
  He watched the shepherd bring
His flock at sundown to the welcome fold,
  The fisherman at daybreak fling
His net across the waters gray and cold,
And all day long the patient reaper swing
His curving sickle through the harvest-gold.
So through the world the foot-path way he trod,
Breathing the air of heaven in every breath;
And in the evening sacrifice of death
Beneath the open sky he gave his soul to God.
Him will I trust, and for my Master take;
Him will I follow; and for his dear sake,
    God of the open air,
   To thee I make my prayer.

VI

From the prison of anxious thought that greed has builded,
From the fetters that envy has wrought and pride has gilded,
From the noise of the crowded ways and the fierce confusion,
From the folly that wastes its days in a world of illusion,
(Ah, but the life is lost that frets and languishes there!)
I would escape and be free in the joy of the open air.

GOD OF THE OPEN AIR

By the breadth of the blue that shines in silence o'er me,
By the length of the mountain-lines that stretch before me,
By the height of the cloud that sails, with rest in motion,
Over the plains and the vales to the measureless ocean,
(Oh, how the sight of the greater things enlarges the eyes!)
Draw me away from myself to the peace of the hills and skies.

While the tremulous leafy haze on the woodland is spreading,
And the bloom on the meadow betrays where May has been treading;
While the birds on the branches above, and the brooks flowing under,
Are singing together of love in a world full of wonder,
(Lo, in the magic of Springtime, dreams are changed into truth!)
Quicken my heart, and restore the beautiful hopes of youth.

By the faith that the wild-flowers show when they bloom unbidden,
By the calm of the river's flow to a goal that is hidden,
By the strength of the tree that clings to its deep foundation,

SONGS OUT OF DOORS

By the courage of birds' light wings on the long migration,
(Wonderful spirit of trust that abides in Nature's breast!)
Teach me how to confide, and live my life, and rest.

For the comforting warmth of the sun that my body embraces,
For the cool of the waters that run through the shadowy places,
For the balm of the breezes that brush my face with their fingers,
For the vesper-hymn of the thrush when the twilight lingers,
For the long breath, the deep breath, the breath of a heart without care,—
I will give thanks and adore thee, God of the open air!

VII

These are the gifts I ask
Of thee, Spirit serene:
Strength for the daily task,
Courage to face the road,
Good cheer to help me bear the traveller's load,
And, for the hours of rest that come between,
An inward joy in all things heard and seen.

GOD OF THE OPEN AIR

    These are the sins I fain
    Would have thee take away:
    Malice, and cold disdain,
    Hot anger, sullen hate,
Scorn of the lowly, envy of the great,
And discontent that casts a shadow gray
On all the brightness of the common day.
    These are the things I prize
    And hold of dearest worth:
    Light of the sapphire skies,
    Peace of the silent hills,
Shelter of forests, comfort of the grass,
Music of birds, murmur of little rills,
Shadows of cloud that swiftly pass,
    And, after showers,
    The smell of flowers
    And of the good brown earth,—
And best of all, along the way, friendship and mirth.
    So let me keep
    These treasures of the humble heart
  In true possession, owning them by love;
  And when at last I can no longer move
    Among them freely, but must part
From the green fields and from the waters clear
    Let me not creep
Into some darkened room and hide
From all that makes the world so bright and dear
    But throw the windows wide

SONGS OUT OF DOORS

To welcome in the light;
And while I clasp a well-belovèd hand,
Let me once more have sight
Of the deep sky and the far-smiling land,—
Then gently fall on sleep,
And breathe my body back to Nature's care,
My spirit out to thee, God of the open air.

1904.

NARRATIVE POEMS

THE TOILING OF FELIX
A LEGEND ON A NEW SAYING OF JESUS

In the rubbish heaps of the ancient city of Oxyrhynchus, near the River Nile, a party of English explorers, in the winter of 1897, discovered a fragment of a papyrus book, written in the second or third century, and hitherto unknown. This single leaf contained parts of seven short sentences of Christ, each introduced by the words, "Jesus says." It is to the fifth of these Sayings of Jesus that the following poem refers.

THE TOILING OF FELIX

I

PRELUDE

HEAR a word that Jesus spake
    Nineteen hundred years ago,
    Where the crimson lilies blow
Round the blue Tiberian lake:
There the bread of life He brake,
    Through the fields of harvest walking
    With His lowly comrades, talking
    Of the secret thoughts that feed
    Weary souls in time of need.
Art thou hungry? Come and take;
Hear the word that Jesus spake!
'Tis the sacrament of labour, bread and wine divinely blest;
Friendship's food and sweet refreshment, strength and courage, joy and rest.

But this word the Master said
    Long ago and far away,
    Silent and forgotten lay
Buried with the silent dead,
Where the sands of Egypt spread
    Sea-like, tawny billows heaping
    Over ancient cities sleeping,

NARRATIVE POEMS

While the River Nile between
Rolls its summer flood of green
Rolls its autumn flood of red:
There the word the Master said,
Written on a frail papyrus, wrinkled, scorched by fire,
  and torn,
Hidden by God's hand was waiting for its resurrection
  morn.

Now at last the buried word
  By the delving spade is found,
  Sleeping in the quiet ground.
Now the call of life is heard:
Rise again, and like a bird,
  Fly abroad on wings of gladness
  Through the darkness and the sadness,
  Of the toiling age, and sing
  Sweeter than the voice of Spring,
Till the hearts of men are stirred
By the music of the word,—
Gospel for the heavy-laden, answer to the labourer's cry:
"*Raise the stone, and thou shalt find me; cleave the wood
  and there am I.*"

THE TOILING OF FELIX

II

LEGEND

Brother-men who look for Jesus, long to see Him close and clear,
Hearken to the tale of Felix, how he found the Master near.

Born in Egypt, 'neath the shadow of the crumbling gods of night,
He forsook the ancient darkness, turned his young heart toward the Light.

Seeking Christ, in vain he waited for the vision of the Lord;
Vainly pondered many volumes where the creeds of men were stored;

Vainly shut himself in silence, keeping vigil night and day;
Vainly haunted shrines and churches where the Christians came to pray.

One by one he dropped the duties of the common life of care,
Broke the human ties that bound him, laid his spirit waste and bare,

NARRATIVE POEMS

Hoping that the Lord would enter that deserted dwelling-place,
And reward the loss of all things with the vision of His face.

Still the blessed vision tarried; still the light was unrevealed;
Still the Master, dim and distant, kept His countenance concealed.

Fainter grew the hope of finding, wearier grew the fruitless quest;
Prayer and penitence and fasting gave no comfort, brought no rest.

Lingering in the darkened temple, ere the lamp of faith went out,
Felix knelt before the altar, lonely, sad, and full of doubt.

"Hear me, O my Lord and Master," from the altar-step he cried,
"Let my one desire be granted, let my hope be satisfied!

"Only once I long to see Thee, in the fulness of Thy grace:
Break the clouds that now enfold Thee, with the sunrise of Thy face!

THE TOILING OF FELIX

"All that men desire and treasure have I counted loss for Thee;
Every hope have I forsaken, save this one, my Lord to see.

"Loosed the sacred bands of friendship, solitary stands my heart;
Thou shalt be my sole companion when I see Thee as Thou art.

"From Thy distant throne in glory, flash upon my inward sight,
Fill the midnight of my spirit with the splendour of Thy light.

"All Thine other gifts and blessings, common mercies, I disown;
Separated from my brothers, I would see Thy face alone.

"I have watched and I have waited as one waiteth for the morn:
Still the veil is never lifted, still Thou leavest me forlorn.

"Now I seek Thee in the desert, where the holy hermits dwell;
There, beside the saint Serapion, I will find a lonely cell.

NARRATIVE POEMS

"There at last Thou wilt be gracious; there Thy presence,
    long-concealed,
In the solitude and silence to my heart shall be revealed.

"Thou wilt come, at dawn or twilight, o'er the rolling
    waves of sand;
I shall see Thee close beside me, I shall touch Thy pierced
    hand.

"Lo, Thy pilgrim kneels before Thee; bless my journey
    with a word;
Tell me now that if I follow, I shall find Thee, O my
    Lord!"

Felix listened: through the darkness, like a murmur of
    the wind,
Came a gentle sound of stillness: "Never faint, and thou
    shalt find."

Long and toilsome was his journey through the heavy
    land of heat,
Egypt's blazing sun above him, blistering sand beneath
    his feet.

Patiently he plodded onward, from the pathway never
    erred,
Till he reached the river-headland called the Mountain
    of the Bird.

THE TOILING OF FELIX

There the tribes of air assemble, once a year, their noisy flock,
Then, departing, leave a sentinel perched upon the highest rock.

Far away, on joyful pinions, over land and sea they fly;
But the watcher on the summit lonely stands against the sky.

There the eremite Serapion in a cave had made his bed;
There the faithful bands of pilgrims sought his blessing, brought him bread.

Month by month, in deep seclusion, hidden in the rocky cleft,
Dwelt the hermit, fasting, praying; once a year the cave he left.

On that day a happy pilgrim, chosen out of all the band,
Won a special sign of favour from the holy hermit's hand.

Underneath the narrow window, at the doorway closely sealed,
While the afterglow of sunset deepened round him, Felix kneeled.

NARRATIVE POEMS

"Man of God, of men most holy, thou whose gifts cannot
    be priced!
Grant me thy most precious guerdon; tell me how to
    find the Christ."

Breathless, Felix bent and listened, but no answering
    voice he heard;
Darkness folded, dumb and deathlike, round the Moun-
    tain of the Bird.

Then he said, "The saint is silent; he would teach my
    soul to wait:
I will tarry here in patience, like a beggar at his gate."

Near the dwelling of the hermit Felix found a rude
    abode,
In a shallow tomb deserted, close beside the pilgrim-
    road.

So the faithful pilgrims saw him waiting there without
    complaint,—
Soon they learned to call him holy, fed him as they fed
    the saint.

Day by day he watched the sunrise flood the distant plain
    with gold,
While the River Nile beneath him, silvery coiling, sea-
    ward rolled.

THE TOILING OF FELIX

Night by night he saw the planets range their glittering court on high,
Saw the moon, with queenly motion, mount her throne and rule the sky.

Morn advanced and midnight fled, in visionary pomp attired;
Never morn and never midnight brought the vision long-desired.

Now at last the day is dawning when Serapion makes his gift;
Felix kneels before the threshold, hardly dares his eyes to lift.

Now the cavern door uncloses, now the saint above him stands,
Blesses him without a word, and leaves a token in his hands.

'Tis the guerdon of thy waiting! Look, thou happy pilgrim, look!
Nothing but a tattered fragment of an old papyrus book.

Read! perchance the clue to guide thee hidden in the words may lie:
"*Raise the stone, and thou shalt find me; cleave the wood, and there am I.*"

NARRATIVE POEMS

Can it be the mighty Master spake such simple words as these?
Can it be that men must seek Him at their toil 'mid rocks and trees?

Disappointed, heavy-hearted, from the Mountain of the Bird
Felix mournfully descended, questioning the Master's word.

Not for him a sacred dwelling, far above the haunts of men:
He must turn his footsteps backward to the common life again.

From a quarry near the river, hollowed out amid the hills,
Rose the clattering voice of labour, clanking hammers, clinking drills.

Dust, and noise, and hot confusion made a Babel of the spot:
There, among the lowliest workers, Felix sought and found his lot.

Now he swung the ponderous mallet, smote the iron in the rock—
Muscles quivering, tingling, throbbing—blow on blow and shock on shock;

THE TOILING OF FELIX

Now he drove the willow wedges, wet them till they swelled and split,
With their silent strength, the fragment, sent it thundering down the pit.

Now the groaning tackle raised it; now the rollers made it slide;
Harnessed men, like beasts of burden, drew it to the river-side.

Now the palm-trees must be riven, massive timbers hewn and dressed;
Rafts to bear the stones in safety on the rushing river's breast.

Axe and auger, saw and chisel, wrought the will of man in wood:
'Mid the many-handed labour Felix toiled, and found it good.

Every day the blood ran fleeter through his limbs and round his heart;
Every night he slept the sweeter, knowing he had done his part.

Dreams of solitary saintship faded from him; but, instead,
Came a sense of daily comfort in the toil for daily bread.

NARRATIVE POEMS

Far away, across the river, gleamed the white walls of
    the town
Whither all the stones and timbers day by day were
    floated down.

There the workman saw his labour taking form and bear-
    ing fruit,
Like a tree with splendid branches rising from a humble
    root.

Looking at the distant city, temples, houses, domes, and
    towers,
Felix cried in exultation: "All that mighty work is
    ours.

"Every toiler in the quarry, every builder on the shore,
Every chopper in the palm-grove, every raftsman at the
    oar,

"Hewing wood and drawing water, splitting stones and
    cleaving sod,
All the dusty ranks of labour, in the regiment of
    God,

"March together toward His triumph, do the task His
    hands prepare:
Honest toil is holy service; faithful work is praise and
    prayer."

THE TOILING OF FELIX

While he bore the heat and burden Felix felt the sense of rest
Flowing softly like a fountain, deep within his weary breast;

Felt the brotherhood of labour, rising round him like a tide,
Overflow his heart and join him to the workers at his side.

Oft he cheered them with his singing at the breaking of the light,
Told them tales of Christ at noonday, taught them words of prayer at night.

Once he bent above a comrade fainting in the mid-day heat,
Sheltered him with woven palm-leaves, gave him water, cool and sweet.

Then it seemed, for one swift moment, secret radiance filled the place;
Underneath the green palm-branches flashed a look of Jesus' face.

Once again, a raftsman, slipping, plunged beneath the stream and sank;
Swiftly Felix leaped to rescue, caught him, drew him toward the bank—

NARRATIVE POEMS

Battling with the cruel river, using all his strength to save—
Did he dream? or was there One beside him walking on the wave?

Now at last the work was ended, grove deserted, quarry stilled;
Felix journeyed to the city that his hands had helped to build.

In the darkness of the temple, at the closing hour of day,
As of old he sought the altar, as of old he knelt to pray:

"Hear me, O Thou hidden Master! Thou hast sent a word to me;
It is written—Thy commandment—I have kept it faithfully.

"Thou hast bid me leave the visions of the solitary life,
Bear my part in human labour, take my share in human strife.

"I have done Thy bidding, Master; raised the rock and felled the tree,
Swung the axe and plied the hammer, working every day for Thee.

THE TOILING OF FELIX

"Once it seemed I saw Thy presence through the bending palm-leaves gleam;
Once upon the flowing water— Nay, I know not; 'twas a dream!

"This I know: Thou hast been near me: more than this I dare not ask.
Though I see Thee not, I love Thee. Let me do Thy humblest task!"

Through the dimness of the temple slowly dawned a mystic light;
There the Master stood in glory, manifest to mortal sight:

Hands that bore the mark of labour, brow that bore the print of care;
Hands of power, divinely tender; brow of light, divinely fair.

"Hearken, good and faithful servant, true disciple, loyal friend!
Thou hast followed me and found me; I will keep thee to the end.

"Well I know thy toil and trouble; often weary, fainting, worn,
I have lived the life of labour, heavy burdens I have borne.

NARRATIVE POEMS

"Never in a prince's palace have I slept on golden bed,
Never in a hermit's cavern have I eaten unearned bread.

"Born within a lowly stable, where the cattle round me stood,
Trained a carpenter in Nazareth, I have toiled, and found it good.

"They who tread the path of labour follow where my feet have trod;
They who work without complaining do the holy will of God.

"Where the many toil together, there am I among my own;
Where the tired workman sleepeth, there am I with him alone.

"I, the peace that passeth knowledge, dwell amid the daily strife;
I, the bread of heaven, am broken in the sacrament of life.

"Every task, however simple, sets the soul that does it free;
Every deed of love and mercy, done to man, is done to me.

THE TOILING OF FELIX

"Thou hast learned the open secret; thou hast come to me for rest;
With thy burden, in thy labour, thou art Felix, doubly blest.

"Nevermore thou needest seek me; I am with thee everywhere;
Raise the stone, and thou shalt find me; cleave the wood, and I am there."

III

ENVOY

The legend of Felix is ended, the toiling of Felix is done;
The Master has paid him his wages, the goal of his journey is won;
He rests, but he never is idle; a thousand years pass like a day,
In the glad surprise of that Paradise where work is sweeter than play.

Yet often the King of that country comes out from His tireless host,
And walks in this world of the weary as if He loved it the most;
For here in the dusty confusion, with eyes that are heavy and dim,
He meets again the labouring men who are looking and longing for Him.

NARRATIVE POEMS

He cancels the curse of Eden, and brings them a blessing
  instead:
Blessed are they that labour, for Jesus partakes of their
  bread.
He puts His hand to their burdens, He enters their homes
  at night:
Who does his best shall have as a guest the Master of
  life and light.

And courage will come with His presence, and patience
  return at His touch,
And manifold sins be forgiven to those who love Him
  much;
The cries of envy and anger will change to the songs of
  cheer,
The toiling age will forget its rage when the Prince of
  Peace draws near.

This is the gospel of labour, ring it, ye bells of the kirk!
The Lord of Love came down from above, to live with
  the men who work.
This is the rose that He planted, here in the thorn-curst
  soil:
Heaven is blest with perfect rest, but the blessing of
  Earth is toil.

1898.

VERA

I

A SILENT world,—yet full of vital joy
Uttered in rhythmic movements manifold,
And sunbeams flashing on the face of things
Like sudden smilings of divine delight,—
A world of many sorrows too, revealed
In fading flowers and withering leaves and dark
Tear-laden clouds, and tearless, clinging mists
That hung above the earth too sad to weep,—
A world of fluent change, and changeless flow,
And infinite suggestion of new thought,
Reflected in the crystal of the heart,—
A world of many meanings but no words,
A silent world was Vera's home.

                              For her
The inner doors of sound were closely sealed
The outer portals, delicate as shells
Suffused with faintest rose of far-off morn,
Like underglow of daybreak in the sea,—
The ear-gates of the garden of her soul,
Shaded by drooping tendrils of brown hair,—
Waited in vain for messengers to pass,
And thread the labyrinth with flying feet,
And swiftly knock upon the inmost door,
And enter in, and speak the mystic word.

NARRATIVE POEMS

But through those gates no message ever came.
Only with eyes did she behold and see,—
With eyes as luminous and bright and brown
As waters of a woodland river,—eyes
That questioned so they almost seemed to speak,
And answered so they almost seemed to hear,—
Only with wondering eyes did she behold
The silent splendour of a living world.

She saw the great wind ranging freely down
Interminable archways of the wood,
While tossing boughs and bending tree-tops hailed
His coming: but no sea-toned voice of pines,
No roaring of the oaks, no silvery song
Of poplars or of birches, followed him.
He passed; they waved their arms and clapped their hands;
There was no sound.
                       The torrents from the hills
Leaped down their rocky pathways, like wild steeds
Breaking the yoke and shaking manes of foam.
The lowland brooks coiled smoothly through the fields,
And softly spread themselves in glistening lakes
Whose ripples merrily danced among the reeds.
The standing waves that ever keep their place
In the swift rapids, curled upon themselves,
And seemed about to break and never broke;
And all the wandering waves that fill the sea

VERA

Came buffeting in along the stony shore,
Or plunging in along the level sands,
Or creeping in along the winding creeks
And inlets. Yet from all the ceaseless flow
And turmoil of the restless element
Came neither song of joy nor sob of grief;
For there were many waters, but no voice.

Silent the actors all on Nature's stage
Performed their parts before her watchful eyes,
Coming and going, making war and love,
Working and playing, all without a sound.
The oxen drew their load with swaying necks;
The cows came sauntering home along the lane;
The nodding sheep were led from field to fold
In mute obedience. Down the woodland track
The hounds with panting sides and lolling tongues
Pursued their flying prey in noiseless haste.
The birds, the most alive of living things,
Mated, and built their nests, and reared their young
And swam the flood of air like tiny ships
Rising and falling over unseen waves,
And, gathering in great navies, bore away
To North or South, without a note of song.

All these were Vera's playmates; and she loved
To watch them, wondering oftentimes how well
They knew their parts, and how the drama moved

NARRATIVE POEMS

So swiftly, smoothly on from scene to scene
Without confusion. But she sometimes dreamed
There must be something hidden in the play
Unknown to her, an utterance of life
More clear than action and more deep than looks.
And this she felt most deeply when she watched
Her human comrades and the throngs of men,
Who met and parted oft with moving lips
That had a meaning more than she could see.
She saw a lover bend above a maid,
With moving lips; and though he touched her not
A sudden rose of joy bloomed in her face.
She saw a hater stand before his foe
And move his lips; whereat the other shrank
As if he had been smitten on the mouth.
She saw the regiments of toiling men
Marshalled in ranks and led by moving lips.
And once she saw a sight more strange than all:
A crowd of people sitting charmed and still
Around a little company of men
Who touched their hands in measured, rhythmic time
To curious instruments; a woman stood
Among them, with bright eyes and heaving breast,
And lifted up her face and moved her lips.
Then Vera wondered at the idle play,
But when she looked around, she saw the glow
Of deep delight on every face, as if
Some visitor from a celestial world

VERA

Had brought glad tidings. But to her alone
No angel entered, for the choir of sound
Was vacant in the temple of her soul,
And worship lacked her golden crown of song.

So when by vision baffled and perplexed
She saw that all the world could not be seen,
And knew she could not know the whole of life
Unless a hidden gate should be unsealed,
She felt imprisoned. In her heart there grew
The bitter creeping plant of discontent,
The plant that only grows in prison soil,
Whose root is hunger and whose fruit is pain.
The springs of still delight and tranquil joy
Were drained as dry as desert dust to feed
That never-flowering vine, whose tendrils clung
With strangling touch around the bloom of life
And made it wither. Vera could not rest
Within the limits of her silent world;
Along its dumb and desolate paths she roamed
A captive, looking sadly for escape.

Now in those distant days, and in that land
Remote, there lived a Master wonderful,
Who knew the secret of all life, and could,
With gentle touches and with potent words,
Open all gates that ever had been sealed,
And loose all prisoners whom Fate had bound.

NARRATIVE POEMS

Obscure he dwelt, not in the wilderness,
But in a hut among the throngs of men,
Concealed by meekness and simplicity.
And ever as he walked the city streets,
Or sat in quietude beside the sea,
Or trod the hillsides and the harvest fields,
The multitude passed by and knew him not.
But there were some who knew, and turned to him
For help; and unto all who asked, he gave.
Thus Vera came, and found him in the field,
And knew him by the pity in his face.
She knelt to him and held him by one hand,
And laid the other hand upon her lips
In mute entreaty. Then she lifted up
The coils of hair that hung about her neck,
And bared the beauty of the gates of sound,—
Those virgin gates through which no voice had passed
She made them bare before the Master's sight,
And looked into the kindness of his face
With eyes that spoke of all her prisoned pain,
And told her great desire without a word.

The Master waited long in silent thought,
As one reluctant to bestow a gift,
Not for the sake of holding back the thing
Entreated, but because he surely knew
Of something better that he fain would give
If only she would ask it. Then he stooped

VERA

To Vera, smiling, touched her ears and spoke:
"Open, fair gates, and you, reluctant doors,
Within the ivory labyrinth of the ear,
Let fall the bar of silence and unfold!
Enter, you voices of all living things,
Enter the garden sealed,—but softly, slowly,
Not with a noise confused and broken tumult,—
Come in an order sweet as I command you,
And bring the double gift of speech and hearing."

Vera began to hear. At first the wind
Breathed a low prelude of the birth of sound,
As if an organ far away were touched
By unseen fingers; then the little stream
That hurried down the hillside, swept the harp
Of music into merry, tinkling notes;
And then the lark that poised above her head
On wings a-quiver, overflowed the air
With showers of song; and one by one the tones
Of all things living, in an order sweet,
Without confusion and with deepening power,
Entered the garden sealed. And last of all
The Master's voice, the human voice divine,
Passed through the gates and called her by her name
And Vera heard.

NARRATIVE POEMS

II

        What rapture of new life
Must come to one for whom a silent world
Is suddenly made vocal, and whose heart
By the same magic is awaked at once,
Without the learner's toil and long delay,
Out of a night of dumbly moving dreams,
Into a day that overflows with music!
This joy was Vera's; and to her it seemed
As if a new creative morn had risen
Upon the earth, and after the full week
When living things unfolded silently,
And after the long, quiet Sabbath day,
When all was still, another day had dawned,
And through the calm expectancy of heaven
A secret voice had said, "Let all things speak."
The world responded with an instant joy;
And all the unseen avenues of sound
Were thronged with varying forms of viewless life

To every living thing a voice was given
Distinct and personal. The forest trees
Were not more varied in their shades of green
Than in their tones of speech; and every bird
That nested in their branches had a song
Unknown to other birds and all his own.
The waters spoke a hundred dialects

VERA

Of one great language; now with pattering fall
Of raindrops on the glistening leaves, and now
With steady roar of rivers rushing down
To meet the sea, and now with rhythmic throb
And measured tumult of tempestuous waves,
And now with lingering lisp of creeping tides,—
The manifold discourse of many waters.
But most of all the human voice was full
Of infinite variety, and ranged
Along the scale of life's experience
With changing tones, and notes both sweet and sad
All fitted to express some unseen thought,
Some vital motion of the hidden heart.
So Vera listened with her new-born sense
To all the messengers that passed the gates,
In measureless delight and utter trust,
Believing that they brought a true report
From every living thing of its true life,
And hoping that at last they would make clear
The mystery and the meaning of the world.

But soon there came a trouble in her joy,
A note discordant that dissolved the chord
And broke the bliss of hearing into pain.
Not from the harsher sounds and voices wild
Of anger and of anguish, that reveal
The secret strife in nature, and confess
The touch of sorrow on the heart of life,—

NARRATIVE POEMS

From these her trouble came not. For in these,
However sad, she felt the note of truth,
And truth, though sad, is always musical.
The raging of the tempest-ridden sea,
The crash of thunder, and the hollow moan
Of winds complaining round the mountain-crags,
The shrill and quavering cry of birds of prey,
The fiercer roar of conflict-loving beasts,—
All these wild sounds are potent in their place
Within life's mighty symphony; the charm
Of truth attunes them, and the hearing ear
Finds pleasure in their rude sincerity.
Even the broken and tumultuous noise
That rises from great cities, where the heart
Of human toil is beating heavily
With ceaseless murmurs of the labouring pulse,
Is not a discord; for it speaks to life
Of life unfeigned, and full of hopes and fears,
And touched through all the trouble of its notes
With something real and therefore glorious.

One voice alone of all that sound on earth,
Is hateful to the soul, and full of pain,—
The voice of falsehood. So when Vera heard
This mocking voice, and knew that it was false;
When first she learned that human lips can speak
The thing that is not, and betray the ear
Of simple trust with treachery of words;

VERA

The joy of hearing withered in her heart.
For now she felt that faithless messengers
Could pass the open and unguarded gates
Of sound, and bring a message all untrue,
Or half a truth that makes the deadliest lie,
Or idle babble, neither false nor true,
But hollow to the heart, and meaningless.
She heard the flattering voices of deceit,
That mask the hidden purposes of men
With fair attire of favourable words,
And hide the evil in the guise of good:
The voices vain and decorous and smooth,
That fill the world with empty-hearted talk;
The foolish voices, wandering and confused,
That never clearly speak the thing they would,
But ramble blindly round their true intent
And tangle sense in hopeless coils of sound,—
All these she heard, and with a deep mistrust
Began to doubt the value of her gift.
It seemed as if the world, the living world,
Sincere, and vast, and real, were still concealed
And she, within the prison of her soul,
Still waiting silently to hear the voice
Of perfect knowledge and of perfect peace.

So with the burden of her discontent
She turned to seek the Master once again,
And found him sitting in the market-place,

NARRATIVE POEMS

Half-hidden in the shadow of a porch,
Alone among the careless crowd.

                        She spoke:
"Thy gift was great, dear Master, and my heart
Has thanked thee many times because I hear
But I have learned that hearing is not all;
For underneath the speech of men, there flows
Another current of their hidden thoughts;
Behind the mask of language I perceive
The eyes of things unsaid.

                        Touch me again,
O Master, with thy liberating hand,
And free me from the bondage of deceit.
Open another gate, and let me hear
The secret thoughts and purposes of men;
For only thus my heart will be at rest,
And only thus, at last, I shall perceive
The mystery and the meaning of the world."

The Master's face was turned aside from her;
His eyes looked far away, as if he saw
Something beyond her sight; and yet she knew
That he was listening; for her pleading voice
No sooner ceased than he put forth his hand
To touch her brow, and very gently spoke:
"Thou seekest for thyself a wondrous gift,—
The opening of the second gate, a gift
That many wise men have desired in vain:

VERA

But some have found it,—whether well or ill
For their own peace, they have attained the power
To hear unspoken thoughts of other men.
And thou hast begged this gift? Thou shalt receive,-
Not knowing what thou seekest,—it is thine:
The second gate is open! Thou shalt hear
All that men think and feel within their hearts:
Thy prayer is granted, daughter, go thy way!
But if thou findest sorrow on this path,
Come back again,—there is a path to peace."

III

Beyond our power of vision, poets say,
There is another world of forms unseen,
Yet visible to purer eyes than ours.
And if the crystal of our sight were clear,
We should behold the mountain-slopes of cloud,
The moving meadows of the untilled sea,
The groves of twilight and the dales of dawn,
And every wide and lonely field of air,
More populous than cities, crowded close
With living creatures of all shapes and hues.
But if that sight were ours, the things that now
Engage our eyes would seem but dull and dim
Beside the wonders of our new-found world,
And we should be amazed and overwhelmed
Not knowing how to use the plenitude
Of vision.

NARRATIVE POEMS

So in Vera's soul, at first,
The opening of the second gate of sound
Let in confusion like a whirling flood.
The murmur of a myriad-throated mob;
The trampling of an army through a place
Where echoes hide; the sudden, whistling flight
Of an innumerable flock of birds
Along the highway of the midnight sky;
The many-whispered rustling of the reeds
Beneath the passing feet of all the winds;
The long-drawn, inarticulate, wailing cry
Of million-pebbled beaches when the lash
Of stormy waves is drawn across their back,—
All these were less bewildering than to hear
What now she heard at once: the tangled sound
Of all that moves within the minds of men.
For now there was no measured flow of words
To mark the time; nor any interval
Of silence to repose the listening ear.
But through the dead of night, and through the calm
Of weary noon-tide, through the solemn hush
That fills the temple in the pause of praise,
And through the breathless awe in rooms of death,
She heard the ceaseless motion and the stir
Of never-silent hearts, that fill the world
With interwoven thoughts of good and ill,
With mingled music of delight and grief,
With songs of love, and bitter cries of hate,

VERA

With hymns of faith, and dirges of despair,
And murmurs deeper and more vague than all,—
Thoughts that are born and die without a name,
Or rather, never die, but haunt the soul,
With sad persistence, till a name is given.
These Vera heard, at first with mind perplexed
And half-benumbed by the disordered sound.
But soon a clearer sense began to pierce
The cloudy turmoil with discerning power.
She learned to know the tones of human thought
As plainly as she knew the tones of speech.
She could divide the evil from the good,
Interpreting the language of the mind,
And tracing every feeling like a thread
Within the mystic web the passions weave
From heart to heart around the living world.

But when at last the Master's second gift
Was perfected within her, and she heard
And understood the secret thoughts of men,
A sadness fell upon her, and the load
Of insupportable knowledge pressed her down
With weary wishes to know more, or less.
For all she knew was like a broken word
Inscribed upon the fragment of a ring;
And all she heard was like a broken strain
Preluding music that is never played.

NARRATIVE POEMS

Then she remembered in her sad unrest
The Master's parting word,—"a path to peace,"—
And turned again to seek him with her grief.
She found him in a hollow of the hills,
Beside a little spring that issued forth
Beneath the rocks and filled a mossy cup
With never-failing water. There he sat,
With waiting looks that welcomed her afar.
"I know that thou hast heard, my child," he said,
"For all the wonder of the world of sound
Is written in thy face. But hast thou heard,
Among the many voices, one of peace?
And is thy heart that hears the secret thoughts,
The hidden wishes and desires of men,
Content with hearing? Art thou satisfied?"
"Nay, Master," she replied, "thou knowest well
That I am not at rest, nor have I heard
The voice of perfect peace; but what I hear
Brings me disquiet and a troubled mind.
The evil voices in the souls of men,
Voices of rage and cruelty and fear
Have not dismayed me; for I have believed
The voices of the good, the kind, the true,
Are more in number and excel in strength.
There is more love than hate, more hope than fear
In the deep throbbing of the human heart.
But while I listen to the troubled sound,
One thing torments me, and destroys my rest

VERA

And presses me with dull, unceasing pain.
For out of all the minds of all mankind,
There rises evermore a questioning voice
That asks the meaning of this mighty world
And finds no answer,—asks, and asks again,
With patient pleading or with wild complaint,
But wakens no response, except the sound
Of other questions, wandering to and fro,
From other souls in doubt. And so this voice
Persists above all others that I hear,
And binds them up together into one,
Until the mingled murmur of the world
Sounds through the inner temple of my heart
Like an eternal question, vainly asked
By every human soul that thinks and feels.
This is the heaviness that weighs me down,
And this the pain that will not let me rest.
Therefore, dear Master, shut the gates again,
And let me live in silence as before!
Or else,—and if there is indeed a gate
Unopened yet, through which I might receive
An answer in the voice of perfect peace—"

She ceased; and in her upward faltering tone
The question echoed.
                Then the Master said:
"There is another gate, not yet unclosed.
For through the outer portal of the ear

NARRATIVE POEMS

Only the outer voice of things may pass;
And through the middle doorway of the mind
Only the half-formed voice of human thoughts,
Uncertain and perplexed with endless doubt;
But through the inmost gate the spirit hears
The voice of that great Spirit who is Life.
Beneath the tones of living things He breathes
A deeper tone than ever ear hath heard;
And underneath the troubled thoughts of men
He thinks forever, and His thought is peace.
Behold, I touch thee once again, my child:
The third and last of those three hidden gates
That closed around thy soul and shut thee in,
Is open now, and thou shalt truly hear."

Then Vera heard. The spiritual gate
Was opened softly as a full-blown flower
Unfolds its heart to welcome in the dawn,
And on her listening face there shone a light
Of still amazement and completed joy
In the full gift of hearing.

                              What she heard
I cannot tell; nor could she ever tell
In words; because all human words are vain.
There is no speech nor language, to express
The secret messages of God, that make
Perpetual music in the hearing heart.
Below the voice of waters, and above

VERA

The wandering voice of winds, and underneath
The song of birds, and all the varying tones
Of living things that fill the world with sound,
God spoke to her, and what she heard was peace.

So when the Master questioned, "Dost thou hear?"
She answered, "Yea, at last I hear." And then
He asked her once again, "What hearest thou?
What means the voice of Life?" She answered, "Love!
For love is life, and they who do not love
Are not alive. But every soul that loves,
Lives in the heart of God and hears Him speak."

1898.

ANOTHER CHANCE

A DRAMATIC LYRIC

Come, give me back my life again, you heavy-handed Death!
Uncrook your fingers from my throat, and let me draw my breath.
You do me wrong to take me now—too soon for me to die—
Ah, loose me from this clutching pain, and hear the reason why.

I know I've had my forty years, and wasted every one;
And yet, I tell you honestly, my life is just begun;
I've walked the world like one asleep, a dreamer in a trance;
But now you've gripped me wide awake—I want another chance.

My dreams were always beautiful, my thoughts were high and fine;
No life was ever lived on earth to match those dreams of mine.
And would you wreck them unfulfilled? What folly, nay, what crime!
You rob the world, you waste a soul; give me a little time.

ANOTHER CHANCE

You'll hear me? Yes, I'm sure you will, my hope is not
    in vain:
I feel the even pulse of peace, the sweet relief from
    pain;
The black fog rolls away from me; I'm free once more
    to plan:
Another chance is all I need to prove myself a man!

The world is full of warfare 'twixt the evil and the
    good;
I watched the battle from afar as one who understood
The shouting and confusion, the bloody, blundering
    fight—
How few there are that see it clear, how few that wage
    it right!

The captains flushed with foolish pride, the soldiers pale
    with fear,
The faltering flags, the feeble fire from ranks that swerve
    and veer,
The wild mistakes, the dismal doubts, the coward hearts
    that flee—
The good cause needs a nobler knight to win the victory.

A man whose soul is pure and strong, whose sword is
    bright and keen,
Who knows the splendour of the fight and what its issues
    mean;

NARRATIVE POEMS

Who never takes one step aside, nor halts, though hope be dim,
But cleaves a pathway thro' the strife, and bids men follow him.

No blot upon his stainless shield, no weakness in his arm;
No sign of trembling in his face to break his valour's charm:
A man like this could stay the flight and lead the wavering line;
Ah, give me but a year of life—I'll make that glory mine!

. . . .

Religion? Yes, I know it well; I've heard its prayers and creeds,
And seen men put them all to shame with poor, half-hearted deeds.
They follow Christ, but far away; they wander and they doubt.
I'll serve him in a better way, and live his precepts out.

You see, I waited just for this; I could not be content
To own a feeble, faltering faith with human weakness blent.
Too many runners in the race move slowly, stumble, fall;
But I will run so straight and swift I shall outstrip them all.

ANOTHER CHANCE

Oh, think what it will mean to men, amid their foolish strife,
To see the clear, unshadowed light of one true Christian life,
Without a touch of selfishness, without a taint of sin,—
With one short month of such a life a new world would begin!

. . . .

And love!—I often dream of that—the treasure of the earth;
How little they who use the coin have realised its worth!
'Twill pay all debts, enrich all hearts, and make all joys secure.
But love, to do its perfect work, must be sincere and pure.

My heart is full of virgin gold. I'll pour it out and spend
My hidden wealth with open hand on all who call me friend.
Not one shall miss the kindly deed, the largess of relief,
The generous fellowship of joy, the sympathy of grief.

I'll say the loyal, helpful things that make life sweet and fair,
I'll pay the gratitude I owe for human love and care.
Perhaps I've been at fault sometimes—I'll ask to be forgiven,
And make this little room of mine seem like a bit of heaven.

NARRATIVE POEMS

For one by one I'll call my friends to stand beside my bed;
I'll speak the true and tender words so often left unsaid;
And every heart shall throb and glow, all coldness melt away
Around my altar-fire of love—ah, give me but one day!

. . . .

What's that? I've had another day, and wasted it again?
A priceless day in empty dreams, another chance in vain?
Thou fool—this night—it's very dark—the last—this choking breath—
One prayer—have mercy on a dreamer's soul—God, this is death!

A LEGEND OF SERVICE

It pleased the Lord of Angels (praise His name!)
To hear, one day, report from those who came
With pitying sorrow, or exultant joy,
To tell of earthly tasks in His employ.
For some were grieved because they saw how slow
The stream of heavenly love on earth must flow;
And some were glad because their eyes had seen,
Along its banks, fresh flowers and living green.
At last, before the whiteness of the throne
The youngest angel, Asmiel, stood alone;
Nor glad, nor sad, but full of earnest thought,
And thus his tidings to the Master brought·
"Lord, in the city Lupon I have found
"Three servants of thy holy name, renowned
"Above their fellows. One is very wise,
"With thoughts that ever range beyond the skies;
"And one is gifted with the golden speech
"That makes men gladly hear when he will teach;
"And one, with no rare gift or grace endued,
"Has won the people's love by doing good.
"With three such saints Lupon is trebly blest;
"But, Lord, I fain would know, which loves Thee best?"
Then spake the Lord of Angels, to whose look
The hearts of all are like an open book:
"In every soul the secret thought I read,

NARRATIVE POEMS

"And well I know who loves me best indeed.
"But every life has pages vacant still,
"Whereon a man may write the thing he will;
"Therefore I read the record, day by day,
"And wait for hearts untaught to learn my way.
"But thou shalt go to Lupon, to the three
"Who serve me there, and take this word from me:
"Tell each of them his Master bids him go
"Alone to Spiran's huts, across the snow;
"There he shall find a certain task for me:
"But what, I do not tell to them nor thee.
"Give thou the message, make my word the test,
"And crown for me the one who loves me best."
Silent the angel stood, with folded hands,
To take the imprint of his Lord's commands;
Then drew one breath, obedient and elate,
And passed the self-same hour, through Lupon's gate

. . . .

First to the Temple door he made his way;
And there, because it was a holy-day,
He saw the folk in thousands thronging, stirred
By ardent thirst to hear the preacher's word.
Then, while the people whispered Bernol's name,
Through aisles that hushed behind him Bernol came;
Strung to the keenest pitch of conscious might,
With lips prepared and firm, and eyes alight.
One moment at the pulpit step he knelt
In silent prayer, and on his shoulder felt

A LEGEND OF SERVICE

The angel's hand:—"The Master bids thee go
"Alone to Spiran's huts, across the snow,
"To serve Him there." Then Bernol's hidden face
Went white as death, and for about the space
Of ten slow heart-beats there was no reply;
Till Bernol looked around and whispered, "*Why?*"
But answer to his question came there none;
The angel sighed, and with a sigh was gone.

. . . .

Within the humble house where Malvin spent
His studious years, on holy things intent,
Sweet stillness reigned; and there the angel found
The saintly sage immersed in thought profound,
Weaving with patient toil and willing care
A web of wisdom, wonderful and fair:
A seamless robe for Truth's great bridal meet,
And needing but one thread to be complete.
Then Asmiel touched his hand, and broke the thread
Of fine-spun thought, and very gently said,
"The One of whom thou thinkest bids thee go
"Alone to Spiran's huts, across the snow,
"To serve Him there." With sorrow and surprise
Malvin looked up, reluctance in his eyes.
The broken thought, the strangeness of the call,
The perilous passage of the mountain-wall,
The solitary journey, and the length
Of ways unknown, too great for his frail strength,
Appalled him. With a doubtful brow

NARRATIVE POEMS

He scanned the doubtful task, and muttered *"How?"*
But Asmiel answered, as he turned to go,
With cold, disheartened voice, "I do not know."

. . . .

Now as he went, with fading hope, to seek
The third and last to whom God bade him speak,
Scarce twenty steps away whom should he meet
But Fermor, hurrying cheerful down the street,
With ready heart that faced his work like play,
And joyed to find it greater every day!
The angel stopped him with uplifted hand,
And gave without delay his Lord's command:
"He whom thou servest here would have thee go
"Alone to Spiran's huts, across the snow,
"To serve Him there." Ere Asmiel breathed again
The eager answer leaped to meet him, *"When?"*

The angel's face with inward joy grew bright,
And all his figure glowed with heavenly light;
He took the golden circlet from his brow
And gave the crown to Fermor, answering, "Now!
"For thou hast met the Master's hidden test,
"And I have found the man who loves Him best.
"Not thine, nor mine, to question or reply
"When He commands us, asking 'how?' or 'why?'
"He knows the cause; His ways are wise and just;
"Who serves the King must serve with perfect trust

February, 1902.

THE WHITE BEES

I

LEGEND

Long ago Apollo called to Aristæus, youngest of the
   shepherds,
   Saying, "I will make you keeper of my bees."
Golden were the hives and golden was the honey; golden,
   too, the music
   Where the honey-makers hummed among the trees.

Happy Aristæus loitered in the garden, wandered in the
   orchard,
   Careless and contented, indolent and free;
Lightly took his labour, lightly took his pleasure, till the
   fated moment
   When across his pathway came Eurydice.

Then her eyes enkindled burning love within him; drove
   him wild with longing
   For the perfect sweetness of her flower-like face;
Eagerly he followed, while she fled before him, over mead
   and mountain,
   On through field and forest, in a breathless race.

But the nymph, in flying, trod upon a serpent; like a
   dream she vanished;
   Pluto's chariot bore her down among the dead!

NARRATIVE POEMS

Lonely Aristæus, sadly home returning, found his garden empty,
  All the hives deserted, all the music fled.

Mournfully bewailing,—"Ah, my honey-makers, where have you departed?"
  Far and wide he sought them over sea and shore;
Foolish is the tale that says he ever found them, brought them home in triumph,—
  Joys that once escape us fly for evermore.

Yet I dream that somewhere, clad in downy whiteness, dwell the honey-makers,
  In aërial gardens that no mortal sees:
And at times returning, lo, they flutter round us, gathering mystic harvest,—
  So I weave the legend of the long-lost bees.

II

THE SWARMING OF THE BEES

Who can tell the hiding of the white bees' nest?
  Who can trace the guiding of their swift home flight?
Far would be his riding on a life-long quest:
  Surely ere it ended would his beard grow white.

Never in the coming of the rose-red Spring,
  Never in the passing of the wine-red Fall,

THE WHITE BEES

May you hear the humming of the white bee's wing
  Murmur o'er the meadow ere the night bells call.

Wait till winter hardens in the cold gray sky,
  Wait till leaves are fallen and the brooks all freeze
Then above the gardens where the dead flowers lie,
  Swarm the merry millions of the wild white bees.

> Out of the high-built airy hive,
> Deep in the clouds that veil the sun,
> Look how the first of the swarm arrive;
> Timidly venturing, one by one,
> Down through the tranquil air,
> Wavering here and there,
> Large, and lazy in flight,—
> Caught by a lift of the breeze,
> Tangled among the naked trees,—
> Dropping then, without a sound,
> Feather-white, feather-light,
> To their rest on the ground.
>
> Thus the swarming is begun.
> Count the leaders, every one
> Perfect as a perfect star
> Till the slow descent is done.
> Look beyond them, see how far
> Down the vistas dim and gray,
> Multitudes are on the way.

NARRATIVE POEMS

    Now a sudden brightness
    Dawns within the sombre day,
    Over fields of whiteness;
    And the sky is swiftly alive
    With the flutter and the flight
    Of the shimmering bees, that pour
    From the hidden door of the hive
    Till you can count no more.

Now on the branches of hemlock and pine
Thickly they settle and cluster and swing,
Bending them low; and the trellised vine
And the dark elm-boughs are traced with a line
Of beauty wherever the white bees cling.
Now they are hiding the wrecks of the flowers,
    Softly, softly, covering all,
Over the grave of the summer hours
    Spreading a silver pall.
Now they are building the broad roof ledge,
Into a cornice smooth and fair,
Moulding the terrace, from edge to edge,
Into the sweep of a marble stair.
Wonderful workers, swift and dumb,
Numberless myriads, still they come,
Thronging ever faster, faster, faster!
Where is their queen? Who is their master?
The gardens are faded, the fields are frore,—
What is the honey they toil to store

THE WHITE BEES

In the desolate day, where no blossoms gleam?
Forgetfulness and a dream!

But now the fretful wind awakes;
I hear him girding at the trees;
He strikes the bending boughs, and shakes
The quiet clusters of the bees
    To powdery drift;
  He tosses them away,
  He drives them like spray;
He makes them veer and shift
  Around his blustering path.
  In clouds blindly whirling,
  In rings madly swirling,
  Full of crazy wrath,
So furious and fast they fly
They blur the earth and blot the sky
    In wild, white mirk.
They fill the air with frozen wings
And tiny, angry, icy stings;
They blind the eyes, and choke the breath,
They dance a maddening dance of death
    Around their work,
Sweeping the cover from the hill,
Heaping the hollows deeper still,
Effacing every line and mark,
And swarming, storming in the dark
    Through the long night;

NARRATIVE POEMS

Until, at dawn, the wind lies down
  Weary of fight;
The last torn cloud, with trailing gown,
Passes the open gates of light;
And the white bees are lost in flight.

Look how the landscape glitters wide and still,
  Bright with a pure surprise!
The day begins with joy, and all past ill,
  Buried in white oblivion, lies
Beneath the snow-drifts under crystal skies.
New hope, new love, new life, new cheer,
  Flow in the sunrise beam,—
  The gladness of Apollo when he sees,
Upon the bosom of the wintry year,
The honey-harvest of his wild white bees,
  Forgetfulness and a dream!

III

LEGEND

Listen, my beloved, while the silver morning, like a tranquil vision,
  Fills the world around us and our hearts with peace;
Quiet is the close of Aristæus' legend, happy is the ending—
  Listen while I tell you how he found release.

THE WHITE BEES

Many months he wandered far away in sadness, desolately thinking
 Only of the vanished joys he could not find;
Till the great Apollo, pitying his shepherd, loosed him from the burden
 Of a dark, reluctant, backward-looking mind.

Then he saw around him all the changeful beauty of the changing seasons,
 In the world-wide regions where his journey lay;
Birds that sang to cheer him, flowers that bloomed beside him, stars that shone to guide him,—
 Traveller's joy was plenty all along the way!

Everywhere he journeyed strangers made him welcome, listened while he taught them
 Secret lore of field and forest he had learned:
How to train the vines and make the olives fruitful; how to guard the sheepfolds;
 How to stay the fever when the dog-star burned.

Friendliness and blessing followed in his footsteps; richer were the harvests,
 Happier the dwellings, wheresoe'er he came;
Little children loved him, and he left behind him, in the hour of parting,
 Memories of kindness and a god-like name.

NARRATIVE POEMS

So he travelled onward, desolate no longer, patient in
    his seeking,
  Reaping all the wayside comfort of his quest;
Till at last in Thracia, high upon Mount Hæmus, far from
    human dwelling,
  Weary Aristæus laid him down to rest.

Then the honey-makers, clad in downy whiteness, flut-
    tered soft around him,
  Wrapt him in a dreamful slumber pure and deep.
This is life, beloved: first a sheltered garden, then a
    troubled journey,
  Joy and pain of seeking,—and at last we sleep!

1905.

NEW YEAR'S EVE

I

The other night I had a dream, most clear
And comforting, complete
In every line, a crystal sphere,
And full of intimate and secret cheer.
Therefore I will repeat
That vision, dearest heart, to you,
As of a thing not feigned, but very true,
Yes, true as ever in my life befell;
And you, perhaps, can tell
Whether my dream was really sad or sweet.

II

The shadows flecked the elm-embowered street
I knew so well, long, long ago;
And on the pillared porch where Marguerite
Had sat with me, the moonlight lay like snow
But she, my comrade and my friend of youth,
Most gaily wise,
Most innocently loved,—
She of the blue-gray eyes
That ever smiled and ever spoke the truth,—
From that familiar dwelling, where she moved
Like mirth incarnate in the years before,
Had gone into the hidden house of Death.

NARRATIVE POEMS

I thought the garden wore
White mourning for her blessed innocence,
And the syringa's breath
Came from the corner by the fence
Where she had made her rustic seat,
With fragrance passionate, intense,
As if it breathed a sigh for Marguerite.
My heart was heavy with a sense
Of something good for ever gone. I sought
Vainly for some consoling thought,
Some comfortable word that I could say
To her sad father, whom I visited again
For the first time since she had gone away.
The bell rang shrill and lonely,—then
The door was opened, and I sent my name
To him,—but ah! 'twas Marguerite who came!
There in the dear old dusky room she stood
Beneath the lamp, just as she used to stand,
In tender mocking mood.
"You did not ask for me," she said,
"And so I will not let you take my hand;
"But I must hear what secret talk you planned
"With father. Come, my friend, be good,
"And tell me your affairs of state:
"Why you have stayed away and made me wait
"So long. Sit down beside me here,—
"And, do you know, it seems a year
"Since we have talked together,—why so late?"

NEW YEAR'S EVE

Amazed, incredulous, confused with joy
I hardly dared to show,
And stammering like a boy,
I took the place she showed me at her side;
And then the talk flowed on with brimming tide
Through the still night,
While she with influence light
Controlled it, as the moon the flood.
She knew where I had been, what I had done,
What work was planned, and what begun;
My troubles, failures, fears she understood,
And touched them with a heart so kind,
That every care was melted from my mind,
And every hope grew bright,
And life seemed moving on to happy ends.
(Ah, what self-beggared fool was he
That said a woman cannot be
The very best of friends?)
Then there were memories of old times,
Recalled with many a gentle jest;
And at the last she brought the book of rhymes
We made together, trying to translate
The Songs of Heine (hers were always best).
"Now come," she said,
"To-night we will collaborate
"Again; I'll put you to the test.
"Here's one I never found the way to do,—
"The simplest are the hardest ones, you know,—

139

NARRATIVE POEMS

"I give this song to you."
And then she read:
> *Mein Kind, wir waren Kinder,*
> *Zwei Kinder, jung und froh.*

. . . .

But all the while, a silent question stirred
Within me, though I dared not speak the word:
"Is it herself, and is she truly here,
"And was I dreaming when I heard
"That she was dead last year?
"Or was it true, and is she but a shade
"Who brings a fleeting joy to eye and ear,
"Cold though so kind, and will she gently fade
"When her sweet ghostly part is played
"And the light-curtain falls at dawn of day?"

But while my heart was troubled by this fear
So deeply that I could not speak it out,
Lest all my happiness should disappear,
I thought me of a cunning way
To hide the question and dissolve the doubt.
"Will you not give me now your hand,
"Dear Marguerite," I asked, "to touch and hold
"That by this token I may understand
"You are the same true friend you were of old?
She answered with a smile so bright and calm
It seemed as if I saw the morn arise
In the deep heaven of her eyes;

NEW YEAR'S EVE

And smiling so, she laid her palm
In mine. Dear God, it was not cold
But warm with vital heat!
"You live!" I cried, "you live, dear Marguerite!"
Then I awoke; but strangely comforted,
Although I knew again that she was dead.

III

Yes, there's the dream! And was it sweet or sad?
Dear mistress of my waking and my sleep,
Present reward of all my heart's desire,
Watching with me beside the winter fire,
Interpret now this vision that I had.
But while you read the meaning, let me keep
The touch of you: for the Old Year with storm
Is passing through the midnight, and doth shake
The corners of the house,—and oh! my heart would break
Unless both dreaming and awake
My hand could feel your hand was warm, warm, warm!

1905.

THE VAIN KING

In robes of Tyrian blue the King was drest,
A jewelled collar shone upon his breast,
A giant ruby glittered in his crown:
Lord of rich lands and many a splendid town,
In him the glories of an ancient line
Of sober kings, who ruled by right divine,
Were centred; and to him with loyal awe
The people looked for leadership and law.
Ten thousand knights, the safeguard of the land,
Were like a single sword within his hand;
A hundred courts, with power of life and death,
Proclaimed decrees of justice by his breath;
And all the sacred growths that men had known
Of order and of rule upheld his throne.

Proud was the King: yet not with such a heart
As fits a man to play a royal part.
Not his the pride that honours as a trust
The right to rule, the duty to be just:
Not his the dignity that bends to bear
The monarch's yoke, the master's load of care,
And labours like the peasant at his gate,
To serve the people and protect the State.
Another pride was his, and other joys:
To him the crown and sceptre were but toys,

142

THE VAIN KING

With which he played at glory's idle game,
To please himself and win the wreaths of fame.
The throne his fathers held from age to age,
To his ambition seemed a fitting stage
Built for King Martın to display at will,
His mighty strength and universal skill.
No conscious child, that, spoiled with praising, tries
At every step to win admiring eyes,
No favourite mountebank, whose acting draws
From gaping crowds the thunder of applause,
Was vainer than the King: his only thirst
Was to be hailed, in every race, the first.
When tournament was held, in knightly guise
The King would ride the lists and win the prize;
When music charmed the court, with golden lyre
The King would take the stage and lead the choir;
In hunting, his the lance to slay the boar;
In hawking, see his falcon highest soar;
In painting, he would wield the master's brush;
In high debate,—"the King is speaking! Hush!"
Thus, with a restless heart, in every field
He sought renown, and made his subjects yield.
But while he played the petty games of life
His kingdom fell a prey to inward strife;
Corruption through the court unheeded crept,
And on the seat of honour justice slept.
The strong trod down the weak; the helpless poor
Groaned under burdens grievous to endure;

NARRATIVE POEMS

The nation's wealth was spent in vain display,
And weakness wore the nation's heart away.

Yet think not Earth is blind to human woes—
Man has more friends and helpers than he knows;
And when a patient people are oppressed,
The land that bore them feels it in her breast.
Spirits of field and flood, of heath and hill,
Are grieved and angry at the spreading ill;
The trees complain together in the night,
Voices of wrath are heard along the height,
And secret vows are sworn, by stream and strand,
To bring the tyrant low and free the land.

But little recked the pampered King of these;
He heard no voice but such as praise and please.
Flattered and fooled, victor in every sport,
One day he wandered idly with his court
Beside the river, seeking to devise
New ways to show his skill to wondering eyes.
There in the stream a patient angler stood,
And cast his line across the rippling flood.
His silver spoil lay near him on the green:
"Such fish," the courtiers cried, "were never seen!
"Three salmon longer than a cloth-yard shaft—
"This man must be the master of his craft!"
"An easy art!" the jealous King replied:
"Myself could learn it better, if I tried,

THE VAIN KING

"And catch a hundred larger fish a week—
"Wilt thou accept the challenge, fellow? Speak!"
The angler turned, came near, and bent his knee
"'Tis not for kings to strive with such as me;
"Yet if the King commands it, I obey.
"But one condition of the strife I pray:
"The fisherman who brings the least to land
"Shall do whate'er the other may command."
Loud laughed the King: "A foolish fisher thou!
'For I shall win, and rule thee then as now."

Then to Prince John, a sober soul, sedate
And slow, King Martin left the helm of State,
While to the novel game with eager zest
He all his time and all his powers addressed.
Sure such a sight was never seen before!
In robe and crown the monarch trod the shore;
His golden hooks were decked with feathers fine,
His jewelled reel ran out a silken line.
With kingly strokes he flogged the crystal stream
Far-off the salmon saw his tackle gleam;
Careless of kings, they eyed with calm disdain
The gaudy lure, and Martin fished in vain.
On Friday, when the week was almost spent,
He scanned his empty creel with discontent,
Called for a net, and cast it far and wide,
And drew—a thousand minnows from the tide!
Then came the angler to conclude the match,

NARRATIVE POEMS

And at the monarch's feet spread out his catch—
A hundred salmon, greater than before.
"I win!" he cried: "the King must pay the score
Then Martin, angry, threw his tackle down:
"Rather than lose this game I'd lose my crown!"
"Nay, thou hast lost them both," the angler said;
And as he spoke a wondrous light was shed
Around his form; he dropped his garments mean,
And in his place the River-god was seen.
"Thy vanity has brought thee in my power,
"And thou must pay the forfeit at this hour:
"For thou hast shown thyself a royal fool,
"Too proud to angle, and too vain to rule,
"Eager to win in every trivial strife,—
"Go! Thou shalt fish for minnows all thy life!"
Wrathful, the King the magic sentence heard;
He strove to answer, but he only *chirr-r-ed*:
His royal robe was changed to wings of blue,
His crown a ruby crest,—away he flew!

So every summer day along the stream
The vain King-fisher darts, an azure gleam,
And scolds the angler with a mocking scream.

April, 1904.

THE FOOLISH FIR-TREE

A tale that the poet Rückert told
To German children, in days of old;
Disguised in a random, rollicking rhyme
Like a merry mummer of ancient time,
And sent, in its English dress, to please
The little folk of the Christmas trees.

A LITTLE fir grew in the midst of the wood
Contented and happy, as young trees should.
His body was straight and his boughs were clean;
And summer and winter the bountiful sheen
Of his needles bedecked him, from top to root,
In a beautiful, all-the-year, evergreen suit.

But a trouble came into his heart one day,
When he saw that the other trees were gay
In the wonderful raiment that summer weaves
Of manifold shapes and kinds of leaves:
He looked at his needles so stiff and small,
And thought that his dress was the poorest of all
Then jealousy clouded the little tree's mind,
And he said to himself, "It was not very kind
"To give such an ugly old dress to a tree!
"If the fays of the forest would only ask me,
"I'd tell them how I should like to be dressed,—
"In a garment of gold, to bedazzle the rest!"
So he fell asleep, but his dreams were bad.

NARRATIVE POEMS

When he woke in the morning, his heart was glad
For every leaf that his boughs could hold
Was made of the brightest beaten gold.
I tell you, children, the tree was proud;
He was something above the common crowd;
And he tinkled his leaves, as if he would say
To a pedlar who happened to pass that way,
"Just look at me! Don't you think I am fine?
"And wouldn't you like such a dress as mine?"
"Oh, yes!" said the man, "and I really guess
"I must fill my pack with your beautiful dress."
So he picked the golden leaves with care,
And left the little tree shivering there.

"Oh, why did I wish for golden leaves?"
The fir-tree said, "I forgot that thieves
"Would be sure to rob me in passing by.
"If the fairies would give me another try,
"I'd wish for something that cost much less,
"And be satisfied with glass for my dress!"
Then he fell asleep; and, just as before,
The fairies granted his wish once more.
When the night was gone, and the sun rose clear,
The tree was a crystal chandelier;
And it seemed, as he stood in the morning light,
That his branches were covered with jewels bright.
"Aha!" said the tree. "This is something great!"
And he held himself up, very proud and straight;

THE FOOLISH FIR-TREE

But a rude young wind through the forest dashed,
In a reckless temper, and quickly smashed
The delicate leaves. With a clashing sound
They broke into pieces and fell on the ground,
Like a silvery, shimmering shower of hail,
And the tree stood naked and bare to the gale.

Then his heart was sad; and he cried, "Alas
"For my beautiful leaves of shining glass!
"Perhaps I have made another mistake
"In choosing a dress so easy to break.
"If the fairies only would hear me again
"I'd ask them for something both pretty and plain
"It wouldn't cost much to grant my request,—
"In leaves of green lettuce I'd like to be dressed!"
By this time the fairies were laughing, I know;
But they gave him his wish in a second; and so
With leaves of green lettuce, all tender and sweet,
The tree was arrayed, from his head to his feet.
"I knew it!" he cried, "I was sure I could find
"The sort of a suit that would be to my mind.
"There's none of the trees has a prettier dress,
"And none as attractive as I am, I guess."
But a goat, who was taking an afternoon walk,
By chance overheard the fir-tree's talk.
So he came up close for a nearer view;—
"My salad!" he bleated, "I think so too!
"You're the most attractive kind of a tree,

NARRATIVE POEMS

"And I want your leaves for my five-o'clock tea."
So he ate them all without saying grace,
And walked away with a grin on his face;
While the little tree stood in the twilight dim,
With never a leaf on a single limb.

Then he sighed and groaned; but his voice was weak
He was so ashamed that he could not speak.
He knew at last he had been a fool,
To think of breaking the forest rule,
And choosing a dress himself to please,
Because he envied the other trees.
But it couldn't be helped, it was now too late,
He must make up his mind to a leafless fate!
So he let himself sink in a slumber deep,
But he moaned and he tossed in his troubled sleep,
Till the morning touched him with joyful beam,
And he woke to find it was all a dream.
For there in his evergreen dress he stood,
A pointed fir in the midst of the wood!
His branches were sweet with the balsam smell,
His needles were green when the white snow fell.
And always contented and happy was he,—
The very best kind of a Christmas tree.

"GRAN' BOULE"

A SEAMAN'S TALE OF THE SEA

WE men that go down for a livin' in ships to the sea,—
We love it a different way from you poets that 'bide on the land.
We are fond of it, sure! But, you take it as comin' from me,
There's a fear and a hate in our love that a landsman can't understand.

Oh, who could help likin' the salty smell, and the blue
Of the waves that are lazily breathin' as if they dreamed in the sun?
She's a Sleepin' Beauty, the sea,—but you can't tell what she'll do;
And the seamen never trust her,—they know too well what she's done!

She's a wench like one that I saw in a singin'-play,—
Carmen they called her,—Lord, what a life her lovers did lead!
She'd cuddle and kiss you, and sing you and dance you away;
And then,—she'd curse you, and break you, and throw you down like a weed.

NARRATIVE POEMS

You may chance it awhile with the girls like that, if you please;
But you want a woman to trust when you settle down with a wife;
And a seaman's thought of growin' old at his ease
Is a snug little house on the land to shelter the rest of his life.

So that was old Poisson's dream,—did you know the Cap'?
A brown little Frenchman, clever, and brave, and quick as a fish,—
Had a wife and kids on the other side of the map,—
And a rose-covered cottage for them and him was his darlin' wish.

"I 'ave sail," says he, in his broken-up Frenchy talk,
"Mos' forty-two year; I 'ave go on all part of de worl' dat ees wet.
I'm seeck of de boat and de water. I rader walk
Wid ma Josephine in one garden; an' eef we get tire', we set!

"You see dat *bateau, Sainte Brigitte?* I bring 'er dh'are
From de Breton coas', by gar, jus' feefteen year bifore.
She ole w'en she come on Kebec, but *Holloway Frères*
Dey buy 'er, an' hire me run 'er along dat dam' Nort' Shore.

"GRAN' BOULE"

"Dose engine one leetl' bit cranky,—too ole, you see,—
She roll and peetch in de wave'. But I lak' 'er pretty
  well;
An' dat sheep she lak' 'er captaine, sure, dat's me!
Wit' forty ton coal in de bunker, I tek' dat sheep t'rou'
  hell.

"But I don' wan' risk it no more; I had *bonne chance*:
I save already ten t'ousan' dollar', dat's plenty I s'pose!
Nex' winter I buy dat house wid de garden on France
An' I tell *adieu* to de sea, and I leev' on de lan' in ripose."

All summer he talked of his house,—you could see the
  flowers
Abloom, and the pear-trees trained on the garden-wall
  so trim,
And the Captain awalkin' and smokin' away the hours,—
He thought he had done with the sea, but the sea hadn't
  done with him!

It was late in the fall when he made the last regular
  run,
Clear down to the Esquimault Point and back with his
  rickety ship;
She hammered and pounded a lot, for the storms had
  begun;
But he drove her,—and went for his season's pay at the
  end of the trip.

NARRATIVE POEMS

Now the Holloway Brothers are greedy and thin little
    men,
With their eyes set close together, and money's their
    only God;
So they told the Cap' he must run the "Bridget" again,
To fetch a cargo from Moisie, two thousand quintals of
    cod.

He said the season was over. They said: "Not yet.
You finish the whole of your job, old man, or you don't
    draw a cent!"
(They had the "Bridget" insured for all they could get.)
And the Captain objected, and cursed, and cried. But
    he *went*.

They took on the cargo at Moisie, and folks beside,—
Three traders, a priest, and a couple of nuns, and a
    girl
For a school at Quebec,—when the Captain saw her he
    sighed,
And said: "Ma littl' Fifi got hair lak' dat, all curl!"

The snow had fallen a foot, and the wind was high,
When the "Bridget" butted her way thro' the billows
    on Moisie bar.
The darkness grew with the gale, not a star in the sky,
And the Captain swore: "We mus' make *Sept Isles* to-
    night, by gar!"

"GRAN' BOULE"

He couldn't go back, for he didn't dare to turn;
The sea would have thrown the ship like a mustang noosed with a rope;
For the monstrous waves were leapin' high astern,
And the shelter of Seven Island Bay was the only hope.

There's a bunch of broken hills half sunk in the mouth
Of the bay, with their jagged peaks afoam; and the Captain thought
He could pass to the north; but the sea kept shovin' him south,
With her harlot hands, in the snow-blind murk, till she had him caught.

She had waited forty years for a night like this,—
Did he think he could leave her now, and live in a cottage, the fool?
She headed him straight for the island he couldn't miss;
And heaved his boat in the dark,—and smashed it against *Gran' Boule.*

How the Captain and half of the people clambered ashore,
Through the surf and the snow in the gloom of that horrible night,
There's no one ever will know. For two days more
The death-white shroud of the tempest covered the island from sight.

NARRATIVE POEMS

How they suffered, and struggled, and died, will never
    be told;
We discovered them all at last when we reached *Gran'
    Boule* with a boat;
The drowned and the frozen were lyin' stiff and cold,
And the poor little girl with the curls was wrapped in
    the Captain's coat.

Go write your song of the sea as the landsmen do,
And call her your "great sweet mother," your "bride,"
    and all the rest;
She was made to be loved,—but remember, she won't
    love you,—
The men who trust her the least are the sailors who know
    her the best.

HEROES OF THE "TITANIC"

Honour the brave who sleep
  Where the lost "Titanic" lies,
The men who knew what a man must do
  When he looks Death in the eyes.

"Women and children first,"—
  Ah, strong and tender cry!
The sons whom women had borne and nursed
  Remembered,—and dared to die.

The boats crept off in the dark:
  The great ship groaned: and then,—
O stars of the night, who saw that sight,
  Bear witness, *These were men!*

November 9, 1912.

THE STANDARD-BEARER

I

"How can I tell," Sir Edmund said,
  "Who has the right or the wrong o' this thing?
  Cromwell stands for the people's cause,
  Charles is crowned by the ancient laws;
English meadows are sopping red,
Englishmen striking each other dead,—
  Times are black as a raven's wing.
Out of the ruck and the murk I see
    Only one thing!
The King has trusted his banner to me,
  And I must fight for the King."

II

Into the thick of the Edgehill fight
  Sir Edmund rode with a shout; and the ring
  Of grim-faced, hard-hitting Parliament men
  Swallowed him up,—it was one against ten!
He fought for the standard with all his might,
Never again did he come to sight—
  Victor, hid by the raven's wing!
After the battle had passed we found
    Only one thing,—
The hand of Sir Edmund gripped around
  The banner-staff of his King.

1914.

THE PROUD LADY

When Stävoren town was in its prime
    And queened the Zuyder Zee,
Her ships went out to every clime
    With costly merchantry.

A lady dwelt in that rich town,
    The fairest in all the land;
She walked abroad in a velvet gown,
    With many rings on her hand.

Her hair was bright as the beaten gold,
    Her lips as coral red,
Her roving eyes were blue and bold,
    And her heart with pride was fed.

For she was proud of her father's ships,
    As she watched them gaily pass;
And pride looked out of her eyes and lips
    When she saw herself in the glass.

"Now come," she said to the captains ten
    Who were ready to put to sea,
"Ye are all my men and my father's men
    And what will ye do for me?"

NARRATIVE POEMS

"Go north and south, go east and west,
  And get me gifts," she said.
"And he who bringeth me home the best,
  With that man will I wed."

So they all fared forth, and sought with care
  In many a famous mart,
For satins and silks and jewels rare,
  To win that lady's heart.

She looked at them all with never a thought,
  And careless put them by;
"I am not fain of the things ye brought,
  Enough of these have I."

The last that came was the head of the fleet,
  His name was Jan Borel;
He bent his knee at the lady's feet,—
  In truth he loved her well.

"I've brought thee home the best i' the world
  A shipful of Danzig corn!"
She stared at him long; her red lips curled,
  Her blue eyes filled with scorn.

"Now out on thee, thou feckless kerl,
  A loon thou art," she said.
"Am I a starving beggar girl?
  Shall I ever lack for bread?"

THE PROUD LADY

"Go empty all thy sacks of grain
  Into the nearest sea,
And never show thy face again
  To make a mock of me."

Young Jan Borel, he answered naught,
  But in the harbour cast
The sacks of golden corn he brought,
  And groaned when fell the last.

Then Jan Borel, he hoisted sail,
  And out to sea he bore;
He passed the Helder in a gale
  And came again no more.

But the grains of corn went drifting down
  Like devil-scattered seed,
To sow the harbour of the town
  With a wicked growth of weed.

The roots were thick and the silt and sand
  Were gathered day by day,
Till not a furlong out from land
  A shoal had barred the way.

Then Stävoren town saw evil years,
  No ships could out or in,
The boats lay rotting at the piers,
  And the mouldy grain in the bin.

NARRATIVE POEMS

The grass-grown streets were all forlorn,
  The town in ruin stood,
The lady's velvet gown was torn,
  Her rings were sold for food.

Her father had perished long ago,
  But the lady held her pride,
She walked with a scornful step and slow,
  Till at last in her rags she died.

Yet still on the crumbling piers of the town
  When the midnight moon shines free,
A woman walks in a velvet gown
  And scatters corn in the sea.

1917.

LYRICS OF
LABOUR AND ROMANCE

A MILE WITH ME

O who will walk a mile with me
  Along life's merry way?
A comrade blithe and full of glee,
Who dares to laugh out loud and free,
And let his frolic fancy play,
Like a happy child, through the flowers gay
That fill the field and fringe the way
  Where he walks a mile with me.

And who will walk a mile with me
  Along life's weary way?
A friend whose heart has eyes to see
The stars shine out o'er the darkening lea,
And the quiet rest at the end o' the day,—
A friend who knows, and dares to say,
The brave, sweet words that cheer the way
  Where he walks a mile with me.

With such a comrade, such a friend,
I fain would walk till journeys end,
Through summer sunshine, winter rain,
And then?—Farewell, we shall meet again!

THE THREE BEST THINGS

I
WORK

Let me but do my work from day to day,
  In field or forest, at the desk or loom,
  In roaring market-place or tranquil room;
Let me but find it in my heart to say,
When vagrant wishes beckon me astray,
  "This is my work; my blessing, not my doom
  "Of all who live, I am the one by whom
"This work can best be done in the right way."

Then shall I see it not too great, nor small,
  To suit my spirit and to prove my powers;
  Then shall I cheerful greet the labouring hours
And cheerful turn, when the long shadows fall
At eventide, to play and love and rest,
Because I know for me my work is best.

THE THREE BEST THINGS

II

LOVE

Let me but love my love without disguise,
  Nor wear a mask of fashion old or new,
  Nor wait to speak till I can hear a clue,
Nor play a part to shine in others' eyes,
Nor bow my knees to what my heart denies;
  But what I am, to that let me be true,
  And let me worship where my love is due,
And so through love and worship let me rise

For love is but the heart's immortal thirst
  To be completely known and all forgiven,
  Even as sinful souls that enter Heaven:
So take me, dear, and understand my worst,
And freely pardon it, because confessed,
And let me find in loving thee, my best.

LABOUR AND ROMANCE

III

LIFE

Let me but live my life from year to year,
  With forward face and unreluctant soul;
  Not hurrying to, nor turning from, the goal;
Not mourning for the things that disappear
In the dim past, nor holding back in fear
  From what the future veils; but with a whole
  And happy heart, that pays its toll
To Youth and Age, and travels on with cheer.

So let the way wind up the hill or down,
  O'er rough or smooth, the journey will be joy
  Still seeking what I sought when but a boy,
New friendship, high adventure, and a crown,
My heart will keep the courage of the quest,
And hope the road's last turn will be the best.

RELIANCE

Not to the swift, the race:
    Not to the strong, the fight:
Not to the righteous, perfect grace
    Not to the wise, the light.

But often faltering feet
    Come surest to the goal;
And they who walk in darkness meet
    The sunrise of the soul.

A thousand times by night
    The Syrian hosts have died;
A thousand times the vanquished right
    Hath risen, glorified.

The truth the wise men sought
    Was spoken by a child;
The alabaster box was brought
    In trembling hands defiled.

Not from my torch, the gleam,
    But from the stars above:
Not from my heart, life's crystal stream
    But from the depths of Love.

DOORS OF DARING

THE mountains that inclose the vale
   With walls of granite, steep and high,
Invite the fearless foot to scale
   Their stairway toward the sky.

The restless, deep, dividing sea
   That flows and foams from shore to shore
Calls to its sunburned chivalry,
   "Push out, set sail, explore!"

The bars of life at which we fret,
   That seem to prison and control,
Are but the doors of daring, set
   Ajar before the soul.

Say not, "Too poor," but freely give;
   Sigh not, "Too weak," but boldly try;
You never can begin to live
   Until you dare to die.

THE CHILD IN THE GARDEN

When to the garden of untroubled thought
　I came of late, and saw the open door,
　And wished again to enter, and explore
The sweet, wild ways with stainless bloom inwrought
And bowers of innocence with beauty fraught,
　It seemed some purer voice must speak before
　I dared to tread that garden loved of yore,
That Eden lost unknown and found unsought.

Then just within the gate I saw a child,—
　A stranger-child, yet to my heart most dear;
He held his hands to me, and softly smiled
　With eyes that knew no shade of sin or fear:
"Come in," he said, "and play awhile with me;
"I am the little child you used to be."

LOVE'S REASON

For that thy face is fair I love thee not;
  Nor yet because thy brown benignant eyes
  Have sudden gleams of gladness and surprise,
Like woodland brooks that cross a sunlit spot:
Nor for thy body, born without a blot,
  And loveliest when it shines with no disguise
  Pure as the star of Eve in Paradise,—
For all these outward things I love thee not:

But for a something in thy form and face,
  Thy looks and ways, of primal harmony;
A certain soothing charm, a vital grace
  That breathes of the eternal womanly,
And makes me feel the warmth of Nature's breast
When in her arms, and thine, I sink to rest.

THE ECHO IN THE HEART

It's little I can tell
  About the birds in books;
And yet I know them well,
  By their music and their looks:
    When May comes down the lane
    Her airy lovers throng
    To welcome her with song,
    And follow in her train:
    Each minstrel weaves his part
    In that wild-flowery strain,
    And I know them all again
    By their echo in my heart.

It's little that I care
  About my darling's place
In books of beauty rare,
  Or heraldries of race:
    For when she steps in view,
    It matters not to me
    What her sweet type may be,
    Of woman, old or new.
    I can't explain the art,
    But I know her for my own,
    Because her lightest tone
    Wakes an echo in my heart.

"UNDINE"

'Twas far away and long ago,
  When I was but a dreaming boy,
This fairy tale of love and woe
  Entranced my heart with tearful joy;
And while with white Undine I wept
  Your spirit,—ah, how strange it seems,—
Was cradled in some star, and slept,
  Unconscious of her coming dreams.

"RENCONTRE"

Oh, was I born too soon, my dear, or were you born too late,
That I am going out the door while you come in the gate?
For you the garden blooms galore, the castle is *en fête;*
You are the coming guest, my dear,—for me the horses wait.

I know the mansion well, my dear, its rooms so rich and wide;
If you had only come before I might have been your guide,
And hand in hand with you explore the treasures that they hide;
But you have come to stay, my dear, and I prepare to ride.

Then walk with me an hour, my dear, and pluck the reddest rose
Amid the white and crimson store with which your garden glows,—
A single rose,—I ask no more of what your love bestows;
It is enough to give, my dear,—a flower to him who goes.

LABOUR AND ROMANCE

The House of Life is yours, my dear, for many and many a day,
But I must ride the lonely shore, the Road to Far Away:
So bring the stirrup-cup and pour a brimming draught, I pray,
And when you take the road, my dear, I'll meet you on the way.

LOVE IN A LOOK

Let me but feel thy look's embrace
  Transparent, pure, and warm,
And I'll not ask to touch thy face,
  Or fold thee in mine arm.
For in thine eyes a girl doth rise,
  Arrayed in candid bliss,
And draws me to her with a charm
  More close than any kiss.

A loving-cup of golden wine,
  Songs of a silver brook,
And fragrant breaths of eglantine,
  Are mingled in thy look.
More fair they are than any star,
  Thy topaz eyes divine—
And deep within their trysting-nook
  Thy spirit blends with mine.

MY APRIL LADY

WHEN down the stair at morning
  The sunbeams round her float,
Sweet rivulets of laughter
  Are rippling in her throat;
The gladness of her greeting
  Is gold without alloy;
And in the morning sunlight
  I think her name is Joy.

When in the evening twilight
  The quiet book-room lies,
We read the sad old ballads,
  While from her hidden eyes
The tears are falling, falling,
  That give her heart relief;
And in the evening twilight,
  I think her name is Grief.

My little April lady,
  Of sunshine and of showers
She weaves the old spring magic,
  And my heart breaks in flowers!
But when her moods are ended,
  She nestles like a dove;
Then, by the pain and rapture,
  I know her name is Love.

A LOVER'S ENVY

I ENVY every flower that blows
Along the meadow where she goes,
  And every bird that sings to her,
  And every breeze that brings to her
    The fragrance of the rose.

I envy every poet's rhyme
That moves her heart at eventime,
  And every tree that wears for her
  Its brightest bloom, and bears for her
    The fruitage of its prime.

I envy every Southern night
That paves her path with moonbeams white
  And silvers all the leaves for her,
  And in their shadow weaves for her
    A dream of dear delight.

I envy none whose love requires
Of her a gift, a task that tires:
  I only long to live to her,
  I only ask to give to her,
    All that her heart desires.

FIRE-FLY CITY

Like a long arrow through the dark the train is darting,
   Bearing me far away, after a perfect day of love's delight:
Wakeful with all the sad-sweet memories of parting,
   I lift the narrow window-shade and look out on the night.

Lonely the land unknown, and like a river flowing,
   Forest and field and hill are gliding backward still athwart my dream;
Till in that country strange, and ever stranger growing,
   A magic city full of lights begins to glow and gleam.

Wide through the landscape dim the lamps are lit in millions;
   Long avenues unfold clear-shining lines of gold across the green;
Clusters and rings of light, and luminous pavilions,—
   Oh, who will tell the city's name, and what these wonders mean?

Why do they beckon me, and what have they to show me?
   Crowds in the blazing street, mirth where the feasters meet, kisses and wine:

FIRE-FLY CITY

Many to laugh with me, but never one to know me:
   A cityful of stranger-hearts and none to beat with mine!

Look how the glittering lines are wavering and lifting,—
   Softly the breeze of night scatters the vision bright:
      and, passing fair,
Over the meadow-grass and through the forest drifting,
The Fire-Fly City of the Dark is lost in empty air!

THE GENTLE TRAVELLER

"Through many a land your journey ran,
   And showed the best the world can boast
Now tell me, traveller, if you can,
   The place that pleased you most."

She laid her hands upon my breast,
   And murmured gently in my ear,
"The place I loved and liked the best
   Was in your arms, my dear!"

NEPENTHE

Yes, it was like you to forget,
And cancel in the welcome of your smile
My deep arrears of debt,
And with the putting forth of both your hands
To sweep away the bars my folly set
Between us—bitter thoughts, and harsh demands
And reckless deeds that seemed untrue
To love, when all the while
My heart was aching through and through
For you, sweet heart, and only you.

Yet, as I turned to come to you again,
I thought there must be many a mile
Of sorrowful reproach to cross,
And many an hour of mutual pain
To bear, until I could make plain
That all my pride was but the fear of loss,
And all my doubt the shadow of despair
To win a heart so innocent and fair;
And even that which looked most ill
Was but the fever-fret and effort vain
To dull the thirst which you alone could still.

But as I turned, the desert miles were crossed,
And when I came, the weary hours were sped!

LABOUR AND ROMANCE

For there you stood beside the open door,
Glad, gracious, smiling as before,
And with bright eyes and tender hands outspread
Restored me to the Eden I had lost.
Never a word of cold reproof,
No sharp reproach, no glances that accuse
The culprit whom they hold aloof,—
Ah, 'tis not thus that other women use
The empire they have won!
For there is none like you, belovèd,—none
Secure enough to do what you have done.
Where did you learn this heavenly art,—
You sweetest and most wise of all that live,—
With silent welcome to impart
Assurance of the royal heart
That never questions where it would forgive?

None but a queen could pardon me like this!
My sovereign lady, let me lay
Within each rosy palm a loyal kiss
Of penitence, then close the fingers up,
Thus—thus! Now give the cup
Of full nepenthe in your crimson mouth,
And come—the garden blooms with bliss,
The wind is in the south,
The rose of love with dew is wet—
Dear, it was like you to forget!

DAY AND NIGHT

How long is the night, brother,
 And how long is the day?
Oh, the day's too short for a happy task,
 And the day's too short for play;
And the night's too short for the bliss of love,—
 For look, how the edge of the sky grows gray
While the stars die out in the blue above,
 And the wan moon fades away.

How short is the day, brother,
 And how short is the night?
Oh, the day's too long for a heavy task,
 And long, long, long is the night,
When the wakeful hours are filled with pain,
 And the sad heart waits for the thing it fears
And sighs for the dawn to come again,—
 The night is a thousand years!

How long is a life, dear God,
 And how fast does it flow?
The measure of life is a flame in the soul:
 It is neither swift nor slow.
But the vision of time is the shadow cast
 By the fleeting world on the body's wall;
When it fades there is neither future nor past,
 But love is all in all.

HESPER

Her eyes are like the evening air
 Her voice is like a rose,
Her lips are like a lovely song,
 That ripples as it flows,
And she herself is sweeter than
 The sweetest thing she knows.

A slender, haunting, twilight form
 Of wonder and surprise,
She seemed a fairy or a child,
 Till, deep within her eyes,
I saw the homeward-leading star
 Of womanhood arise.

ARRIVAL

Across a thousand miles of sea, a hundred leagues of land,
Along a path I had not traced and could not understand,
I travelled fast and far for this,—to take thee by the hand.

A pilgrim knowing not the shrine where he would bend his knee,
A mariner without a dream of what his port would be,
So fared I with a seeking heart until I came to thee.

O cooler than a grove of palm in some heat-weary place,
O fairer than an isle of calm after the wild sea race,
The quiet room adorned with flowers where first I saw thy face!

Then furl the sail, let fall the oar, forget the paths of foam!
The fate that made me wander far at last has brought me home
To thee, dear haven of my heart, and I no more will roam.

DEPARTURE

Oh, why are you shining so bright, big Sun,
   And why is the garden so gay?
Do you know that my days of delight are done,
   Do you know I am going away?
If you covered your face with a cloud, I'd dream
   You were sorry for me in my pain,
And the heavily drooping flowers would seem
   To be weeping with me in the rain.

But why is your head so low, sweet heart,
   And why are your eyes overcast?
Are you crying because you know we must part,
   Do you think this embrace is our last?
Then kiss me again, and again, and again,
   Look up as you bid me good-bye!
For your face is too dear for the stain of a tear,
   And your smile is the sun in my sky.

THE BLACK BIRDS

I

Once, only once, I saw it clear,—
That Eden every human heart has dreamed
A hundred times, but always far away!
Ah, well do I remember how it seemed,
Through the still atmosphere
Of that enchanted day,
To lie wide open to my weary feet:
A little land of love and joy and rest,
With meadows of soft green,
Rosy with cyclamen, and sweet
With delicate breath of violets unseen,—
And, tranquil 'mid the bloom
As if it waited for a coming guest,
A little house of peace and joy and love
Was nested like a snow-white dove.

II

From the rough mountain where I stood,
Homesick for happiness,
Only a narrow valley and a darkling wood
To cross, and then the long distress
Of solitude would be forever past,—
I should be home at last.

LABOUR AND ROMANCE

But not too soon! oh, let me linger here
And feed my eyes, hungry with sorrow,
On all this loveliness, so near,
And mine to-morrow!

III

Then, from the wood, across the silvery blue,
A dark bird flew,
Silent, with sable wings.
Close in his wake another came,—
Fragments of midnight floating through
The sunset flame,—
Another and another, weaving rings
Of blackness on the primrose sky,—
Another, and another, look, a score,
A hundred, yes, a thousand rising heavily
From that accursed, dumb, and ancient wood,
They boiled into the lucid air
Like smoke from some deep caldron of despair!
And more, and more, and ever more,
The numberless, ill-omened brood
Flapping their ragged plumes,
Possessed the landscape and the evening light
With menaces and glooms.
Oh, dark, dark, dark they hovered o'er the place
Where once I saw the little house so white
Amid the flowers, covering every trace

THE BLACK BIRDS

Of beauty from my troubled sight,—
And suddenly it was night!

IV

At break of day I crossed the wooded vale;
And while the morning made
A trembling light among the tree-tops pale,
I saw the sable birds on every limb,
Clinging together closely in the shade,
And croaking placidly their surly hymn.
But, oh, the little land of peace and love
That those night-loving wings had poised above,
Where was it gone?
Lost, lost, forevermore!
Only a cottage, dull and gray,
In the cold light of dawn,
With iron bars across the door:
Only a garden where the drooping head
Of one sad rose, foreboding its decay,
Hung o'er a barren bed:
Only a desolate field that lay
Untilled beneath the desolate day,—
Where Eden seemed to bloom I found but these
So, wondering, I passed along my way,
With anger in my heart, too deep for words,
Against that grove of evil-sheltering trees,
And the black magic of the croaking birds.

WITHOUT DISGUISE

If I have erred in showing all my heart,
   And lost your favour by a lack of pride;
   If standing like a beggar at your side
With naked feet, I have forgot the art
Of those who bargain well in passion's mart,
   And win the thing they want by what they hide
   Be mine the fault as mine the hope denied,
Be mine the lover's and the loser's part.

The sin, if sin it was, I do repent,
   And take the penance on myself alone;
Yet after I have borne the punishment,
   I shall not fear to stand before the throne
Of Love with open heart, and make this plea:
"At least I have not lied to her nor Thee!"

AN HOUR

You only promised me a single hour:
　But in that hour I journeyed through a year
　Of life: the joy of finding you,—the fear
Of losing you again,—the sense of power
To make you all my own,—the sudden shower
　Of tears that came because you were more dear
　Than words could ever tell you,—then,—the clear
Soft rapture when I plucked love's crimson flower.

An hour,—a year,—I felt your bosom rise
　And fall with mystic tides, and saw the gleam
Of undiscovered stars within your eyes,—
　A year,—an hour? I knew not, for the stream
Of love had carried me to Paradise,
　Where all the forms of Time are like a dream.

"RAPPELLE–TOI"

Remember, when the timid light
 Through the enchanted hall of dawn is gleaming;
Remember, when the pensive night
 Beneath her silver-sprinkled veil walks dreaming;
  When pleasure calls thee and thy heart beats high
  When tender joys through evening shades draw nigh
   Hark, from the woodland deeps
   A gentle whisper creeps,
    Remember!

Remember, when the hand of fate
 My life from thine forevermore has parted;
When sorrow, exile, and the weight
 Of lonely years have made me heavy-hearted;
  Think of my loyal love, my last adieu;
  Absence and time are naught, if we are true;
   Long as my heart shall beat,
   To thine it will repeat,
    Remember!

"RAPPELLE-TOI"

Remember, when the cool, dark tomb
  Receives my heart into its quiet keeping,
And some sweet flower begins to bloom
  Above the grassy mound where I am sleeping
    Ah then, my face thou nevermore shalt see
    But still my soul will linger close to thee,
      And in the holy place of night,
      The litany of love recite,—
        Remember!

Freely rendered from the French of Alfred de Musset.

LOVE'S NEARNESS

I THINK of thee when golden sunbeams glimmer
    Across the sea;
And when the waves reflect the moon's pale shimmer
    I think of thee.

I see thy form when down the distant highway
    The dust-clouds rise;
In darkest night, above the mountain by-way
    I see thine eyes.

I hear thee when the ocean-tides returning
    Aloud rejoice;
And on the lonely moor in silence yearning
    I hear thy voice.

I dwell with thee; though thou art far removèd,
    Yet thou art near.
The sun goes down, the stars shine out,—Belovèd
    If thou wert here!

From the German of Goethe, 1898.

TWO SONGS OF HEINE

I

"EIN FICHTENBAUM"

A FIR-TREE standeth lonely
On a barren northern height,
Asleep, while winter covers
His rest with robes of white.

In dreams, he sees a palm-tree
In the golden morning-land;
She droops alone and silent
In burning wastes of sand.

II

"DU BIST WIE EINE BLUME"

Fair art thou as a flower
  And innocent and shy:
I look on thee and sorrow;
  I grieve, I know not why.

I long to lay, in blessing,
  My hand upon thy brow,
And pray that God may keep thee
  As fair and pure as now.

1872.

EIGHT ECHOES FROM THE POEMS OF AUGUSTE ANGELLIER

I

THE IVORY CRADLE

The cradle I have made for thee
Is carved of orient ivory,
And curtained round with wavy silk
More white than hawthorn-bloom or milk.

A twig of box, a lilac spray,
Will drive the goblin-horde away;
And charm thy childlike heart to keep
Her happy dream and virgin sleep.

Within that pure and fragrant nest,
I'll rock thy gentle soul to rest,
With tender songs we need not fear
To have a passing angel hear.

Ah, long and long I fain would hold
The snowy curtain's guardian fold
Around thy crystal visions, born
In clearness of the early morn.

But look, the sun is glowing red
With triumph in his golden bed;

ECHOES FROM AUGUSTE ANGELLIER

Aurora's virgin whiteness dies
In crimson glory of the skies.

The rapid flame will burn its way
Through these white curtains, too, one day;
The ivory cradle will be left
Undone, and broken, and bereft.

LABOUR AND ROMANCE

II

DREAMS

Often I dream your big blue eyes,
   Though loth their meaning to confess,
Regard me with a clear surprise
   Of dawning tenderness.

Often I dream you gladly hear
   The words I hardly dare to breathe,—
The words that falter in their fear
   To tell what throbs beneath.

Often I dream your hand in mine
   Falls like a flower at eventide,
And down the path we leave a line
   Of footsteps side by side.

But ah, in all my dreams of bliss,
   In passion's hunger, fever's drouth,
I never dare to dream of this:
   My lips upon your mouth.

And so I dream your big blue eyes,
   That look on me with tenderness,
Grow wide, and deep, and sad, and wise
   And dim with dear distress.

ECHOES FROM AUGUSTE ANGELLIER

III

THE GARLAND OF SLEEP

A wreath of poppy flowers,
  With leaves of lotus blended,
Is carved on Life's façade of hours,
  From night to night suspended.

Along the columned wall,
  From birth's low portal starting,
It flows, with even rise and fall,
  To death's dark door of parting.

How short each measured arc,
  How brief the columns' number!
The wreath begins and ends in dark,
  And leads from sleep to slumber.

The marble garland seems,
  With braided leaf and bloom,
To deck the palace of our dreams
  As if it were a tomb.

LABOUR AND ROMANCE

IV

TRANQUIL HABIT

Dear tranquil Habit, with her silent hands,
  Doth heal our deepest wounds from day to day
  With cooling, soothing oil, and firmly lay
Around the broken heart her gentle bands.

Her nursing is as calm as Nature's care;
  She doth not weep with us; yet none the less
  Her quiet fingers weave forgetfulness,—
We fall asleep in peace when she is there.

Upon the mirror of the mind her breath
  Is like a cloud, to hide the fading trace
  Of that dear smile, of that remembered face,
Whose presence were the joy and pang of death.

And he who clings to sorrow overmuch,
  Weeping for withered grief, has cause to bless,
  More than all cries of pity and distress,—
Dear tranquil Habit, thy consoling touch!

ECHOES FROM AUGUSTE ANGELLIER

V

THE OLD BRIDGE

On the old, old bridge, with its crumbling stones
All covered with lichens red and gray,
Two lovers were talking in sweet low tones:
    And we were they!

As he leaned to breathe in her willing ear
The love that he vowed would never die,
He called her his darling, his dove most dear:
    And he was I!

She covered her face from the pale moonlight
With her trembling hands, but her eyes looked through
And listened and listened with long delight:
    And she was you!

On the old, old bridge, where the lichens rust,
Two lovers are learning the same old lore;
He tells his love, and she looks her trust:
    But we,—no more!

LABOUR AND ROMANCE

VI

EYES AND LIPS

1

Our silent eyes alone interpreted
   The new-born feeling in the heart of each:
   In yours I read your sorrow without speech,
Your lonely struggle in their tears unshed.
Behind their dreamy sweetness, as a veil,
   I saw the moving lights of trouble shine;
   And then my eyes were brightened as with wine
My spirit reeled to see your face grow pale!

Our deepening love, that is not yet allowed
   Another language than the eyes, doth learn
To speak it perfectly: above the crowd
Our looks exchange avowals and desires,—
   Like wave-divided beacon lights that burn,
And talk to one another by their fires.

2

When I embrace her in a fragrant shrine
   Of climbing roses, my first kiss shall fall
   On you, sweet eyes, that mutely told me all,—
Through you my soul will rise to make her mine.
Upon your drooping lids, blue-veined and fair,
   The touch of tenderness I first will lay,

ECHOES FROM AUGUSTE ANGELLIER

You springs of joy, lights of my gloomy day,
Whose dear discovered secret bade me dare!

And when you open, eyes of my fond dove,
　Your look will shine with new delight, made sure
By this forerunner of a faithful love.
　'Tis just, dear eyes, so pensive and so pure,
That you should bear the sealing kisses true
Of love unhoped that came to me through you.

3

This was my thought; but when beneath the rose
　That hides the lonely bench where lovers rest,
　In friendly dusk I held her on my breast
For one brief moment,—while I saw you close,
Dear, yielding eyes, as if your lids, blue-veined
　And pure, were meekly fain at last to bear
　The proffered homage of my wistful prayer,—
In that high moment, by your grace obtained,

Forgetting your avowals, your alarms,
　Your anguish and your tears, sweet weary eyes,
Forgetting that you gave her to my arms,
I broke my promise; and my first caress,
　Ungrateful, sought her lips in sweet surprise,—
Her lips, which breathed a word of tenderness!

LABOUR AND ROMANCE

VII

AN EVOCATION

When first upon my brow I felt your kiss,
   A sudden splendour filled me, like the ray
That promptly runs to crown the hills with bliss
   Of purple dawn before the golden day,
And ends the gloom it crosses at one leap.
   My brow was not unworthy your caress;
For some foreboding joy had bade me keep
   From all affront the place your lips would bless

Yet when your mouth upon my mouth did lay
   The royal touch, no rapture made me thrill,
   But I remained confused, ashamed, and still.
   Beneath your kiss, my queen without a stain,
I felt,—like ghosts who rise at Judgment Day,—
   A throng of ancient kisses vile and vain!

ECHOES FROM AUGUSTE ANGELLIER

VIII

RESIGNATION

1

Well, you will triumph, dear and noble friend!
   The holy love that wounded you so deep
   Will bring you balm, and on your heart asleep
The fragrant dew of healing will descend.
   Your children,—ah, how quickly they will grow
   Between us, like a wall that fronts the sun,
   Lifting a screen with rosy buds o'errun,
To hide the shaded path where I must go.

You'll walk in light; and dreaming less and less
   Of him who droops in gloom beyond the wall,
Your mother-soul will fill with happiness
   When first you hear your grandchild's babbling call,
Beneath the braided bloom of flower and leaf
That life has wrought to veil your vanished grief.

2

Then I alone shall suffer! I shall bear
   The double burden of our grief alone,
While I enlarge my soul to take your share
   Of pain and hold it close beside my own.
Our love is torn asunder; but the crown
   Of thorns that love has woven I will make

LABOUR AND ROMANCE

My relic sacrosanct, and press it down
  Upon my bleeding heart that will not break.

Ah, that will be the depth of solitude!
  For my regret, that evermore endures,
  Will know that new-born hope has conquered yours
And when the evening comes, no gentle brood
Of wondering children, gathered at my side,
Will soothe away the tears I cannot hide.

Freely rendered from the French, 1911.

RAPPEL D'AMOUR

Come home, my love, come home!
  The twilight is falling,
  The whippoorwill calling,
  The night is very near,
  And the darkness full of fear,
Come home to my arms, come home!

Come home, my love, come home!
  In folly we parted,
  And now, lonely hearted,
  I know you look in vain
  For a love like mine again;
Come home to my arms, come home!

Come home, dear love, come home!
  I've much to forgive you,
  And more yet to give you.
  I'll put a little light
  In the window every night,—
Come home to my arms, come home.

THE RIVER OF DREAMS

The river of dreams runs quietly down
    From its hidden home in the forest of sleep
    With a measureless motion calm and deep;
And my boat slips out on the current brown,
    In a tranquil bay where the trees incline
    Far over the waves, and creepers twine
    Far over the boughs, as if to steep
    Their drowsy bloom in the tide that goes
    By a secret way that no man knows,
Under the branches bending,
Under the shadows blending,
    And the body rests, and the passive soul
    Is drifted along to an unseen goal,
While the river of dreams runs down.

The river of dreams runs gently down,
    With a leisurely flow that bears my bark
    Out of the visionless woods of dark,
Into a glory that seems to crown
    Valley and hill with light from far,
    Clearer than sun or moon or star,
    Luminous, wonderful, weird, oh, mark
    How the radiance pulses everywhere,
    In the shadowless vault of lucid air!
Over the mountains shimmering,
Up from the fountains glimmering,—

THE RIVER OF DREAMS

'Tis the mystical glow of the inner light,
That shines in the very noon of night,
While the river of dreams runs down.

The river of dreams runs murmuring down,
Through the fairest garden that ever grew;
And now, as my boat goes drifting through,
A hundred voices arise to drown
The river's whisper, and charm my ear
With a sound I have often longed to hear,—
A magical music, strange and new,
The wild-rose ballad, the lilac-song,
The virginal chant of the lilies' throng,
Blue-bells silverly ringing,
Pansies merrily singing,—
For all the flowers have found their voice;
And I feel no wonder, but only rejoice,
While the river of dreams runs down.

The river of dreams runs broadening down,
Away from the peaceful garden-shore,
With a current that deepens more and more
By the league-long walls of a mighty town;
And I see the hurrying crowds of men
Gather like clouds and dissolve again;
But never a face I have seen before.
They come and go, they shift and change,
Their ways and looks are wild and strange,—

LABOUR AND ROMANCE

This is a city haunted,
A multitude enchanted!
    At the sight of the throng I am dumb with fear
    And never a sound from their lips I hear,
While the river of dreams runs down.

The river of dreams runs darkly down
    Into the heart of a desolate land,
    With ruined temples half-buried in sand,
And riven hills, whose black brows frown
    Over the shuddering, lonely wave.
    The air grows dim with the dust of the grave;
    No sign of life on the dreary strand;
    No ray of light on the mountain's crest;
    And a weary wind that cannot rest
Comes down the valley creeping,
Lamenting, wailing, weeping,—
    I strive to cry out, but my fluttering breath
    Is choked with the clinging fog of death,
While the river of dreams runs down.

The river of dreams runs trembling down,
    Out of the valley of nameless fear,
    Into a country calm and clear,
With a mystical name of high renown,—
    A name that I know, but may not tell,—
    And there the friends that I loved so well,
    Old companions forever dear,

THE RIVER OF DREAMS

    Come beckoning down to the river shore,
    And hail my boat with the voice of yore.
Fair and sweet are the places
Where I see their unchanged faces!
    And I feel in my heart with a secret thrill,
    That the loved and lost are living still,
While the river of dreams runs down.

The river of dreams runs dimly down
    By a secret way that no man knows;
    But the soul lives on while the river flows
Through the gardens bright and the forests brown
    And I often think that our whole life seems
    To be more than half made up of dreams.
    The changing sights and the passing shows,
    The morning hopes and the midnight fears,
    Are left behind with the vanished years;
Onward, with ceaseless motion,
The life-stream flows to the ocean,
    While we follow the tide, awake or asleep,
    Till we see the dawn on Love's great deep,
    And the shadows melt, and the soul is free,—
    The river of dreams has reached the sea.

1900.

SONGS OF
HEARTH AND ALTAR

A HOME SONG

I READ within a poet's book
    A word that starred the page:
"Stone walls do not a prison make,
    Nor iron bars a cage!"

Yes, that is true, and something more
    You'll find, where'er you roam,
That marble floors and gilded walls
    Can never make a home.

But every house where Love abides,
    And Friendship is a guest,
Is surely home, and home-sweet-home:
    For there the heart can rest.

"LITTLE BOATIE"

A SLUMBER-SONG FOR THE FISHERMAN'S CHILD

Furl your sail, my little boatie;
    Here's the haven still and deep,
Where the dreaming tides in-streaming
    Up the channel creep.
Now the sunset breeze is dying;
Hear the plover, landward flying,
Softly down the twilight crying;
    Come to anchor, little boatie,
    In the port of Sleep.

Far away, my little boatie,
    Roaring waves are white with foam;
Ships are striving, onward driving,
    Day and night they roam.
Father's at the deep-sea trawling,
In the darkness, rowing, hauling,
While the hungry winds are calling,—
    God protect him, little boatie,
    Bring him safely home!

Not for you, my little boatie,
    Is the wide and weary sea;
You're too slender, and too tender,
    You must bide with me.

"LITTLE BOATIE"

All day long you have been straying
Up and down the shore and playing;
Come to harbour, no delaying!
    Day is over, little boatie,
        Night falls suddenly.

Furl your sail, my little boatie,
    Fold your wings, my weary dove.
Dews are sprinkling, stars are twinkling
    Drowsily above.
Cease from sailing, cease from rowing;
Rock upon the dream-tide, knowing
Safely o'er your rest are glowing,
    All the night, my little boatie,
        Harbour-lights of love.

1897.

A MOTHER'S BIRTHDAY

Lord Jesus, Thou hast known
  A mother's love and tender care:
    And Thou wilt hear,
      While for my own
    Mother most dear
      I make this birthday prayer.

Protect her life, I pray,
  Who gave the gift of life to me;
    And may she know,
      From day to day,
    The deepening glow
      Of joy that comes from Thee

As once upon her breast
  Fearless and well content I lay,
    So let her heart,
      On Thee at rest,
    Feel fear depart
      And trouble fade away.

Ah, hold her by the hand,
  As once her hand held mine;
    And though she may
      Not understand
    Life's winding way,
      Lead her in peace divine.

A MOTHER'S BIRTHDAY

I cannot pay my debt
   For all the love that she has given;
   But Thou, love's Lord,
      Wilt not forget
      Her due reward,—
         Bless her in earth and heaven

TRANSFORMATION

ONLY a little shrivelled seed,
It might be flower, or grass, or weed;
Only a box of earth on the edge
Of a narrow, dusty window-ledge;
Only a few scant summer showers;
Only a few clear shining hours;
That was all. Yet God could make
Out of these, for a sick child's sake,
A blossom-wonder, fair and sweet
As ever broke at an angel's feet.

Only a life of barren pain,
Wet with sorrowful tears for rain,
Warmed sometimes by a wandering gleam
Of joy, that seemed but a happy dream;
A life as common and brown and bare
As the box of earth in the window there;
Yet it bore, at last, the precious bloom
Of a perfect soul in that narrow room;
Pure as the snowy leaves that fold
Over the flower's heart of gold.

RENDEZVOUS

I count that friendship little worth
  Which has not many things untold,
  Great longings that no words can hold,
And passion-secrets waiting birth.

Along the slender wires of speech
  Some message from the heart is sent;
  But who can tell the whole that's meant?
Our dearest thoughts are out of reach.

I have not seen thee, though mine eyes
  Hold now the image of thy face;
  In vain, through form, I strive to trace
The soul I love: that deeper lies.

A thousand accidents control
  Our meeting here. Clasp hand in hand,
  And swear to meet me in that land
Where friends hold converse soul to soul.

GRATITUDE

"Do you give thanks for this?—or that?" No, God be
   thanked
         I am not grateful
In that cold, calculating way, with blessings ranked
  As one, two, three, and four,—that would be hateful.

I only know that every day brings good above
         My poor deserving;
I only feel that in the road of Life true Love
  Is leading me along and never swerving.

Whatever gifts and mercies to my lot may fall,
         I would not measure
As worth a certain price in praise, or great or small;
  But take and use them all with simple pleasure.

For when we gladly eat our daily bread, we bless
         The Hand that feeds us;
And when we tread the road of Life in cheerfulness,
  Our very heart-beats praise the Love that leads us.

PEACE

With eager heart and will on fire,
I strove to win my great desire.
"Peace shall be mine," I said; but life
Grew bitter in the barren strife.

My soul was weary, and my pride
Was wounded deep; to Heaven I cried
"God grant me peace or I must die;"
The dumb stars glittered no reply.

Broken at last, I bowed my head,
Forgetting all myself, and said,
"Whatever comes, His will be done;"
And in that moment peace was won.

SANTA CHRISTINA

SAINTS are God's flowers, fragrant souls
　That His own hand hath planted,
Not in some far-off heavenly place,
　Or solitude enchanted,
But here and there and everywhere,—
　In lonely field, or crowded town,
　God sees a flower when He looks down.

Some wear the lily's stainless white,
　And some the rose of passion,
And some the violet's heavenly blue,
　But each in its own fashion,
With silent bloom and soft perfume,
　Is praising Him who from above
　Beholds each lifted face of love.

One such I knew,—and had the grace
　To thank my God for knowing:
The beauty of her quiet life
　Was like a rose in blowing,
So fair and sweet, so all-complete
　And all unconscious, as a flower,
　That light and fragrance were her dower

SANTA CHRISTINA

No convent-garden held this rose,
  Concealed like secret treasure;
No royal terrace guarded her
  For some sole monarch's pleasure.
She made her shrine, this saint of mine,
  In a bright home where children played;
  And there she wrought and there she prayed

In sunshine, when the days were glad,
  She had the art of keeping
The clearest rays, to give again
  In days of rain and weeping;
Her blessed heart could still impart
  Some portion of its secret grace,
  And charity shone in her face.

In joy she grew from year to year;
  And sorrow made her sweeter;
And every comfort, still more kind;
  And every loss, completer.
Her children came to love her name,—
  "Christina,"—'twas a lip's caress;
  And when they called, they seemed to bless.

HEARTH AND ALTAR

No more they call, for she is gone
    Too far away to hear them;
And yet they often breathe her name
    As if she lingered near them;
They cannot reach her with love's speech,
    But when they say "Christina" now
    'Tis like a prayer or like a vow:

A vow to keep her life alive
    In deeds of pure affection,
So that her love shall find in them
    A daily resurrection;
A constant prayer that they may wear
    Some touch of that supernal light
    With which she blossoms in God's sight

THE BARGAIN

What shall I give for thee,
   Thou Pearl of greatest price?
For all the treasures I possess
   Would not suffice.

I give my store of gold;
   It is but earthly dross:
But thou wilt make me rich, beyond
   All fear of loss.

Mine honours I resign;
   They are but small at best:
Thou like a royal star wilt shine
   Upon my breast.

My worldly joys I give,
   The flowers with which I played;
Thy beauty, far more heavenly fair,
   Shall never fade.

Dear Lord, is that enough?
   Nay, not a thousandth part.
Well, then, I have but one thing more
   Take Thou my heart.

TO THE CHILD JESUS

I

THE NATIVITY

Could every time-worn heart but see Thee once again
A happy human child, among the homes of men,
The age of doubt would pass,—the vision of Thy face
Would silently restore the childhood of the race.

II

THE FLIGHT INTO EGYPT

Thou wayfaring Jesus, a pilgrim and stranger,
  Exiled from heaven by love at thy birth,
Exiled again from thy rest in the manger,
  A fugitive child 'mid the perils of earth,—
Cheer with thy fellowship all who are weary,
  Wandering far from the land that they love;
Guide every heart that is homeless and dreary,
  Safe to its home in thy presence above.

BITTER-SWEET

Just to give up, and trust
  All to a Fate unknown,
Plodding along life's road in the dust,
  Bounded by walls of stone;
Never to have a heart at peace;
Never to see when care will cease;
Just to be still when sorrows fall—
This is the bitterest lesson of all.

Just to give up, and rest
  All on a Love secure,
Out of a world that's hard at the best
  Looking to heaven as sure;
Ever to hope, through cloud and fear,
In darkest night, that the dawn is near;
Just to wait at the Master's feet—
Surely, now, the bitter is sweet.

HYMN OF JOY

TO THE MUSIC OF BEETHOVEN'S NINTH SYMPHONY

Joyful, joyful, we adore Thee,
  God of glory, Lord of love;
Hearts unfold like flowers before Thee,
  Praising Thee their sun above.
Melt the clouds of sin and sadness;
  Drive the dark of doubt away;
Giver of immortal gladness,
  Fill us with the light of day!

All Thy works with joy surround Thee,
  Earth and heaven reflect Thy rays,
Stars and angels sing around Thee,
  Centre of unbroken praise:
Field and forest, vale and mountain,
  Blooming meadow, flashing sea,
Chanting bird and flowing fountain,
  Call us to rejoice in Thee.

Thou art giving and forgiving,
  Ever blessing, ever blest,
Well-spring of the joy of living,
  Ocean-depth of happy rest!
Thou our Father, Christ our Brother,—
  All who live in love are Thine:
Teach us how to love each other,
  Lift us to the Joy Divine.

HYMN OF JOY

Mortals join the mighty chorus,
  Which the morning stars began
Father-love is reigning o'er us,
  Brother-love binds man to man
Ever singing march we onward,
  Victors in the midst of strife;
Joyful music lifts us sunward
  In the triumph song of life.

1908.

SONG OF A PILGRIM-SOUL

MARCH on, my soul, nor like a laggard stay!
March swiftly on. Yet err not from the way
Where all the nobly wise of old have trod,—
The path of faith, made by the sons of God.

Follow the marks that they have set beside
The narrow, cloud-swept track, to be thy guide
Follow, and honour what the past has gained,
And forward still, that more may be attained.

Something to learn, and something to forget:
Hold fast the good, and seek the better yet:
Press on, and prove the pilgrim-hope of youth:
The Creeds are milestones on the road to Truth

ODE TO PEACE

I

IN EXCELSIS

Two dwellings, Peace, are thine.
  One is the mountain-height,
Uplifted in the loneliness of light
  Beyond the realm of shadows,—fine,
And far, and clear,—where advent of the night
Means only glorious nearness of the stars,
And dawn unhindered breaks above the bars
That long the lower world in twilight keep.
Thou sleepest not, and hast no need of sleep,
For all thy cares and fears have dropped away;
The night's fatigue, the fever-fret of day,
Are far below thee; and earth's weary wars,
  In vain expense of passion, pass
Before thy sight like visions in a glass,—
Or like the wrinkles of the storm that creep
  Across the sea and leave no trace
Of trouble on that immemorial face,—
So brief appear the conflicts, and so slight
The wounds men give, the things for which they fight!
Here hangs a fortress on the distant steep,—
  A lichen clinging to the rock.
There sails a fleet upon the deep,—

HEARTH AND ALTAR

A wandering flock
Of snow-winged gulls. And yonder, in the plain,
A marble palace shines,—a grain
Of mica glittering in the rain.
Beneath thy feet the clouds are rolled
By voiceless winds: and far between
The rolling clouds, new shores and peaks are seen
In shimmering robes of green and gold,
And faint aerial hue
That silent fades into the silent blue.
Thou, from thy mountain-hold,
All day in tranquil wisdom looking down
On distant scenes of human toil and strife,
All night, with eyes aware of loftier life
Uplifted to the sky where stars are sown,
Dost watch the everlasting fields grow white
Unto the harvest of the sons of light,
And welcome to thy dwelling-place sublime
The few strong souls that dare to climb
The slippery crags, and find thee on the height.

II

DE PROFUNDIS

But in the depth thou hast another home,
For hearts less daring, or more frail.
Thou dwellest also in the shadowy vale;
And pilgrim-souls that roam

ODE TO PEACE

With weary feet o'er hill and dale,
Bearing the burden and the heat
    Of toilful days,
    Turn from the dusty ways
To find thee in thy green and still retreat.

Here is no vision wide outspread
Before the lonely and exalted seat
Of all-embracing knowledge. Here, instead,
A little cottage, and a garden-nook,
    With outlooks brief and sweet
Across the meadows, and along the brook,—
    A little stream that nothing knows
Of the great sea to which it gladly flows,—
A little field that bears a little wheat
To make a portion of earth's daily bread.

    The vast cloud-armies overhead
    Are marshalled, and the wild wind blows
    Its trumpet, but thou canst not tell
Whence comes the wind nor where it goes;
Nor dost thou greatly care, since all is well.

    Thy daily task is done,
And now the wages of repose are won.
Here friendship lights the fire, and every heart
Sure of itself and sure of all the rest,
Dares to be true, and gladly takes its part
In open converse, bringing forth its best:
And here is music, melting every chain
    Of lassitude and pain:

HEARTH AND ALTAR

And here, at last, is sleep with silent gifts,—
    Kind sleep, the tender nurse who lifts
The soul grown weary of the waking world,
    And lays it, with its thoughts all furled
Its fears forgotten, and its passions still,
On the deep bosom of the Eternal Will.

THREE PRAYERS FOR SLEEP AND WAKING

I

BEDTIME

Ere thou sleepest gently lay
Every troubled thought away:
Put off worry and distress
As thou puttest off thy dress:
Drop thy burden and thy care
In the quiet arms of prayer.

Lord, Thou knowest how I live,
All I've done amiss forgive:
All of good I've tried to do,
Strengthen, bless, and carry through:
All I love in safety keep,
While in Thee I fall asleep.

HEARTH AND ALTAR

II

NIGHT WATCH

If slumber should forsake
  Thy pillow in the dark,
  Fret not thyself to mark
How long thou liest awake.
There is a better way;
  Let go the strife and strain,
  Thine eyes will close again,
If thou wilt only pray.

Lord, Thy peaceful gift restore,
Give my body sleep once more:
While I wait my soul will rest
Like a child upon Thy breast.

THREE PRAYERS

III

NEW DAY

Ere thou risest from thy bed,
Speak to God Whose wings were spread
O'er thee in the helpless night:
Lo, He wakes thee now with light!
Lift thy burden and thy care
In the mighty arms of prayer.

Lord, the newness of this day
Calls me to an untried way :
Let me gladly take the road,
Give me strength to bear my load,
Thou my guide and helper be—
I will travel through with Thee.

The Mission Inn, California, Easter, 1913.

PORTRAIT AND REALITY

If on the closèd curtain of my sight
  My fancy paints thy portrait far away,
  I see thee still the same, by night or day;
Crossing the crowded street, or moving bright
'Mid festal throngs, or reading by the light
  Of shaded lamp some friendly poet's lay,
  Or shepherding the children at their play,—
The same sweet self, and my unchanged delight.

But when I see thee near, I recognize
  In every dear familiar way some strange
Perfection, and behold in April guise
  The magic of thy beauty that doth range
Through many moods with infinite surprise,—
  Never the same, and sweeter with each change

THE WIND OF SORROW

The fire of love was burning, yet so low
    That in the peaceful dark it made no rays,
    And in the light of perfect-placid days
The ashes hid the smouldering embers' glow.
Vainly, for love's delight, we sought to throw
    New pleasures on the pyre to make it blaze:
    In life's calm air and tranquil-prosperous ways
We missed the radiant heat of long ago.

Then in the night, a night of sad alarms,
    Bitter with pain and black with fog of fears
That drove us trembling to each other's arms,
    Across the gulf of darkness and salt tears
Into life's calm the wind of sorrow came,
And fanned the fire of love to clearest flame.

HIDE AND SEEK

I

ALL the trees are sleeping, all the winds are still,
All the fleecy flocks of cloud, gone beyond the hill;
Through the noon-day silence, down the woods of June
Hark, a little hunter's voice, running with a tune.
    "Hide and seek!
    "When I speak,
    "You must answer me:
    "Call again,
    "Merry men,
   "Coo-ee, coo-ee, coo-ee!"

Now I hear his footsteps rustling in the grass:
Hidden in my leafy nook, shall I let him pass?
Just a low, soft whistle,—quick the hunter turns,
Leaps upon me laughing loud, rolls me in the ferns.
    "Hold him fast,
    "Caught at last!
    "Now you're it, you see.
    "Hide your eye,
    "Till I cry,
   Coo-ee, coo-ee, coo-ee!"

HIDE AND SEEK

II

Long ago he left me, long and long ago;
Now I wander thro' the world, seeking high and low.
Hidden safe and happy, in some pleasant place,—
If I could but hear his voice, soon I'd see his face!
    Far away,
    Many a day,
    Where can Barney be?
    Answer, dear,
    Don't you hear?
   Coo-ee, coo-ee, coo-ee!

Birds that every spring-time sung him full of joy,
Flowers he loved to pick for me, mind me of my boy
Somewhere he is waiting till my steps come nigh;
Love may hide itself awhile, but love can never die.
    Heart, be glad,
    The little lad
    Will call again to thee:
    "Father dear,
    "Heaven is here,
   "Coo-ee, coo-ee, coo-ee!"

1898.

AUTUMN IN THE GARDEN

When the frosty kiss of Autumn in the dark
    Makes its mark
On the flowers, and the misty morning grieves
    Over fallen leaves;
Then my olden garden, where the golden soil
    Through the toil
Of a hundred years is mellow, rich, and deep,
    Whispers in its sleep.

'Mid the crumpled beds of marigold and phlox,
    Where the box
Borders with its glossy green the ancient walks,
    There's a voice that talks
Of the human hopes that bloomed and withered here
    Year by year,—
And the dreams that brightened all the labouring hours,
    Fading as the flowers.

Yet the whispered story does not deepen grief;
    But relief
For the loneliness of sorrow seems to flow
    From the Long-Ago,
When I think of other lives that learned, like mine,
    To resign,
And remember that the sadness of the fall
    Comes alike to all.

AUTUMN IN THE GARDEN

What regrets, what longings for the lost were theirs
        And what prayers
For the silent strength that nerves us to endure
        Things we cannot cure!
Pacing up and down the garden where they paced,
        I have traced
All their well-worn paths of patience, till I find
        Comfort in my mind.

Faint and far away their ancient griefs appear:
        Yet how near
Is the tender voice, the careworn, kindly face,
        Of the human race!
Let us walk together in the garden, dearest heart,—
        Not apart!
They who know the sorrows other lives have known
        Never walk alone.

October, 1903.

THE MESSAGE

WAKING from tender sleep,
  My neighbour's little child
Put out his baby hand to me,
  Looked in my face, and smiled.

It seems as if he came
  Home from a happy land,
To bring a message to my heart
  And make me understand.

Somewhere, among bright dreams,
  A child that once was mine
Has whispered wordless love to him,
  And given him a sign.

Comfort of kindly speech,
  And counsel of the wise,
Have helped me less than what I read
  In those deep-smiling eyes.

Sleep sweetly, little friend,
  And dream again of heaven:
With double love I kiss your hand,—
  Your message has been given.

November, 1903.

DULCIS MEMORIA

LONG, long ago I heard a little song,
  (Ah, was it long ago, or yesterday?)
So lowly, slowly wound the tune along,
  That far into my heart it found the way:
A melody consoling and endearing;
And now, in silent hours, I'm often hearing
  The small, sweet song that does not die away.

Long, long ago I saw a little flower—
  (Ah, was it long ago, or yesterday?)
So fair of face and fragrant for an hour,
  That something dear to me it seemed to say,—
A wordless joy that blossomed into being;
And now, in winter days, I'm often seeing
  The friendly flower that does not fade away.

Long, long ago we had a little child,—
  (Ah, was it long ago, or yesterday?)
Into his mother's eyes and mine he smiled
  Unconscious love; warm in our arms he lay.
An angel called! Dear heart, we could not hold him
Yet secretly your arms and mine infold him—
  Our little child who does not go away.

HEARTH AND ALTAR

Long, long ago? Ah, memory, make it clear—
  (It was not long ago, but yesterday,)
So little and so helpless and so dear—
  Let not the song be lost, the flower decay!
His voice, his waking eyes, his gentle sleeping:
The smallest things are safest in thy keeping,—
  Sweet memory, keep our child with us alway

November, 1903.

THE WINDOW

ALL night long, by a distant bell
    The passing hours were notched
On the dark, while her breathing rose and fell;
    And the spark of life I watched
In her face was glowing, or fading,—who could tell?—
    And the open window of the room,
        With a flare of yellow light,
    Was peering out into the gloom,
        Like an eye that searched the night.

Oh, what do you see in the dark, little window, and why do you peer?
"I see that the garden is crowded with creeping forms of fear:
Little white ghosts in the locust-tree, wave in the night-wind's breath,
And low in the leafy laurels the lurking shadow of death."

Sweet, clear notes of a waking bird
    Told of the passing away
Of the dark,—and my darling may have heard;
    For she smiled in her sleep, while the ray
Of the rising dawn spoke joy without a word,
    Till the splendour born in the east outburned
        The yellow lamplight, pale and thin,
    And the open window slowly turned
        To the eye of the morning, looking in.

HEARTH AND ALTAR

*Oh, what do you see in the room, little window, that makes
  you so bright?*
*"I see that a child is asleep on her pillow, soft and white:
With the rose of life on her lips, the pulse of life in her breast,
And the arms of God around her, she quietly takes her rest."*

Neuilly, June, 1909.

CHRISTMAS TEARS

The day returns by which we date our years:
Day of the joy of giving,—that means love;
Day of the joy of living,—that means hope;
Day of the Royal Child,—and day that brings
To older hearts the gift of Christmas tears!

Look, how the candles twinkle through the tree,
The children shout when baby claps his hands,
The room is full of laughter and of song!
Your lips are smiling, dearest,—tell me why
Your eyes are brimming full of Christmas tears?

Was it a silent voice that joined the song?
A vanished face that glimmered once again
Among the happy circle round the tree?
Was it an unseen hand that touched your cheek
And brought the secret gift of Christmas tears?

Not dark and angry like the winter storm
Of selfish grief,—but full of starry gleams,
And soft and still that others may not weep,—
Dews of remembered happiness descend
To bless us with the gift of Christmas tears.

HEARTH AND ALTAR

Ah, lose them not, dear heart,—life has no pearls
More pure than memories of joy love-shared.
See, while we count them one by one with prayer
The Heavenly hope that lights the Christmas tree
Has made a rainbow in our Christmas tears!
1912.

DOROTHEA

1888–1912

A DEEPER crimson in the rose,
A deeper blue in sky and sea,
And ever, as the summer goes,
A deeper loss in losing thee!

A deeper music in the strain
Of hermit-thrush from lonely tree;
And deeper grows the sense of gain
My life has found in having thee.

A deeper love, a deeper rest,
A deeper joy in all I see;
And ever deeper in my breast
A silver song that comes from thee!

Seal Harbour, August 1, 1912.

EPIGRAMS, GREETINGS, AND INSCRIPTIONS

FOR KATRINA'S SUN-DIAL

IN HER GARDEN OF YADDO

   Hours fly,
   Flowers die
   New days,
   New ways,
   Pass by.
   Love stays.

   Time is
Too Slow for those who Wait,
Too Swift for those who Fear,
Too Long for those who Grieve,
Too Short for those who Rejoice
  But for those who Love,
   Time is not.

FOR KATRINA'S WINDOW

IN HER TOWER OF YADDO

THIS is the window's message,
    In silence, to the Queen:
"Thou hast a double kingdom
    And I am set between:
Look out and see the glory,
    On hill and plain and sky:
Look in and see the light of love
    That nevermore shall die!"

L'ENVOI

Window in the Queen's high tower,
This shall be thy magic power!
Shut the darkness and the doubt,
Shut the storm and conflict, out;
Wind and hail and snow and rain
Dash against thee all in vain.
Let in nothing from the night,—
Let in every ray of light!

FOR THE FRIENDS AT HURSTMONT

THE HOUSE

The cornerstone in Truth is laid,
The guardian walls of Honour made,
The roof of Faith is built above,
The fire upon the hearth is Love:
Though rains descend and loud winds call,
This happy house shall never fall.

THE HEARTH

When the logs are burning free,
Then the fire is full of glee:
When each heart gives out its best,
Then the talk is full of zest:
Light your fire and never fear,
Life was made for love and cheer.

THE DOOR

The lintel low enough to keep out pomp and pride:
The threshold high enough to turn deceit aside:
The fastening strong enough from robbers to defend:
This door will open at a touch to welcome every friend

EPIGRAMS AND GREETINGS

THE DIAL

Time can never take
  What Time did not give;
When my shadows have all passed,
  You shall live.

THE SUN-DIAL AT MORVEN

FOR BAYARD AND HELEN STOCKTON

Two hundred years of blessing I record
For Morven's house, protected by the Lord:
And still I stand among old-fashioned flowers
To mark for Morven many sunlit hours.

THE SUN-DIAL AT WELLS COLLEGE

FOR THE CLASS OF 1904

The shadow by my finger cast
Divides the future from the past:
Before it, sleeps the unborn hour,
In darkness, and beyond thy power:
Behind its unreturning line,
The vanished hour, no longer thine:
One hour alone is in thy hands,—
The NOW on which the shadow stands.

March, 1904.

TO MARK TWAIN

I

AT A BIRTHDAY FEAST

With memories old and wishes new
We crown our cups again,
And here's to you, and here's to you
With love that ne'er shall wane!
And may you keep, at sixty-seven,
The joy of earth, the hope of heaven,
And fame well-earned, and friendship true,
And peace that comforts every pain,
And faith that fights the battle through,
And all your heart's unbounded wealth,
And all your wit, and all your health,—
Yes, here's a hearty health to you,
And here's to you, and here's to you,
Long life to you, Mark Twain.

November 30, 1902.

II

AT THE MEMORIAL MEETING

We knew you well, dear Yorick of the West,
The very soul of large and friendly jest!
You loved and mocked the broad grotesque of things
In this new world where all the folk are kings.

TO MARK TWAIN

Your breezy humour cleared the air, with sport
Of shams that haunt the democratic court;
For even where the sovereign people rule,
A human monarch needs a royal fool.

Your native drawl lent flavour to your wit;
Your arrows lingered but they always hit;
Homeric mirth around the circle ran,
But left no wound upon the heart of man.

We knew you kind in trouble, brave in pain;
We saw your honour kept without a stain;
We read this lesson of our Yorick's years,—
True wisdom comes with laughter and with tears

November 30, 1910.

STARS AND THE SOUL

(TO CHARLES A. YOUNG, ASTRONOMER)

"Two things," the wise man said, "fill me with awe
The starry heavens and the moral law."
Nay, add another wonder to thy roll,—
The living marvel of the human soul!

Born in the dust and cradled in the dark,
It feels the fire of an immortal spark,
And learns to read, with patient, searching eyes,
The splendid secret of the unconscious skies.

For God thought Light before He spoke the word;
The darkness understood not, though it heard:
But man looks up to where the planets swim,
And thinks God's thoughts of glory after Him.

What knows the star that guides the sailor's way,
Or lights the lover's bower with liquid ray,
Of toil and passion, danger and distress,
Brave hope, true love, and utter faithfulness?

But human hearts that suffer good and ill,
And hold to virtue with a loyal will,
Adorn the law that rules our mortal strife
With star-surpassing victories of life.

STARS AND THE SOUL

So take our thanks, dear reader of the skies
Devout astronomer, most humbly wise,
For lessons brighter than the stars can give,
And inward light that helps us all to live.

TO JULIA MARLOWE

(READING KEATS' ODE ON A GRECIAN URN)

Long had I loved this "Attic shape," the brede
 Of marble maidens round this urn divine:
But when your golden voice began to read,
 The empty urn was filled with Chian wine.

TO JOSEPH JEFFERSON

May 4th, 1898.—To-day, fishing down the Swiftwater, I found Joseph Jefferson on a big rock in the middle of the brook, casting the fly for trout. He said he had fished this very stream three-and-forty years ago; and near by, in the Paradise Valley, he wrote his famous play.—Leaf from my Diary.

We met on Nature's stage,
 And May had set the scene,
With bishop-caps standing in delicate ranks,
And violets blossoming over the banks,
 While the brook ran full between.

The waters rang your call,
 With frolicsome waves a-twinkle,—
They knew you as boy, and they knew you as man,
And every wave, as it merrily ran,
 Cried, "Enter Rip van Winkle!"

THE MOCKING-BIRD

In mirth he mocks the other birds at noon,
Catching the lilt of every easy tune;
But when the day departs he sings of love,—
His own wild song beneath the listening moon.

THE EMPTY QUATRAIN

A FLAWLESS cup: how delicate and fine
The flowing curve of every jewelled line!
Look, turn it up or down, 'tis perfect still,—
But holds no drop of life's heart-warming wine

PAN LEARNS MUSIC

FOR A SCULPTURE BY SARA GREENE

LIMBER-LIMBED, lazy god, stretched on the rock,
Where is sweet Echo, and where is your flock?
What are you making here? "Listen," said Pan
"Out of a river-reed music for man!"

THE SHEPHERD OF NYMPHS

THE nymphs a shepherd took
To guard their snowy sheep;
He led them down along the brook,
And guided them with pipe and crook,
    Until he fell asleep.

But when the piping stayed,
Across the flowery mead
The milk-white nymphs ran out afraid:
O Thyrsis, wake! Your flock has strayed,—
    The nymphs a shepherd need.

ECHOES FROM THE GREEK ANTHOLOGY

I

STARLIGHT

With two bright eyes, my star, my love,
Thou lookest on the stars above:
Ah, would that I the heaven might be
With a million eyes to look on thee.

Plato.

II

ROSELEAF

A little while the rose,
And after that the thorn;
An hour of dewy morn,
And then the glamour goes.
Ah, love in beauty born,
A little while the rose!

Unknown.

EPIGRAMS AND GREETINGS

III

PHOSPHOR—HESPER

O morning star, farewell!
My love I now must leave;
The hours of day I slowly tell,
And turn to her with the twilight bell,
O welcome, star of eve!

Meleager.

IV

SEASONS

Sweet in summer, cups of snow,
Cooling thirsty lips aglow;
Sweet to sailors winter-bound,
Spring arrives with garlands crowned
Sweeter yet the hour that covers
With one cloak a pair of lovers,
Living lost in golden weather,
While they talk of love together.

Asclepiades.

ECHOES FROM GREEK ANTHOLOGY

V

THE VINE AND THE GOAT

Although you eat me to the root,
I yet shall bear enough of fruit
For wine to sprinkle your dim eyes,
When you are made a sacrifice.

Euenus.

VI

THE PROFESSOR

Seven pupils, in the class
Of Professor Callias,
Listen silent while he drawls,—
Three are benches, four are walls.

Unknown.

ONE WORLD

*"The worlds in which we live are two:
The world 'I am' and the world 'I do.'"*

The worlds in which we live at heart are one,
The world "I am," the fruit of "I have done";
And underneath these worlds of flower and fruit,
The world "I love,"—the only living root.

JOY AND DUTY

"Joy is a Duty,"—so with golden lore
The Hebrew rabbis taught in days of yore,
And happy human hearts heard in their speech
Almost the highest wisdom man can reach.

But one bright peak still rises far above,
And there the Master stands whose name is Love
Saying to those whom weary tasks employ:
"Life is divine when Duty is a Joy."

THE PRISON AND THE ANGEL

Self is the only prison that can ever bind the soul;
Love is the only angel who can bid the gates unroll;
And when he comes to call thee, arise and follow fast;
His way may lie through darkness, but it leads to light
    at last.

THE WAY

Who seeks for heaven alone to save his soul,
May keep the path, but will not reach the goal;
While he who walks in love may wander far,
But God will bring him where the Blessed are.

LOVE AND LIGHT

There are many kinds of love, as many kinds of light,
And every kind of love makes a glory in the night.
There is love that stirs the heart, and love that gives it rest,
But the love that leads life upward is the noblest and the best.

FACTA NON VERBA

Deeds not Words: I say so too!
And yet I find it somehow true,
A word may help a man in need,
To nobler act and braver deed.

FOUR THINGS

Four things a man must learn to do
If he would make his record true:
To think without confusion clearly;
To love his fellow-men sincerely;
To act from honest motives purely;
To trust in God and Heaven securely.

THE GREAT RIVER

"In la sua volontade è nostra pace."

O mighty river! strong, eternal Will,
Wherein the streams of human good and ill
Are onward swept, conflicting, to the sea!
The world is safe because it floats in Thee.

INSCRIPTION FOR A TOMB IN ENGLAND

READ here, O friend unknown,
   Our grief, of her bereft;
Yet think not tears alone
   Within our hearts are left.
The gifts she came to give,
   Her heavenly love and cheer,
Have made us glad to live
   And die without a fear.

1912.

"THE SIGNS"

Dedicated to the Zodiac Club

Who knows how many thousand years ago
The twelvefold Zodiac was made to show
The course of stars above and men below?

The great sun plows his furrow by its "lines":
From all its "houses" mystic meaning shines:
Deep lore of life is written in its "signs."

Aries—Sacrifice.
Snow-white and sacred is the sacrifice
That Heaven demands for what our heart doth prize
The man who fears to suffer, ne'er can rise.

Taurus—Strength.
Rejoice, my friend, if God has made you strong:
Put forth your force to move the world along:
Yet never shame your strength to do a wrong.

Gemini—Brotherhood.
Bitter his life who lives for self alone,
Poor would he be with riches and a throne:
But friendship doubles all we are and own.

EPIGRAMS AND GREETINGS

Cancer—The Wisdom of Retreat.
Learn from the crab, O runner fresh and fleet,
Sideways to move, or backward, when discreet;
Life is not all advance,—sometimes retreat!

Leo—Fire.
The sign of Leo is the sign of fire.
Hatred we hate: but no man should desire
A heart too cold to flame with righteous ire.

Virgo—Love.
Mysterious symbol, words are all in vain
To tell the secret power by which you reign.
The more we love, the less we can explain.

Libra—Justice.
Examine well the scales with which you weigh;
Let justice rule your conduct every day;
For when you face the Judge you'll need fair play

Scorpio—Self-Defense.
There's not a creature in the realm of night
But has the wish to live, likewise the right:
Don't tread upon the scorpion, or he'll fight.

Sagittarius—The Archer.
Life is an arrow, therefore you must know
What mark to aim at, how to use the bow,—
Then draw it to the head and let it go!

"THE SIGNS"

Capricornus—The Goat.
The goat looks solemn, yet he likes to run,
And leap the rocks, and gambol in the sun:
The truly wise enjoy a little fun.

Aquarius—Water.
"Like water spilt upon the ground,"—alas,
Our little lives flow swiftly on and pass;
Yet may they bring rich harvests and green grass!

Pisces—The Fishes.
Last of the sacred signs, you bring to me
A word of hope, a word of mystery,—
We all are swimmers in God's mighty sea.

February 28, 1918.

PRO PATRIA

PATRIA

I WOULD not even ask my heart to say
  If I could love another land as well
  As thee, my country, had I felt the spell
Of Italy at birth, or learned to obey
The charm of France, or England's mighty sway
  I would not be so much an infidel
  As once to dream, or fashion words to tell,
What land could hold my heart from thee away

For like a law of nature in my blood,
  America, I feel thy sovereignty,
    And woven through my soul thy vital sign.
My life is but a wave and thou the flood;
  I am a leaf and thou the mother-tree;
    Nor should I be at all, were I not thine.

June, 1904.

AMERICA

I LOVE thine inland seas,
Thy groves of giant trees,
  Thy rolling plains;
Thy rivers' mighty sweep,
Thy mystic canyons deep,
Thy mountains wild and steep
  All thy domains;

Thy silver Eastern strands,
Thy Golden Gate that stands
  Wide to the West;
Thy flowery Southland fair,
Thy sweet and crystal air,—
O land beyond compare,
  Thee I love best!

March, 1906.

THE ANCESTRAL DWELLINGS

Dear to my heart are the ancestral dwellings of America,
Dearer than if they were haunted by ghosts of royal splendour;
They are simple enough to be great in their friendly dignity,—
Homes that were built by the brave beginners of a nation.

I love the old white farmhouses nestled in New England valleys,
Ample and long and low, with elm-trees feathering over them:
Borders of box in the yard, and lilacs, and old-fashioned roses,
A fan-light above the door, and little square panes in the windows,
The wood-shed piled with maple and birch and hickory ready for winter,
The gambrel-roof with its garret crowded with household relics,—
All the tokens of prudent thrift and the spirit of self-reliance.

I love the weather-beaten, shingled houses that front the ocean;
They seem to grow out of the rocks, there is something indomitable about them:

PRO PATRIA

Their backs are bowed, and their sides are covered with lichens;
Soft in their colour as gray pearls, they are full of a patient courage.
Facing the briny wind on a lonely shore they stand undaunted,
While the thin blue pennant of smoke from the square-built chimney
Tells of a haven for man, with room for a hearth and a cradle.

I love the stately southern mansions with their tall white columns,
They look through avenues of trees, over fields where the cotton is growing;
I can see the flutter of white frocks along their shady porches,
Music and laughter float from the windows, the yards are full of hounds and horses.
Long since the riders have ridden away, yet the houses have not forgotten,
They are proud of their name and place, and their doors are always open,
For the thing they remember best is the pride of their ancient hospitality.

THE ANCESTRAL DWELLINGS

In the towns I love the discreet and tranquil Quaker dwellings,
With their demure brick faces and immaculate marble doorsteps;
And the gabled houses of the Dutch, with their high stoops and iron railings,
(I can see their little brass knobs shining in the morning sunlight);
And the solid self-contained houses of the descendants of the Puritans,
Frowning on the street with their narrow doors and dormer-windows;
And the triple-galleried, many-pillared mansions of Charleston,
Standing open sideways in their gardens of roses and magnolias.

Yes, they are all dear to my heart, and in my eyes they are beautiful;
For under their roofs were nourished the thoughts that have made the nation;
The glory and strength of America come from her ancestral dwellings.

July, 1909.

HUDSON'S LAST VOYAGE

THE SHALLOP ON HUDSON BAY

June 22, 1611

ONE sail in sight upon the lonely sea,
And only one! For never ship but mine
Has dared these waters. We were first,
My men, to battle in between the bergs
And floes to these wide waves. This gulf is mine
I name it! and that flying sail is mine!
And there, hull-down below that flying sail,
The ship that staggers home is mine, mine, mine!
My ship *Discoverie!*

       The sullen dogs
Of mutineers, the bitches' whelps that snatched
Their food and bit the hand that nourished them
Have stolen her. You ingrate Henry Greene,
I picked you from the gutter of Houndsditch,
And paid your debts, and kept you in my house,
And brought you here to make a man of you!
You Robert Juet, ancient, crafty man,
Toothless and tremulous, how many times
Have I employed you as a master's mate
To give you bread? And you Abacuck Prickett,
You sailor-clerk, you salted puritan,
You knew the plot and silently agreed,
Salving your conscience with a pious lie!

HUDSON'S LAST VOYAGE

Yes, all of you—hounds, rebels, thieves! Bring back
My ship!

        Too late,—I rave,—they cannot hear
My voice: and if they heard, a drunken laugh
Would be their answer; for their minds have caught
The fatal firmness of the fool's resolve,
That looks like courage but is only fear.
They'll blunder on, and lose my ship, and drown;
Or blunder home to England and be hanged.
Their skeletons will rattle in the chains
Of some tall gibbet on the Channel cliffs,
While passing mariners look up and say:
"Those are the rotten bones of Hudson's men
"Who left their captain in the frozen North!"

O God of justice, why hast Thou ordained
Plans of the wise and actions of the brave
Dependent on the aid of fools and cowards?

Look,—there she goes,—her topsails in the sun
Gleam from the ragged ocean edge, and drop
Clean out of sight! So let the traitors go
Clean out of mind! We'll think of braver things!
Come closer in the boat, my friends. John King,
You take the tiller, keep her head nor'west.
You Philip Staffe, the only one who chose
Freely to share our little shallop's fate,
Rather than travel in the hell-bound ship,—

PRO PATRIA

Too good an English sailor to desert
Your crippled comrades,—try to make them rest
More easy on the thwarts. And John, my son,
My little shipmate, come and lean your head
Against my knee. Do you remember still
The April morn in Ethelburga's church,
Five years ago, when side by side we kneeled
To take the sacrament with all our men,
Before the *Hopewell* left St. Catherine's docks
On our first voyage? It was then I vowed
My sailor-soul and yours to search the sea
Until we found the water-path that leads
From Europe into Asia.
                        I believe
That God has poured the ocean round His world,
Not to divide, but to unite the lands.
And all the English captains that have dared
In little ships to plough uncharted waves,—
Davis and Drake, Hawkins and Frobisher,
Raleigh and Gilbert,—all the other names,—
Are written in the chivalry of God
As men who served His purpose. I would claim
A place among that knighthood of the sea;
And I have earned it, though my quest should fail!
For, mark me well, the honour of our life
Derives from this: to have a certain aim
Before us always, which our will must seek
Amid the peril of uncertain ways.

HUDSON'S LAST VOYAGE

Then, though we miss the goal, our search is crowned
With courage, and we find along our path
A rich reward of unexpected things.
Press towards the aim: take fortune as it fares!

I know not why, but something in my heart
Has always whispered, "Westward seek your goal!"
Three times they sent me east, but still I turned
The bowsprit west, and felt among the floes
Of ruttling ice along the Greenland coast,
And down the rugged shore of Newfoundland,
And past the rocky capes and wooded bays
Where Gosnold sailed,—like one who feels his way
With outstretched hand across a darkened room,—
I groped among the inlets and the isles,
To find the passage to the Land of Spice.
I have not found it yet,—but I have found
Things worth the finding!
      Son, have you forgot
Those mellow autumn days, two years ago,
When first we sent our little ship *Half-Moon*,—
The flag of Holland floating at her peak,—
Across a sandy bar, and sounded in
Among the channels, to a goodly bay
Where all the navies of the world could ride?
A fertile island that the redmen called
Manhattan, lay above the bay: the land
Around was bountiful and friendly fair.

PRO PATRIA

But never land was fair enough to hold
The seaman from the calling of the sea.
And so we bore to westward of the isle,
Along a mighty inlet, where the tide
Was troubled by a downward-flowing flood
That seemed to come from far away,—perhaps
From some mysterious gulf of Tartary?
Inland we held our course; by palisades
Of naked rock; by rolling hills adorned
With forests rich in timber for great ships;
Through narrows where the mountains shut us in
With frowning cliffs that seemed to bar the stream
And then through open reaches where the banks
Sloped to the water gently, with their fields
Of corn and lentils smiling in the sun.
Ten days we voyaged through that placid land,
Until we came to shoals, and sent a boat
Upstream to find,—what I already knew,—
We travelled on a river, not a strait.

But what a river! God has never poured
A stream more royal through a land more rich.
Even now I see it flowing in my dream,
While coming ages people it with men
Of manhood equal to the river's pride.
I see the wigwams of the redmen changed
To ample houses, and the tiny plots
Of maize and green tobacco broadened out

HUDSON'S LAST VOYAGE

To prosperous farms, that spread o'er hill and dale
The many-coloured mantle of their crops.
I see the terraced vineyard on the slope
Where now the fox-grape loops its tangled vine,
And cattle feeding where the red deer roam,
And wild-bees gathered into busy hives
To store the silver comb with golden sweet;
And all the promised land begins to flow
With milk and honey. Stately manors rise
Along the banks, and castles top the hills,
And little villages grow populous with trade,
Until the river runs as proudly as the Rhine,—
The thread that links a hundred towns and towers
Now looking deeper in my dream, I see
A mighty city covering the isle
They call Manhattan, equal in her state
To all the older capitals of earth,—
The gateway city of a golden world,—
A city girt with masts, and crowned with spires,
And swarming with a million busy men,
While to her open door across the bay
The ships of all the nations flock like doves.
My name will be remembered there, the world
Will say, "This river and this isle were found
By Henry Hudson, on his way to seek
The Northwest Passage."
      Yes, I seek it still,—
My great adventure and my guiding star!

PRO PATRIA

For look ye, friends, our voyage is not done;
We hold by hope as long as life endures!
Somewhere among these floating fields of ice,
Somewhere along this westward widening bay,
Somewhere beneath this luminous northern night
The channel opens to the Farthest East,—
I know it,—and some day a little ship
Will push her bowsprit in, and battle through!
And why not ours,—to-morrow,—who can tell?
The lucky chance awaits the fearless heart!
These are the longest days of all the year;
The world is round and God is everywhere,
And while our shallop floats we still can steer.

So point her up, John King, nor'west by north
We'll keep the honour of a certain aim
Amid the peril of uncertain ways,
And sail ahead, and leave the rest to God.

July, 1909.

SEA-GULLS OF MANHATTAN

Children of the elemental mother,
  Born upon some lonely island shore
Where the wrinkled ripples run and whisper,
  Where the crested billows plunge and roar;
Long-winged, tireless roamers and adventurers,
  Fearless breasters of the wind and sea,
In the far-off solitary places
  I have seen you floating wild and free!

Here the high-built cities rise around you;
  Here the cliffs that tower east and west,
Honeycombed with human habitations,
  Have no hiding for the sea-bird's nest:
Here the river flows begrimed and troubled;
  Here the hurrying, panting vessels fume,
Restless, up and down the watery highway,
  While a thousand chimneys vomit gloom.

Toil and tumult, conflict and confusion,
  Clank and clamour of the vast machine
Human hands have built for human bondage—
  Yet amid it all you float serene;
Circling, soaring, sailing, swooping lightly
  Down to glean your harvest from the wave
In your heritage of air and water,
  You have kept the freedom Nature gave.

PRO PATRIA

Even so the wild-woods of Manhattan
   Saw your wheeling flocks of white and gray;
Even so you fluttered, followed, floated,
   Round the *Half-Moon* creeping up the bay;
Even so your voices creaked and chattered,
   Laughing shrilly o'er the tidal rips,
While your black and beady eyes were glistening
   Round the sullen British prison-ships.

Children of the elemental mother,
   Fearless floaters 'mid the double blue,
From the crowded boats that cross the ferries
   Many a longing heart goes out to you.
Though the cities climb and close around us,
   Something tells us that our souls are free,
While the sea-gulls fly above the harbour,
   While the river flows to meet the sea!

December, 1905.

A BALLAD OF CLAREMONT HILL

    The roar of the city is low,
    Muffled by new-fallen snow,
And the sign of the wintry moon is small and round and
    still.
    Will you come with me to-night,
    To see a pleasant sight
Away on the river-side, at the edge of Claremont Hill?

    "And what shall we see there,
    But streets that are new and bare,
And many a desolate place that the city is coming to fill;
    And a soldier's tomb of stone,
    And a few trees standing alone—
Will you walk for that through the cold, to the edge of
    Claremont Hill?"

    But there's more than that for me,
    In the place that I fain would see:
There's a glimpse of the grace that helps us all to bear
    life's ill,
    A touch of the vital breath
    That keeps the world from death,
A flower that never fades, on the edge of Claremont Hill.

    For just where the road swings round,
    In a narrow strip of ground,

PRO PATRIA

Where a group of forest trees are lingering fondly still,
    There's a grave of the olden time,
    When the garden bloomed in its prime,
And the children laughed and sang on the edge of Claremont Hill.

    The marble is pure and white,
    And even in this dim light,
You may read the simple words that are written there if you will;
    You may hear a father tell
    Of the child he loved so well,
A hundred years ago, on the edge of Claremont Hill.

    The tide of the city has rolled
    Across that bower of old,
And blotted out the beds of the rose and the daffodil;
    But the little playmate sleeps,
    And the shrine of love still keeps
A record of happy days, on the edge of Claremont Hill.

    The river is pouring down
    To the crowded, careless town,
Where the intricate wheels of trade are grinding on like a mill;
    But the clamorous noise and strife
    Of the hurrying waves of life
Flow soft by this haven of peace on the edge of Claremont Hill.

A BALLAD OF CLAREMONT HILL

    And after all, my friend,
    When the tale of our years shall end,
Be it long or short, or lowly or great, as God may will
    What better praise could we hear,
    Than this of the child so dear:
You have made my life more sweet, on the edge of Claremont Hill?

December, 1896.

URBS CORONATA

(Song for the City College of New York)

O YOUNGEST of the giant brood
  Of cities far-renowned;
In wealth and glory thou hast passed
  Thy rivals at a bound;
Thou art a mighty queen, New York;
  And how wilt thou be crowned?

"Weave me no palace-wreath of Pride
  The royal city said;
"Nor forge of frowning fortress-walls
  A helmet for my head;
But let me wear a diadem
  Of Wisdom's towers instead."

She bowed herself, she spent herself,
  She wrought her will forsooth,
And set upon her island height
  A citadel of Truth,
A house of Light, a home of Thought
  A shrine of noble Youth.

URBS CORONATA

Stand here, ye City College towers,
　And look both up and down;
Remember all who wrought for you
　Within the toiling town;
Remember all their hopes for you,
　And *be* the City's Crown.

June, 1908.

MERCY FOR ARMENIA

I

THE TURK'S WAY

STAND back, ye messengers of mercy! Stand
  Far off, for I will save my troubled folk
  In my own way. So the false Sultan spoke;
And Europe, hearkening to his base command,
Stood still to see him heal his wounded land.
  Through blinding snows of winter and through smoke
  Of burning towns, she saw him deal the stroke
Of cruel mercy that his hate had planned.
Unto the prisoners and the sick he gave
  New tortures, horrible, without a name;
    Unto the thirsty, blood to drink; a sword
  Unto the hungry; with a robe of shame
    He clad the naked, making life abhorred;
He saved by slaughter, and denied a grave.

II

AMERICA'S WAY

But thou, my country, though no fault be thine
  For that red horror far across the sea;
  Though not a tortured wretch can point to thee,
And curse thee for the selfishness supine
Of those great Powers that cowardly combine

MERCY FOR ARMENIA

To shield the Turk in his iniquity;
  Yet, since thy hand is innocent and free,
Arise, and show the world the way divine!
Thou canst not break the oppressor's iron rod,
  But thou canst help and comfort the oppressed;
    Thou canst not loose the captive's heavy chain,
    But thou canst bind his wounds and soothe his pain
  Armenia calls thee, Sovereign of the West,
To play the Good Samaritan for God.

1896.

SICILY, DECEMBER, 1908

O GARDEN isle, beloved by Sun and Sea,
   Whose bluest billows kiss thy curving bays,
   Whose light infolds thy hills with golden rays,
Filling with fruit each dark-leaved orange-tree,
What hidden hatred hath the Earth for thee,
   That once again, in these dark, dreadful days,
   Breaks forth in trembling rage, and swiftly lays
Thy beauty waste in wreck and agony!
Is Nature, then, a strife of jealous powers,
   And man the plaything of unconscious fate?
     Not so, my troubled heart! God reigns above
And man is greatest in his darkest hours.
   Walking amid the cities desolate,
     Behold the Son of God in human love!

Tertius and Henry van Dyke.

"COME BACK AGAIN, JEANNE D'ARC"

The land was broken in despair,
  The princes quarrelled in the dark,
When clear and tranquil, through the troubled air
Of selfish minds and wills that did not dare,
      Your star arose, Jeanne d'Arc.

O virgin breast with lilies white,
  O sun-burned hand that bore the lance,
You taught the prayer that helps men to unite,
You brought the courage equal to the fight,
      You gave a heart to France!

Your king was crowned, your country free,
  At Rheims you had your soul's desire:
And then, at Rouen, maid of Domrémy,
The black-robed judges gave your victory
      The martyr's crown of fire.

And now again the times are ill,
  And doubtful leaders miss the mark;
The people lack the single faith and will
To make them one,—your country needs you still
      Come back again, Jeanne d'Arc!

PRO PATRIA

O woman-star, arise once more
  And shine to bid your land advance:
The old heroic trust in God restore,
Renew the brave, unselfish hopes of yore
  And give a heart to France!

Paris, July, 1909.

NATIONAL MONUMENTS

COUNT not the cost of honour to the dead!
  The tribute that a mighty nation pays
  To those who loved her well in former days
Means more than gratitude for glories fled;
For every noble man that she hath bred,
  Lives in the bronze and marble that we raise,
  Immortalised by art's immortal praise,
To lead our sons as he our fathers led.

These monuments of manhood strong and high
  Do more than forts or battle-ships to keep
Our dear-bought liberty. They fortify
  The heart of youth with valour wise and deep
They build eternal bulwarks, and command
Immortal hosts to guard our native land.

February, 1905.

THE MONUMENT OF FRANCIS MAKEMIE

(Presbyter of Christ in America, 1683–1708)

To thee, plain hero of a rugged race,
  We bring the meed of praise too long delayed!
  Thy fearless word and faithful work have made
For God's Republic firmer resting-place
In this New World: for thou hast preached the grace
  And power of Christ in many a forest glade,
  Teaching the truth that leaves men unafraid
Of frowning tyranny or death's dark face.

Oh, who can tell how much we owe to thee,
  Makemie, and to labour such as thine,
  For all that makes America the shrine
Of faith untrammelled and of conscience free?
Stand here, gray stone, and consecrate the sod
Where rests this brave Scotch-Irish man of God!

April, 1908.

THE STATUE OF SHERMAN BY ST. GAUDENS

This is the soldier brave enough to tell
The glory-dazzled world that 'war is hell':
Lover of peace, he looks beyond the strife,
And rides through hell to save his country's life.

April, 1904.

"AMERICA FOR ME"

'Tis fine to see the Old World, and travel up and down
Among the famous palaces and cities of renown,
To admire the crumbly castles and the statues of the
    kings,—
But now I think I've had enough of antiquated things.

So it's home again, and home again, America for me!
My heart is turning home again, and there I long to be,
In the land of youth and freedom beyond the ocean bars,
Where the air is full of sunlight and the flag is full of stars.

Oh, London is a man's town, there's power in the air;
And Paris is a woman's town, with flowers in her hair;
And it's sweet to dream in Venice, and it's great to study
    Rome;
But when it comes to living there is no place like home.

I like the German fir-woods, in green battalions drilled;
I like the gardens of Versailles with flashing fountains
    filled;
But, oh, to take your hand, my dear, and ramble for a
    day
In the friendly western woodland where Nature has her
    way!

"AMERICA FOR ME"

I know that Europe's wonderful, yet something seems to lack:
The Past is too much with her, and the people looking back.
But the glory of the Present is to make the Future free,—
We love our land for what she is and what she is to be.

Oh, it's home again, and home again, America for me!
I want a ship that's westward bound to plough the rolling sea,
To the blessèd Land of Room Enough beyond the ocean bars,
Where the air is full of sunlight and the flag is full of stars.

June, 1909.

THE BUILDERS
ODE FOR THE HUNDRED AND FIFTIETH ANNIVERSARY OF PRINCETON COLLEGE

October 21, 1896

I

Into the dust of the making of man
Spirit was breathed when his life began,
Lifting him up from his low estate,
With masterful passion, the wish to create.
Out of the dust of his making, man
Fashioned his works as the ages ran;
Fortress, and palace, and temple, and tower,
Filling the world with the proof of his power.
Over the dust that awaits him, man,
Building the walls that his pride doth plan,
Dreams they will stand in the light of the sun
Bearing his name till Time is done.

II

The monuments of mortals
  Are as the glory of the grass;
Through Time's dim portals
  A voiceless, viewless wind doth pass,
The blossoms fall before it in a day,

THE BUILDERS

The forest monarchs year by year decay,
And man's great buildings slowly fade away.
    One after one,
      They pay to that dumb breath
      The tribute of their death,
        And are undone.
    The towers incline to dust,
    The massive girders rust,
    The domes dissolve in air,
    The pillars that upbear
The lofty arches crumble, stone by stone,
While man the builder looks about him in despair,
For all his works of pride and power are overthrown

III

    A Voice came from the sky:
    "Set thy desires more high.
      Thy buildings fade away
      Because thou buildest clay.
      Now make the fabric sure
      With stones that will endure!
    Hewn from the spiritual rock,
      The immortal towers of the soul
        At Death's dissolving touch shall mock,
          And stand secure while æons roll."

PRO PATRIA

IV

Well did the wise in heart rejoice
To hear the summons of that Voice,
    And patiently begin
    The builder's work within,
    Houses not made with hands,
    Nor founded on the sands.
And thou, Reverèd Mother, at whose call
We come to keep thy joyous festival,
And celebrate thy labours on the walls of Truth
Through sevenscore years and ten of thine eternal youth—
    A master builder thou,
    And on thy shining brow,
Like Cybele, in fadeless light dost wear
A diadem of turrets strong and fair.

V

I see thee standing in a lonely land,
But late and hardly won from solitude,
    Unpopulous and rude,—
On that far western shore I see thee stand,
Like some young goddess from a brighter strand,
While in thine eyes a radiant thought is born,
Enkindling all thy beauty like the morn.
Sea-like the forest rolled, in waves of green,
And few the lights that glimmered, leagues between

THE BUILDERS

High in the north, for fourscore years alone
Fair Harvard's earliest beacon-tower had shone
When Yale was lighted, and an answering ray
Flashed from the meadows by New Haven Bay.
But deeper spread the forest, and more dark,
Where first Neshaminy received the spark
Of sacred learning to a woodland camp,
And Old Log College glowed with Tennant's lamp.
Thine, Alma Mater, was the larger sight,
That saw the future of that trembling light,
And thine the courage, thine the stronger will,
That built its loftier home on Princeton Hill.

"New light!" men cried, and murmured that it came
From an unsanctioned source with lawless flame;
It shone too free, for still the church and school
Must only shine according to their rule.
But Princeton answered, in her nobler mood,
"God made the light, and all the light is good.
There is no war between the old and new;
The conflict lies between the false and true.
The stars, that high in heaven their courses run,
In glory differ, but their light is one.
The beacons, gleaming o'er the sea of life,
Are rivals but in radiance, not in strife.
Shine on, ye sister-towers, across the night!
I too will build a lasting house of light."

PRO PATRIA

VI

Brave was that word of faith and bravely was it kept;
With never-wearying zeal that faltered not, nor slept,
Our Alma Mater toiled, and while she firmly laid
The deep foundation-walls, at all her toil she prayed.
And men who loved the truth because it made them free,
And clearly saw the twofold Word of God agree,
Reading from Nature's book and from the Bible's page
By the same inward ray that grows from age to age,
Were built like living stones that beacon to uplift,
And drawing light from heaven gave to the world the gift.
Nor ever, while they searched the secrets of the earth,
Or traced the stream of life through mystery to its birth,
Nor ever, while they taught the lightning-flash to bear
The messages of man in silence through the air,
Fell from their home of light one false, perfidious ray
To blind the trusting heart, or lead the life astray.
But still, while knowledge grew more luminous and broad
It lit the path of faith and showed the way to God.

VII

Yet not for peace alone
Labour the builders.
Work that in peace has grown
Swiftly is overthrown,
When in the darkening skies

THE BUILDERS

Storm-clouds of wrath arise,
And through the cannon's crash,
War's deadly lightning-flash
 Smites and bewilders.
Ramparts of strength must frown
Round every placid town
 And city splendid;
All that our fathers wrought
With true prophetic thought,
 Must be defended!

VIII

But who could raise protecting walls for thee,
Thou young, defenceless land of liberty?
Or who could build a fortress strong enough,
Or stretch a mighty bulwark long enough
 To hold thy far-extended coast
 Against the overweening host
That took the open path across the sea,
 And like a tempest poured
 Their desolating horde,
To quench thy dawning light in gloom of tyranny?
 Yet not unguarded thou wert found
 When on thy shore with sullen sound
 The blaring trumpets of an unjust king
Proclaimed invasion. From the ground,
In freedom's darkest hour, there seemed to spring

PRO PATRIA

  Unconquerable walls for her defence;
  Not trembling, like those battlements of stone
  That fell when Joshua's horns were blown;
  But firm and stark the living rampart rose,
  To meet the onset of imperious foes
With a long line of brave, unyielding men.
  This was thy fortress, well-defended land,
  And on these walls, the patient, building hand
  Of Princeton laboured with the force of ten.
  Her sons were foremost in the furious fight;
  Her sons were firmest to uphold the right
  In council-chambers of the new-born State,
And prove that he who would be free must first be great
  In heart, and high in thought, and strong
  In purpose not to do or suffer wrong.
  Such were the men, impregnable to fear,
  Whose souls were framed and fashioned here;
And when war shook the land with threatening shock,
  The men of Princeton stood like muniments of rock.
      Nor has the breath of Time
      Dissolved that proud array
      Of never-broken strength:
      For though the rocks decay,
      And all the iron bands
  Of earthly strongholds are unloosed at length,
  And buried deep in gray oblivion's sands;
      The work that heroes' hands
  Wrought in the light of freedom's natal day

THE BUILDERS

    Shall never fade away,
    But lifts itself, sublime
    Into a lucid sphere,
    For ever calm and clear,
Preserving in the memory of the fathers' deed,
A never-failing fortress for their children's need.
There we confirm our hearts to-day, and read
On many a stone the signature of fame,
The builder's mark, our Alma Mater's name.

IX

Bear with us then a moment, while we turn
From all the present splendours of this place—
The lofty towers that like a dream have grown
Where once old Nassau Hall stood all alone—
Back to that ancient time, with hearts that burn
    In filial gratitude, to trace
The glory of our mother's best degree,
    In that "high son of Liberty,"
    Who like a granite block,
    Riven from Scotland's rock,
Stood loyal here to keep Columbia free.
Born far away beyond the ocean's tide,
He found his fatherland upon this side;
And every drop of ardent blood that ran
Through his great heart, was true American.
He held no fealty to a distant throne,

PRO PATRIA

But made his new-found country's cause his own.
    In peril and distress,
    In toil and weariness,
    When darkness overcast her
    With shadows of disaster,
    And voices of confusion
    Proclaimed her hope delusion,
    Robed in his preacher's gown,
    He dared the danger down;
Like some old prophet chanting an inspired rune
In freedom's councils rang the voice of Witherspoon

  And thou, my country, write it on thy heart:
  Thy sons are they who nobly take thy part;
  Who dedicates his manhood at thy shrine,
  Wherever born, is born a son of thine.
  Foreign in name, but not in soul, they come
  To find in thee their long-desired home;
  Lovers of liberty and haters of disorder,
  They shall be built in strength along thy border.

    Dream not thy future foes
    Will all be foreign-born!
    Turn thy clear look of scorn
    Upon thy children who oppose
Their passions wild and policies of shame
To wreck the righteous splendour of thy name.
  Untaught and overconfident they rise,

THE BUILDERS

With folly on their lips, and envy in their eyes:
Strong to destroy, but powerless to create,
And ignorant of all that made our fathers great,
Their hands would take away thy golden crown,
And shake the pillars of thy freedom down
In Anarchy's ocean, dark and desolate.
  O should that storm descend,
  What fortress shall defend
  The land our fathers wrought for,
  The liberties they fought for?
  What bulwark shall secure
Her shrines of law, and keep her founts of justice pure?
    Then, ah then,
    As in the olden days,
  The builders must upraise
  A rampart of indomitable men.
      And once again,
Dear Mother, if thy heart and hand be true,
There will be building work for thee to do;
  Yea, more than once again,
  Thou shalt win lasting praise,
And never-dying honour shall be thine,
For setting many stones in that illustrious line,
To stand unshaken in the swirling strife,
And guard their country's honour as her life.

PRO PATRIA

X

Softly, my harp, and let me lay the touch
Of silence on these rudely clanging strings;
   For he who sings
Even of noble conflicts overmuch,
Loses the inward sense of better things;
  And he who makes a boast
Of knowledge, darkens that which counts the most,—
  The insight of a wise humility
That reverently adores what none can see.
  The glory of our life below
Comes not from what we do, or what we know,
   But dwells forevermore in what we are.
   There is an architecture grander far
    Than all the fortresses of war,
    More inextinguishably bright
   Than learning's lonely towers of light.
Framing its walls of faith and hope and love
   In souls of men, it lifts above
    The frailty of our earthly home
     An everlasting dome;
The sanctuary of the human host,
The living temple of the Holy Ghost.

THE BUILDERS

XI

If music led the builders long ago,
  When Arthur planned the halls of Camelot,
And made the royal city grow,
  Fair as a flower in that forsaken spot;
What sweeter music shall we bring,
To weave a harmony divine
  Of prayer and holy thought
Into the labours of this loftier shrine,
  This consecrated hill,
Where through so many a year
Our Alma Mater's hand hath wrought,
  With toil serene and still,
  And heavenly hope, to rear
Eternal dwellings for the Only King?
  Here let no martial trumpets blow,
Nor instruments of pride proclaim
The loud exultant notes of fame!
  But let the chords be clear and low,
  And let the anthem deeper grow,
And let it move more solemnly and slow;
    For only such an ode
    Can seal the harmony
    Of that deep masonry
Wherein the soul of man is framed for God's abode

PRO PATRIA

XII

O Thou whose boundless love bestows
  The joy of earth, the hope of Heaven,
And whose unchartered mercy flows
  O'er all the blessings Thou hast given;
Thou by whose light alone we see;
And by whose truth our souls set free
Are made imperishably strong;
Hear Thou the solemn music of our song.

Grant us the knowledge that we need
  To solve the questions of the mind,
And light our candle while we read,
  To keep our hearts from going blind;
Enlarge our vision to behold
The wonders Thou hast wrought of old;
Reveal thyself in every law,
And gild the towers of truth with holy awe

Be Thou our strength if war's wild gust
  Shall rage around us, loud and fierce;
Confirm our souls and let our trust
  Be like a shield that none can pierce;
Renew the courage that prevails,
The steady faith that never fails,
And make us stand in every fight
Firm as a fortress to defend the right.

THE BUILDERS

O God, control us as Thou wilt,
    And guide the labour of our hand;
Let all our work be surely built
    As Thou, the architect, hast planned
But whatso'er thy power shall make
Of these frail lives, do not forsake
Thy dwelling: let thy presence rest
For ever in the temple of our breast.

SPIRIT OF THE EVERLASTING BOY

ODE FOR THE HUNDREDTH ANNIVERSARY OF LAWRENCEVILLE SCHOOL

June 11, 1910

I

The British bard who looked on Eton's walls
Endeared by distance in the pearly gray
And soft aerial blue that ever falls
On English landscape with the dying day,
Beheld in thought his boyhood far away,
Its random raptures and its festivals
    Of noisy mirth,
The brief illusion of its idle joys,
And mourned that none of these can stay
With men, whom life inexorably calls
To face the grim realities of earth.
His pensive fancy pictured there at play
From year to year the careless bands of boys
Unconscious victims kept in golden state,
    While haply they await
The dark approach of disenchanting Fate,
    To hale them to the sacrifice
Of Pain and Penury and Grief and Care,
Slow-withering Age, or Failure's swift despair.
Half-pity and half-envy dimmed the eyes

SPIRIT OF THE EVERLASTING BOY

Of that old poet, gazing on the scene
Where long ago his youth had flowed serene,
And all the burden of his ode was this:
"Where ignorance is bliss,
'Tis folly to be wise."

II

But not for us, O plaintive elegist,
Thine epicedial tone of sad farewell
To joy in wisdom and to thought in youth!
Our western Muse would keep her tryst
With sunrise, not with sunset, and foretell
In boyhood's bliss the dawn of manhood's truth

III

O spirit of the everlasting boy,
Alert, elate,
And confident that life is good,
Thou knockest boldly at the gate,
In hopeful hardihood,
Eager to enter and enjoy
Thy new estate.

Through the old house thou runnest everywhere,
Bringing a breath of folly and fresh air.
Ready to make a treasure of each toy,
Or break them all in discontented mood;

PRO PATRIA

Fearless of Fate,
Yet strangely fearful of a comrade's laugh;
Reckless and timid, hard and sensitive;
In talk a rebel, full of mocking chaff,
　　At heart devout conservative;
In love with love, yet hating to be kissed;
　　　Inveterate optimist,
　　　And judge severe,
In reason cloudy but in feeling clear;
Keen critic, ardent hero-worshipper,
Impatient of restraint in little ways,
　　Yet ever ready to confer
On chosen leaders boundless power and praise;
Adventurous spirit burning to explore
Untrodden paths where hidden danger lies,
And homesick heart looking with wistful eyes
Through every twilight to a mother's door;
Thou daring, darling, inconsistent boy,
　　How dull the world would be
Without thy presence, dear barbarian,
And happy lord of high futurity!
Be what thou art, our trouble and our joy,
Our hardest problem and our brightest hope!
And while thine elders lead thee up the slope
Of knowledge, let them learn from teaching thee
That vital joy is part of nature's plan,
And he who keeps the spirit of the boy
Shall gladly grow to be a happy man.

SPIRIT OF THE EVERLASTING BOY

IV

What constitutes a school?
Not ancient halls and ivy-mantled towers,
  Where dull traditions rule
With heavy hand youth's lightly springing powers
  Not spacious pleasure courts,
And lofty temples of athletic fame,
  Where devotees of sports
Mistake a pastime for life's highest aim;
  Not fashion, nor renown
Of wealthy patronage and rich estate;
  No, none of these can crown
A school with light and make it truly great.
  But masters, strong and wise,
Who teach because they love the teacher's task,
  And find their richest prize
In eyes that open and in minds that ask;
  And boys, with heart aglow
To try their youthful vigour on their work,
  Eager to learn and grow,
And quick to hate a coward or a shirk:
  These constitute a school,—
A vital forge of weapons keen and bright,
  Where living sword and tool
Are tempered for true toil or noble fight!
  But let not wisdom scorn
The hours of pleasure in the playing fields:

PRO PATRIA

There also strength is born,
And every manly game a virtue yields.
Fairness and self-control,
Good-humour, pluck, and patience in the race,
Will make a lad heart-whole
To win with honour, lose without disgrace.
Ah, well for him who gains
In such a school apprenticeship to life:
With him the joy of youth remains
In later lessons and in larger strife!

V

On Jersey's rolling plain, where Washington,
In midnight marching at the head
Of ragged regiments, his army led
To Princeton's victory of the rising sun;
Here in this liberal land, by battle won
For Freedom and the rule
Of equal rights for every child of man,
Arose a democratic school,
To train a virile race of sons to bear
With thoughtful joy the name American,
And serve the God who heard their father's prayer
No cloister, dreaming in a world remote
From that real world wherein alone we live;
No mimic court, where titled names denote
A dignity that only worth can give;

SPIRIT OF THE EVERLASTING BOY

But here a friendly house of learning stood,
With open door beside the broad highway,
And welcomed lads to study and to play
In generous rivalry of brotherhood.
A hundred years have passed, and Lawrenceville,
In beauty and in strength renewed,
Stands with her open portal still,
And neither time nor fortune brings
To her deep spirit any change of mood,
Or faltering from the faith she held of old.
Still to the democratic creed she clings:
That manhood needs nor rank nor gold
To make it noble in our eyes;
That every boy is born with royal right,
From blissful ignorance to rise
To joy more lasting and more bright,
In mastery of body and of mind,
King of himself and servant of mankind.

VI

Old Lawrenceville,
Thy happy bell
Shall ring to-day,
O'er vale and hill,
O'er mead and dell,
While far away,
With silent thrill,

PRO PATRIA

The echoes roll
Through many a soul,
That knew thee well,
In boyhood's day,
And loves thee still.

Ah, who can tell
How far away,
Some sentinel
Of God's good will,
In forest cool,
Or desert gray,
By lonely pool,
Or barren hill,
Shall faintly hear,
With inward ear,
The chiming bell,
Of his old school,
Through darkness pealing;
And lowly kneeling,
Shall feel the spell
Of grateful tears
His eyelids fill;
And softly pray
To Him who hears:
God bless old Lawrenceville!

TEXAS

A DEMOCRATIC ODE *

I

THE WILD-BEES

ALL along the Brazos river,
All along the Colorado,
In the valleys and the lowlands
Where the trees were tall and stately,
In the rich and rolling meadows
Where the grass was full of wild-flowers,
Came a humming and a buzzing,
Came the murmur of a going
To and fro among the tree-tops,
Far and wide across the meadows.
And the red-men in their tepees
Smoked their pipes of clay and listened.
"What is this?" they asked in wonder;
"Who can give the sound a meaning?
Who can understand the language
Of this going in the tree-tops?"
Then the wisest of the Tejas
Laid his pipe aside and answered:
"O my brothers, these are people,
Very little, winged people,

* Read at the Dedication of the Rice Institute, Houston, Texas October, 1912.

PRO PATRIA

Countless, busy, banded people,
Coming humming through the timber
These are tribes of bees, united
By a single aim and purpose,
To possess the Tejas' country,
Gather harvest from the prairies,
Store their wealth among the timber.
These are hive and honey makers,
Sent by Manito to warn us
That the white men now are coming,
With their women and their children.
Not the fiery filibusters
Passing wildly in a moment,
Like a flame across the prairies,
Like a whirlwind through the forest,
Leaving empty lands behind them!
Not the Mexicans and Spaniards,
Indolent and proud hidalgos,
Dwelling in their haciendas,
Dreaming, talking of tomorrow,
While their cattle graze around them,
And their fickle revolutions
Change the rulers, not the people!
Other folk are these who follow
When the wild-bees come to warn us,
These are hive and honey makers,
These are busy, banded people,
Roaming far to swarm and settle,

TEXAS

Working every day for harvest,
Fighting hard for peace and order,
Worshipping as queens their women,
Making homes and building cities
Full of riches and of trouble.
All our hunting-grounds must vanish,
All our lodges fall before them,
All our customs and traditions,
All our happy life of freedom,
Fade away like smoke before them.
Come, my brothers, strike your tepees,
Call your women, load your ponies!
Let us take the trail to westward,
Where the plains are wide and open,
Where the bison-herds are gathered
Waiting for our feathered arrows.
We will live as lived our fathers,
Gleaners of the gifts of nature,
Hunters of the unkept cattle,
Men whose women run to serve them.
If the toiling bees pursue us,
If the white men seek to tame us,
We will fight them off and flee them,
Break their hives and take their honey
Moving westward, ever westward,
There to live as lived our fathers."
So the red-men drove their ponies,
With the tent-poles trailing after,

PRO PATRIA

Out along the path to sunset,
While along the river valleys
Swarmed the wild-bees, the forerunners;
And the white men, close behind them,
Men of mark from old Missouri,
Men of daring from Kentucky,
Tennessee, Louisiana,
Men of many States and races,
Bringing wives and children with them,
Followed up the wooded valleys,
Spread across the rolling prairies,
Raising homes and reaping harvests.
Rude the toil that tried their patience,
Fierce the fights that proved their courage
Rough the stone and tough the timber
Out of which they built their order!
Yet they never failed nor faltered,
And the instinct of their swarming
Made them one and kept them working,
Till their toil was crowned with triumph,
And the country of the Tejas
Was the fertile land of Texas.

TEXAS

II

THE LONE STAR

Behold a star appearing in the South,
A star that shines apart from other stars,
   Ruddy and fierce like Mars!
Out of the reeking smoke of cannon's mouth
That veils the slaughter of the Alamo,
   Where heroes face the foe,
One man against a score, with blood-choked breath
Shouting the watchword, "Victory or Death—"
Out of the dreadful cloud that settles low
   On Goliad's plain,
Where thrice a hundred prisoners lie slain
Beneath the broken word of Mexico—
Out of the fog of factions and of feuds
   That ever drifts and broods
Above the bloody path of border war,
   Leaps the Lone Star!

What light is this that does not dread the dark?
What star is this that fights a stormy way
   To San Jacinto's field of victory?
   It is the fiery spark
   That burns within the breast
Of Anglo-Saxon men, who can not rest
   Under a tyrant's sway;
   The upward-leading ray

PRO PATRIA

That guides the brave who give their lives away
    Rather than not be free!
O question not, but honour every name,
Travis and Crockett, Bowie, Bonham, Ward,
Fannin and King, and all who drew the sword
And dared to die for Texan liberty!
Yea, write them all upon the roll of fame,
But no less love and equal honour give
To those who paid the longer sacrifice—
Austin and Houston, Burnet, Rusk, Lamar
And all the stalwart men who dared to live
Long years of service to the lonely star.

Great is the worth of such heroic souls:
Amid the strenuous turmoil of their deeds,
They clearly speak of something that controls
The higher breeds of men by higher needs
Than bees, content with honey in their hives!
    Ah, not enough the narrow lives
  On profitable toil intent!
And not enough the guerdons of success
Garnered in homes of affluent selfishness!
    A noble discontent
    Cries for a wider scope
To use the wider wings of human hope;
  A vision of the common good
Opens the prison-door of solitude;
    And, once beyond the wall,

TEXAS

Breathing the ampler air,
The heart becomes aware
That life without a country is not life at all.
A country worthy of a freeman's love;
A country worthy of a good man's prayer;
A country strong, and just, and brave, and fair
A woman's form of beauty throned above
The shrine where noble aspirations meet—
To live for her is great, to die is sweet!

Heirs of the rugged pioneers
Who dreamed this dream and made it true,
Remember that they dreamed for you.
They did not fear their fate
In those tempestuous years,
But put their trust in God, and with keen eyes,
Trained in the open air for looking far,
They saw the many-million-acred land
Won from the desert by their hand,
Swiftly among the nations rise,—
Texas a sovereign State,
And on her brow a star!

PRO PATRIA

III

THE CONSTELLATION

How strange that the nature of light is a thing beyond
　　our ken,
　　And the flame of the tiniest candle flows from a foun-
　　　　tain sealed!
How strange that the meaning of life, in the little lives
　　of men,
　　So often baffles our search with a mystery unrevealed!

But the larger life of man, as it moves in its secular
　　sweep,
　　Is the working out of a Sovereign Will whose ways
　　　　appear;
And the course of the journeying stars on the dark blue
　　boundless deep,
　　Is the place where our science rests in the reign of law
　　　　most clear.

I would read the story of Texas as if it were written on
　　high;
　　I would look from afar to follow her path through the
　　　　calms and storms;
With a faith in the worldwide sway of the Reason that
　　rules in the sky,
　　And gathers and guides the starry host in clusters and
　　　　swarms.

TEXAS

When she rose in the pride of her youth, she seemed to be moving apart,
 As a single star in the South, self-limited, self-possessed;
But the law of the constellation was written deep in her heart,
 And she heard when her sisters called, from the North and the East and the West.

They were drawn together and moved by a common hope and aim—
 The dream of a sign that should rule a third of the heavenly arch;
The soul of a people spoke in their call, and Texas came
 To enter the splendid circle of States in their onward march.

So the glory gathered and grew and spread from sea to sea,
 And the stars of the great republic lent each other light;
For all were bound together in strength, and each was free—
 Suddenly broke the tempest out of the ancient night!

It came as a clash of the force that drives and the force that draws;
 And the stars were riven asunder, the heavens were desolate,

PRO PATRIA

While brother fought with brother, each for his country's cause:
  But the country of one was the Nation, the country of other the State.

Oh, who shall measure the praise or blame in a strife so vast?
  And who shall speak of traitors or tyrants when all were true?
We lift our eyes to the sky, and rejoice that the storm is past,
  And we thank the God of all that the Union shines in the blue.

Yea, it glows with the glory of peace and the hope of a mighty race,
  High over the grave of broken chains and buried hates;
And the great, big star of Texas is shining clear in its place
  In the constellate symbol and sign of the free United States.

346

TEXAS

IV
AFTER THE PIONEERS

After the pioneers—
Big-hearted, big-handed lords of the axe and the plow
    and the rifle,
Tan-faced tamers of horses and lands, themselves re-
    maining tameless,
Full of fighting, labour and romance, lovers of rude ad-
    venture—
After the pioneers have cleared the way to their homes
    and graves on the prairies:

After the State-builders—
Zealous and jealous men, dreamers, debaters, often at
    odds with each other,
All of them sure it is well to toil and to die, if need be,
Just for the sake of founding a country to leave to their
    children—
After the builders have done their work and written their
    names upon it:

After the civil war—
Wildest of all storms, cruel and dark and seemingly
    wasteful,
Tearing up by the root the vines that were splitting the
    old foundations,

PRO PATRIA

Washing away with a rain of blood and tears the dust of slavery,
After the cyclone has passed and the sky is fair to the far horizon;
After the era of plenty and peace has come with full hands to Texas,
Then—what then?

Is it to be the life of an indolent heir, fat-witted and self-contented,
Dwelling at ease in the house that others have builded,
Boasting about the country for which he has done nothing?
Is it to be an age of corpulent, deadly-dull prosperity,
Richer and richer crops to nourish a race of Philistines,
Bigger and bigger cities full of the same confusion and sorrow,
The people increasing mightily but no increase of the joy?
Is this what the forerunners wished and toiled to win for you,
This the reward of war and the fruitage of high endeavor,
This the goal of your hopes and the vision that satisfies you?

Nay, stand up and answer—I can read what is in your hearts—
You, the children of those who followed the wild-bees,

TEXAS

You, the children of those who served the Lone Star,
Now that the hives are full and the star is fixed in the constellation,
I know that the best of you still are lovers of sweetness and light!

You hunger for honey that comes from invisible gardens;
Pure, translucent, golden thoughts and feelings and inspirations,
Sweetness of all the best that has bloomed in the mind of man.
You rejoice in the light that is breaking along the borders of science;
The hidden rays that enable a man to look through a wall of stone;
The unseen, fire-filled wings that carry his words across the ocean;
The splendid gift of flight that shines, half-captured, above him;
The gleam of a thousand half-guessed secrets, just ready to be discovered!
You dream and devise great things for the coming race—
Children of yours who shall people and rule the domain of Texas;
They shall know, they shall comprehend more than their fathers,
They shall grow in the vigour of well-rounded manhood and womanhood,

PRO PATRIA

Riper minds, richer hearts, finer souls, the only true wealth of a nation—
The league-long fields of the State are pledged to ensure this harvest!

Your old men have dreamed this dream and your young men have seen this vision.
The age of romance has not gone, it is only beginning;
Greater words than the ear of man has heard are waiting to be spoken,
Finer arts than the eyes of man have seen are sleeping to be awakened:
Science exploring the scope of the world,
Poetry breathing the hope of the world,
Music to measure and lead the onward march of man!

Come, ye honoured and welcome guests from the elder nations,
Princes of science and arts and letters,
Look on the walls that embody the generous dream of one of the old men of Texas,
Enter these halls of learning that rise in the land of the pioneer's log-cabin,
Read the confessions of faith that are carved on the stones around you:
Faith in the worth of the smallest fact and the laws that govern the starbeams,

TEXAS

Faith in the beauty of truth and the truth of perfect beauty,
Faith in the God who creates the souls of men by knowledge and love and worship.

This is the faith of the New Democracy—
Proud and humble, patiently pressing forward,
Praising her heroes of old and training her future leaders,
Seeking her crown in a nobler race of men and women—
After the pioneers, sweetness and light!

October, 1912.

WHO FOLLOW THE FLAG

PHI BETA KAPPA ODE
HARVARD UNIVERSITY
June 30, 1910

I

ALL day long in the city's canyon-street,
  With its populous cliffs alive on either side,
  I saw a river of marching men like a tide
Flowing after the flag: and the rhythmic beat
  Of the drums, and the bugles' resonant blare
Metred the tramp, tramp, tramp of a myriad feet,
While the red-white-and-blue was fluttering everywhere
And the heart of the crowd kept time to a martial air

O brave flag, O bright flag, O flag to lead the free!
  The glory of thy silver stars,
  Engrailed in blue above the bars
  Of red for courage, white for truth,
  Has brought the world a second youth
And drawn a hundred million hearts to follow after thee

II

Old Cambridge saw thee first unfurled,
  By Washington's far-reaching hand,
To greet, in Seventy-six, the wintry morn
Of a new year, and herald to the world

WHO FOLLOW THE FLAG

Glad tidings from a Western land,—
A people and a hope new-born!
The double cross then filled thine azure field,
In token of a spirit loath to yield
The breaking ties that bound thee to a throne.
But not for long thine oriflamme could bear
That symbol of an outworn trust in kings.
The wind that bore thee out on widening wings
Called for a greater sign and all thine own,—
A new device to speak of heavenly laws
And lights that surely guide the people's cause.
Oh, greatly did they hope, and greatly dare,
Who bade the stars in heaven fight for them,
And set upon their battle-flag a fair
New constellation as a diadem!
Along the blood-stained banks of Brandywine
The ragged troops were rallied to this sign;
Through Saratoga's woods it fluttered bright
Amid the perils of the hard-won fight;
O'er Yorktown's meadows broad and green
It hailed the glory of the final scene;
And when at length Manhattan saw
The last invaders' line of scarlet coats
Pass Bowling Green, and fill the waiting boats
    And sullenly withdraw,
    The flag that proudly flew
Above the battered line of buff and blue,
Marching, with rattling drums and shrilling pipes

PRO PATRIA

Along the Bowery and down Broadway,
Was this that leads the great parade to-day,—
The glorious banner of the stars and stripes.

First of the flags of earth to dare
A heraldry so high;
First of the flags of earth to bear
The blazons of the sky;
Long may thy constellation glow,
Foretelling happy fate;
Wider thy starry circle grow,
And every star a State!

III

Pass on, pass on, ye flashing files
Of men who march in militant array;
Ye thrilling bugles, throbbing drums,
Ring out, roll on, and die away;
And fade, ye crowds, with the fading day!
    Around the city's lofty piles
    Of steel and stone
    The lilac veil of dusk is thrown,
Entangled full of sparks of fairy light;
And the never-silent heart of the city hums
To a homeward-turning tune before the night.
But far above, on the sky-line's broken height,
From all the towers and domes outlined

WHO FOLLOW THE FLAG

In gray and gold along the city's crest,
I see the rippling flag still take the wind
With a promise of good to come for all mankind.

IV

    O banner of the west,
    No proud and brief parade,
    That glorifies a nation's holiday
With show of troops for warfare dressed,
    Can rightly measure or display
    The mighty army thou hast made
Loyal to guard thy more than royal sway.
    Millions have come across the sea
    To find beneath thy shelter room to grow;
Millions were born beneath thy folds and know
    No other flag but thee.
And other, darker millions bore the yoke
Of bondage in thy borders till the voice
    Of Lincoln spoke,
And sent thee forth to set the bondmen free.
    Rejoice, dear flag, rejoice!
Since thou hast proved and passed that bitter strife
Richer thy red with blood of heroes wet,
Purer thy white through sacrificial life,
Brighter thy blue wherein new stars are set.
    Thou art become a sign,
Revealed in heaven to speak of things divine:

PRO PATRIA

    Of Truth that dares
      To slay the lie it sheltered unawares;
    Of Courage fearless in the fight,
Yet ever quick its foemen to forgive;
Of Conscience earnest to maintain its right
And gladly grant the same to all who live.
    Thy staff is deeply planted in the fact
      That nothing can ennoble man
    Save his own act,
And naught can make him worthy to be free
But practice in the school of liberty.
The cords are two that lift thee to the sky:
Firm faith in God, the King who rules on high;
      And never-failing trust
In human nature, full of faults and flaws,
Yet ever answering to the inward call
That bids it set the "ought" above the "must,"
In all its errors wiser than it seems,
In all its failures full of generous dreams,
Through endless conflict rising without pause
To self-dominion, charactered in laws
That pledge fair-play alike to great and small,
And equal rights for each beneath the rule of all
    These are thy halyards, banner bold,
      And while these hold,
Thy brightness from the sky shall never fall,
Thy broadening empire never know decrease,—
Thy strength is union and thy glory peace.

WHO FOLLOW THE FLAG

V

Look forth across thy widespread lands,
O flag, and let thy stars to-night be eyes
    To see the visionary hosts
Of men and women grateful to be thine,
    That joyfully arise
From all thy borders and thy coasts,
And follow after thee in endless line!
They lift to thee a forest of saluting hands;
They hail thee with a rolling ocean-roar
    Of cheers; and as the echo dies,
There comes a sweet and moving song
Of treble voices from the childish throng
Who run to thee from every school-house door
Behold thine army! Here thy power lies:
The men whom freedom has made strong,
And bound to follow thee by willing vows;
    The women greatened by the joys
Of motherhood to rule a happy house;
    The vigorous girls and boys,
Whose eager faces and unclouded brows
Foretell the future of a noble race,
Rich in the wealth of wisdom and true worth!
While millions such as these to thee belong,
    What foe can do thee wrong,
What jealous rival rob thee of thy place
    Foremost of all the flags of earth?

PRO PATRIA

VI

My vision darkens as the night descends;
And through the mystic atmosphere
I feel the creeping coldness that portends
    A change of spirit in my dream
The multitude that moved with song and cheer
    Have vanished, yet a living stream
    Flows on and follows still the flag,
But silent now, with leaden feet that lag
    And falter in the deepening gloom,—
A weird battalion bringing up the rear.
Ah, who are these on whom the vital bloom
Of life has withered to the dust of doom?
These little pilgrims prematurely worn
And bent as if they bore the weight of years?
These childish faces, pallid and forlorn,
Too dull for laughter and too hard for tears?
Is this the ghost of that insane crusade
That led ten thousand children long ago,
A flock of innocents, deceived, betrayed,
Yet pressing on through want and woe
To meet their fate, faithful and unafraid?

    Nay, for a million children now
Are marching in the long pathetic line,
With weary step and early wrinkled brow;
And at their head appears no holy sign
    Of hope in heaven;
    For unto them is given

WHO FOLLOW THE FLAG

No cross to carry, but a cross to drag.
Before their strength is ripe they bear
The load of labour, toiling underground
In dangerous mines and breathing heavy air
Of crowded shops; their tender lives are bound
To service of the whirling, clattering wheels
That fill the factories with dust and noise;
    They are not girls and boys,
But little "hands" who blindly, dumbly feed
With their own blood the hungry god of Greed
    Robbed of their natural joys,
And wounded with a scar that never heals,
They stumble on with heavy-laden soul,
And fall by thousands on the highway lined
With little graves; or reach at last their goal
Of stunted manhood and embittered age,
To brood awhile with dark and troubled mind,
Beside the smouldering fire of sullen rage,
On life's unfruitful work and niggard wage.
Are these the regiments that Freedom rears
    To serve her cause in coming years?
Nay, every life that Avarice doth maim
And beggar in the helpless days of youth,
    Shall surely claim
A just revenge, and take it without ruth;
And every soul denied the right to grow
Beneath the flag, shall be its secret foe.
Bow down, dear land, in penitence and shame!

PRO PATRIA

Remember now thine oath, so nobly sworn,
    To guard an equal lot
For every child within thy borders born!
These are thy children whom thou hast forgot
They have the bitter right to live, but not
The blessed right to look for happiness.
O lift thy liberating hand once more,
To loose thy little ones from dark duress;
The vital gladness to their hearts restore
In healthful lessons and in happy play;
And set them free to climb the upward way
That leads to self-reliant nobleness.
Speak out, my country, speak at last,
    As thou hast spoken in the past,
    And clearly, bravely say:
    "I will defend
"The coming race on whom my hopes depend
"Beneath my flag and on my sacred soil
"No child shall bear the crushing yoke of toil.

WHO FOLLOW THE FLAG

VII

Look up, look up, ye downcast eyes!
    The night is almost gone:
Along the new horizon flies
    The banner of the dawn;
The eastern sky is banded low
    With white and crimson bars,
While far above the morning glow
    The everlasting stars.

O bright flag, O brave flag, O flag to lead the free!
    The hand of God thy colours blent,
    And heaven to earth thy glory lent,
    To shield the weak, and guide the strong
    To make an end of human wrong,
And draw a countless human host to follow after thee!

STAIN NOT THE SKY

Ye gods of battle, lords of fear,
  Who work your iron will as well
As once ye did with sword and spear,
  With rifled gun and rending shell,—
Masters of sea and land, forbear
The fierce invasion of the inviolate air!

With patient daring man hath wrought
  A hundred years for power to fly;
And will you make his wingéd thought
  A hovering horror in the sky,
Where flocks of human eagles sail,
Dropping their bolts of death on hill and dale?

Ah no, the sunset is too pure,
  The dawn too fair, the noon too bright
For wings of terror to obscure
  Their beauty, and betray the night
That keeps for man, above his wars,
The tranquil vision of untroubled stars.

STAIN NOT THE SKY

Pass on, pass on, ye lords of fear!
  Your footsteps in the sea are red,
And black on earth your paths appear
  With ruined homes and heaps of dead.
Pass on to end your transient reign,
And leave the blue of heaven without a stain

The wrong ye wrought will fall to dust,
  The right ye shielded will abide;
The world at last will learn to trust
  In law to guard, and love to guide;
And Peace of God that answers prayer
Will fall like dew from the inviolate air.

March 5, 1914.

PEACE-HYMN OF THE REPUBLIC

O LORD our God, Thy mighty hand
Hath made our country free;
From all her broad and happy land
May praise arise to Thee.
Fulfill the promise of her youth,
Her liberty defend;
By law and order, love and truth,
America befriend!

The strength of every State increase
In Union's golden chain;
Her thousand cities fill with peace,
Her million fields with grain.
The virtues of her mingled blood
In one new people blend;
By unity and brotherhood,
America befriend!

PEACE-HYMN OF THE REPUBLIC

O suffer not her feet to stray;
But guide her untaught might,
That she may walk in peaceful day,
And lead the world in light.
Bring down the proud, lift up the poor,
Unequal ways amend;
By justice, nation-wide and sure,
America befriend!

Thro' all the waiting land proclaim
Thy gospel of good-will;
And may the music of Thy name
In every bosom thrill.
O'er hill and vale, from sea to sea,
Thy holy reign extend;
By faith and hope and charity,
America befriend!

THE RED FLOWER
AND
GOLDEN STARS

These verses were written during the terrible world-war, and immediately after. The earlier ones had to be unsigned because America was still "neutral" and I held a diplomatic post. The rest of them were printed after I had resigned, and was free to speak out, and to take active service in the Navy, when America entered the great conflict for liberty and peace on earth.

Avalon, February 22, 1920.

THE RED FLOWER
June, 1914

In the pleasant time of Pentecost,
  By the little river Kyll,
I followed the angler's winding path
  Or waded the stream at will,
And the friendly fertile German land
  Lay round me green and still.

But all day long on the eastern bank
  Of the river cool and clear,
Where the curving track of the double rails
  Was hardly seen though near,
The endless trains of German troops
  Went rolling down to Trier.

They packed the windows with bullet heads
  And caps of hodden gray;
They laughed and sang and shouted loud
  When the trains were brought to a stay;
They waved their hands and sang again
  As they went on their iron way.

THE RED FLOWER

No shadow fell on the smiling land,
  No cloud arose in the sky;
I could hear the river's quiet tune
  When the trains had rattled by;
But my heart sank low with a heavy sense
  Of trouble,—I knew not why.

Then came I into a certain field
  Where the devil's paint-brush spread
'Mid the gray and green of the rolling hills
  A flaring splotch of red,—
An evil omen, a bloody sign,
  And a token of many dead.

I saw in a vision the field-gray horde
  Break forth at the devil's hour,
And trample the earth into crimson mud
  In the rage of the Will to Power,—
All this I dreamed in the valley of Kyll,
  At the sign of the blood-red flower.

A SCRAP OF PAPER

Will you go to war just for a scrap of paper?"—Question of the German Chancellor to the British Ambassador, August 5, 1914.

A MOCKING question! Britain's answer came
Swift as the light and searching as the flame.

"Yes, for a scrap of paper we will fight
Till our last breath, and God defend the right!

"A scrap of paper where a name is set
Is strong as duty's pledge and honor's debt.

"A scrap of paper holds for man and wife
The sacrament of love, the bond of life.

"A scrap of paper may be Holy Writ
With God's eternal word to hallow it.

"A scrap of paper binds us both to stand
Defenders of a neutral neighbor land.

"By God, by faith, by honor, yes! We fight
To keep our name upon that paper white."

September, 1914.

STAND FAST

Stand fast, Great Britain!
Together England, Scotland, Ireland stand
One in the faith that makes a mighty land,—
True to the bond you gave and will not break
And fearless in the fight for conscience' sake!
Against the Giant Robber clad in steel,
With blood of trampled Belgium on his heel,
Striding through France to strike you down at last
    Britain, stand fast!

Stand fast, brave land!
The Huns are thundering toward the citadel;
They prate of Culture but their path is Hell;
Their light is darkness, and the bloody sword
They wield and worship is their only Lord.
O land where reason stands secure on right,
O land where freedom is the source of light,
Against the mailed Barbarians' deadly blast,
    Britain, stand fast!

STAND FAST

    Stand fast, dear land!
Thou island mother of a world-wide race,
Whose children speak thy tongue and love thy face,
Their hearts and hopes are with thee in the strife,
Their hands will break the sword that seeks thy life
Fight on until the Teuton madness cease;
Fight bravely on, until the word of peace
Is spoken in the English tongue at last,—
    Britain, stand fast!

September, 1914.

LIGHTS OUT

(1915)

"LIGHTS out" along the land,
"Lights out" upon the sea.
The night must put her hiding hand
O'er peaceful towns where children sleep,
And peaceful ships that darkly creep
Across the waves, as if they were not free.

The dragons of the air,
The hell-hounds of the deep,
Lurking and prowling everywhere,
Go forth to seek their helpless prey,
Not knowing whom they maim or slay—
Mad harvesters, who care not what they reap

Out with the tranquil lights,
Out with the lights that burn
For love and law and human rights!
Set back the clock a thousand years:
All they have gained now disappears,
And the dark ages suddenly return.

LIGHTS OUT

Kaiser, who loosed wild death,
And terror in the night,
God grant you draw no quiet breath,
Until the madness you began
Is ended, and long-suffering man,
Set free from war lords, cries, "Let there be Light.'

October, 1915.

Read at the meeting of the American Academy, Boston, November 1915.

REMARKS ABOUT KINGS

"God said I am tired of kings."—EMERSON.

GOD said, "I am tired of kings,"—
But that was a long while ago!
And meantime man said, "No,—
I like their looks in their robes and rings."
So he crowned a few more,
And they went on playing the game as before,
Fighting and spoiling things.

Man said, "I am tired of kings!
Sons of the robber-chiefs of yore,
They make me pay for their lust and their war
I am the puppet, they pull the strings;
The blood of my heart is the wine they drink.
I will govern myself for awhile I think,
And see what that brings!"

Then God, who made the first remark,
Smiled in the dark.

October, 1915.

Read at the meeting of the American Academy, Boston, November, 1915.

MIGHT AND RIGHT

IF Might made Right, life were a wild-beasts' cage
If Right made Might, this were the golden age;
But now, until we win the long campaign,
Right must gain Might to conquer and to reign.

July 1, 1915.

THE PRICE OF PEACE

PEACE without Justice is a low estate,—
A coward cringing to an iron Fate!
But Peace through Justice is the great ideal,—
We'll pay the price of war to make it real.

December 28, 1916.

STORM-MUSIC

O Music hast thou only heard
The laughing river, the singing bird,
The murmuring wind in the poplar-trees,—
Nothing but Nature's melodies?
  Nay, thou hearest all her tones,
    As a Queen must hear!
    Sounds of wrath and fear,
    Mutterings, shouts, and moans,
  Madness, tumult, and despair,—
  All she has that shakes the air
  With voices fierce and wild!
Thou art a Queen and not a dreaming child,—
Put on thy crown and let us hear thee reign
Triumphant in a world of storm and strain!

  Echo the long-drawn sighs
Of the mounting wind in the pines;
And the sobs of the mounting waves that rise
  In the dark of the troubled deep
To break on the beach in fiery lines.
  Echo the far-off roll of thunder,
    Rumbling loud
  And ever louder, under
  The blue-black curtain of cloud,
  Where the lightning serpents gleam.

STORM-MUSIC

   Echo the moaning
  Of the forest in its sleep
  Like a giant groaning
In the torment of a dream.

  Now an interval of quiet
  For a moment holds the air
  In the breathless hush
  Of a silent prayer.

Then the sudden rush
  Of the rain, and the riot
  Of the shrieking, tearing gale
Breaks loose in the night,
  With a fusillade of hail!
Hear the forest fight,
With its tossing arms that crack and clash
  In the thunder's cannonade,
  While the lightning's forkèd flash
Brings the old hero-trees to the ground with a crash!
Hear the breakers' deepening roar,
  Driven like a herd of cattle
  In the wild stampede of battle,
Trampling, trampling, trampling, to overwhelm the shore!

THE RED FLOWER

Is it the end of all?
Will the land crumble and fall?
Nay, for a voice replies
Out of the hidden skies,
"Thus far, O sea, shalt thou go,
So long, O wind, shalt thou blow:
Return to your bounds and cease,
And let the earth have peace!"

O Music, lead the way—
    The stormy night is past,
Lift up our hearts to greet the day,
    And the joy of things that last.

The dissonance and pain
    That mortals must endure,
Are changed in thine immortal strain
    To something great and pure.

True love will conquer strife,
    And strength from conflict flows,
For discord is the thorn of life
    And harmony the rose.

May, 1916.

THE BELLS OF MALINES

August 17, 1914

The gabled roofs of old Malines
Are russet red and gray and green,
And o'er them in the sunset hour
Looms, dark and huge, St. Rombold's tower
High in that rugged nest concealed,
The sweetest bells that ever pealed,
The deepest bells that ever rung,
The lightest bells that ever sung,
Are waiting for the master's hand
To fling their music o'er the land.

And shall they ring to-night, Malines?
In nineteen hundred and fourteen,
The frightful year, the year of woe,
When fire and blood and rapine flow
Across the land from lost Liége,
Storm-driven by the German rage?
The other carillons have ceased:
Fallen is Hasselt, fallen Diest,
From Ghent and Bruges no voices come,
Antwerp is silent, Brussels dumb!

THE RED FLOWER

But in thy belfry, O Malines,
The master of the bells unseen
Has climbed to where the keyboard stands
To-night his heart is in his hands!
Once more, before invasion's hell
Breaks round the tower he loves so well,
Once more he strikes the well-worn keys,
And sends aërial harmonies
Far-floating through the twilight dim
In patriot song and holy hymn.

O listen, burghers of Malines!
Soldier and workman, pale béguine,
And mother with a trembling flock
Of children clinging to thy frock,—
Look up and listen, listen all!
What tunes are these that gently fall
Around you like a benison?
"The Flemish Lion," "Brabançonne,"
"O brave Liége," and all the airs
That Belgium in her bosom bears.

Ring up, ye silvery octaves high,
Whose notes like circling swallows fly;
And ring, each old sonorous bell,—
"Jesu," "Maria," "Michaël!"

THE BELLS OF MALINES

Weave in and out, and high and low,
The magic music that you know,
And let it float and flutter down
To cheer the heart of the troubled town.
Ring out, "Salvator," lord of all,—
"Roland" in Ghent may hear thee call!

O brave bell-music of Malines,
In this dark hour how much you mean!
The dreadful night of blood and tears
Sweeps down on Belgium, but she hears
Deep in her heart the melody
Of songs she learned when she was free.
She will not falter, faint, nor fail,
But fight until her rights prevail
And all her ancient belfries ring
"The Flemish Lion," "God Save the King!"

JEANNE D'ARC RETURNS*

1914-1916

What hast thou done, O womanhood of France,
  Mother and daughter, sister, sweetheart, wife,
  What hast thou done, amid this fateful strife,
To prove the pride of thine inheritance
In this fair land of freedom and romance?
  I hear thy voice with tears and courage rife,—
  Smiling against the swords that seek thy life,—
Make answer in a noble utterance:
"I give France all I have, and all she asks.
  Would it were more! Ah, let her ask and take:
My hands to nurse her wounded, do her tasks,—
  My feet to run her errands through the dark,—
My heart to bleed in triumph for her sake,—
  And all my soul to follow thee, Jeanne d'Arc!"

April 16, 1916.

* This sonnet belongs with the poem on page 309, "Come Back Again Jeanne D'Arc."

THE NAME OF FRANCE

Give us a name to fill the mind
With the shining thoughts that lead mankind
The glory of learning, the joy of art,—
A name that tells of a splendid part
In the long, long toil and the strenuous fight
Of the human race to win its way
From the feudal darkness into the day
Of Freedom, Brotherhood, Equal Right,—
A name like a star, a name of light.
    I give you *France!*

Give us a name to stir the blood
With a warmer glow and a swifter flood,
At the touch of a courage that conquers fear,-
A name like the sound of a trumpet, clear,
And silver-sweet, and iron-strong,
That calls three million men to their feet,
Ready to march, and steady to meet
The foes who threaten that name with wrong
A name that rings like a battle-song.
    I give you *France!*

THE RED FLOWER

Give us a name to move the heart
With the strength that noble griefs impart,
A name that speaks of the blood outpoured
To save mankind from the sway of the sword,—
A name that calls on the world to share
In the burden of sacrificial strife
When the cause at stake is the world's free life
And the rule of the people everywhere,—
A name like a vow, a name like a prayer.
    I give you *France!*

The Hague, September, 1916.

AMERICA'S PROSPERITY

They tell me thou art rich, my country: gold
  In glittering flood has poured into thy chest;
  Thy flocks and herds increase, thy barns are pressed
With harvest, and thy stores can hardly hold
Their merchandise; unending trains are rolled
  Along thy network rails of East and West;
  Thy factories and forges never rest;
Thou art enriched in all things bought and sold!

But dost *thou* prosper? Better news I crave.
  O dearest country, is it well with thee
    Indeed, and is thy soul in health?
A nobler people, hearts more wisely brave,
  And thoughts that lift men up and make them free,—
    These are prosperity and vital wealth!

The Hague, October 1, 1916.

THE GLORY OF SHIPS

The glory of ships is an old, old song,
  since the days when the sea-rovers ran,
In their open boats through the roaring surf,
  and the spread of the world began;
The glory of ships is a light on the sea,
  and a star in the story of man.

When Homer sang of the galleys of Greece
  that conquered the Trojan shore,
And Solomon lauded the barks of Tyre
  that brought great wealth to his door,
'Twas little they knew, those ancient men,
  what would come of the sail and the oar.

The Greek ships rescued the West from the East,
  when they harried the Persians home;
And the Roman ships were the wings of strength
  that bore up the empire, Rome;
And the ships of Spain found a wide new world,
  far over the fields of foam.

THE GLORY OF SHIPS

Then the tribes of courage at last saw clear
  that the ocean was not a bound,
But a broad highway, and a challenge to seek
  for treasure as yet unfound;
So the fearless ships fared forth to the search,
  in joy that the globe was round.

Their hulls were heightened, their sails spread out
  they grew with the growth of their quest;
They opened the secret doors of the East,
  and the golden gates of the West;
And many a city of high renown
  was proud of a ship on its crest.

The fleets of England and Holland and France
  were at strife with each other and Spain;
And battle and storm sent a myriad ships
  to sleep in the depths of the main;
But the seafaring spirit could never be drowned,
  and it filled up the fleets again.

They greatened and grew, with the aid of steam,
  to a wonderful, vast array,
That carries the thoughts and the traffic of men
  into every harbor and bay;
And now in the world-wide work of the ships
  'tis England that leads the way.

THE RED FLOWER

O well for the leading that follows the law
  of a common right on the sea!
But ill for the leader who tries to hold
  what belongs to mankind in fee!
The way of the ships is an open way,
  and the ocean must ever be free!

Remember, O first of the maritime folk,
  how the rise of your greatness began.
It will live if you safeguard the round-the-world road
  from the shame of a selfish ban;
For the glory of ships is a light on the sea,
  and a star in the story of man!

September 12, 1916.

MARE LIBERUM

I

You dare to say with perjured lips,
"We fight to make the ocean free"?
You, whose black trail of butchered ships
Bestrews the bed of every sea
Where German submarines have wrought
Their horrors! Have you never thought,—
What you call freedom, men call piracy!

II

Unnumbered ghosts that haunt the wave,
Where you have murdered, cry you down;
And seamen whom you would not save,
Weave now in weed-grown depths a crown
Of shame for your imperious head,
A dark memorial of the dead
Women and children whom you sent to drown

THE RED FLOWER

III

Nay, not till thieves are set to guard
The gold, and corsairs called to keep
O'er peaceful commerce watch and ward,
And wolves to herd the helpless sheep,
Shall men and women look to thee,
Thou ruthless Old Man of the Sea,
To safeguard law and freedom on the deep!

IV

In nobler breeds we put our trust:
The nations in whose sacred lore
The "Ought" stands out above the "Must,'
And honor rules in peace and war.
With these we hold in soul and heart,
With these we choose our lot and part,
Till Liberty is safe on sea and shore.

London Times, February 12, 1917.

"LIBERTY ENLIGHTENING THE WORLD"

Thou warden of the western gate, above Manhattan Bay,
The fogs of doubt that hid thy face are driven clean away:
Thine eyes at last look far and clear, thou liftest high thy hand
To spread the light of liberty world-wide for every land.

No more thou dreamest of a peace reserved alone for thee,
While friends are fighting for thy cause beyond the guardian sea:
The battle that they wage is thine; thou fallest if they fall;
The swollen flood of Prussian pride will sweep unchecked o'er all.

O cruel is the conquer-lust in Hohenzollern brains:
The paths they plot to gain their goal are dark with shameful stains;
No faith they keep, no law revere, no god but naked Might;
They are the foemen of mankind. Up, Liberty, and smite!

THE RED FLOWER

Britain, and France, and Italy, and Russia newly born,
Have waited for thee in the night. Oh, come as comes
  the morn!
Serene and strong and full of faith, America, arise,
With steady hope and mighty help to join thy brave
  Allies.

O dearest country of my heart, home of the high desire,
Make clean thy soul for sacrifice on Freedom's altar-
  fire:
For thou must suffer, thou must fight, until the war-
  lords cease,
And all the peoples lift their heads in liberty and peace.
London Times, April 12, 1917.

THE OXFORD THRUSHES

February, 1917

I NEVER thought again to hear
The Oxford thrushes singing clear,
Amid the February rain,
Their sweet, indomitable strain.

A wintry vapor lightly spreads
Among the trees, and round the beds
Where daffodil and jonquil sleep;
Only the snowdrop wakes to weep.

It is not springtime yet. Alas,
What dark, tempestuous days must pass
Till England's trial by battle cease,
And summer comes again with peace.

The lofty halls, the tranquil towers,
Where Learning in untroubled hours
Held her high court, serene in fame,
Are lovely still, yet not the same.

The novices in fluttering gown
No longer fill the ancient town;
But fighting men in khaki drest,
And in the Schools the wounded rest.

THE RED FLOWER

Ah, far away, 'neath stranger skies
Full many a son of Oxford lies,
And whispers from his warrior grave,
"I died to keep the faith you gave."

The mother mourns, but does not fail
Her courage and her love prevail
O'er sorrow, and her spirit hears
The promise of triumphant years.

Then sing, ye thrushes, in the rain
Your sweet indomitable strain.
Ye bring a word from God on high
And voices in our hearts reply.

HOMEWARD BOUND

Home, for my heart still calls me;
  Home, through the danger zone;
Home, whatever befalls me,
  I will sail again to my own!

Wolves of the sea are hiding
  Closely along the way,
Under the water biding
  Their moment to rend and slay.

Black is the eagle that brands them,
  Black are their hearts as the night
Black is the hate that sends them
  To murder but not to fight.

Flower of the German Culture,
  Boast of the Kaiser's Marine,
Choose for your emblem the vulture,
  Cowardly, cruel, obscene!

Forth from her sheltered haven
  Our peaceful ship glides slow,
Noiseless in flight as a raven,
  Gray as a hoodie crow.

THE RED FLOWER

She doubles and turns in her bearing
  Like a twisting plover she goes;
The way of her westward faring
  Only the captain knows.

In a lonely bay concealing
  She lingers for days, and slips
At dusk from her covert, stealing
  Thro' channels feared by the ships.

Brave are the men, and steady,
  Who guide her over the deep,—
British mariners, ready
  To face the sea-wolf's leap.

Lord of the winds and waters,
  Bring our ship to her mark,
Safe from this game of hide-and-seek
  With murderers in the dark!

On the S. S. *Baltic*, May, 1917.

THE WINDS OF WAR-NEWS

The winds of war-news change and veer:
Now westerly and full of cheer,
Now easterly, depressing, sour
With tidings of the Teutons' power.

But thou, America, whose heart
With brave Allies has taken part,
Be not a weathercock to change
With these wild winds that shift and range.

Be thou a compass ever true,
Through sullen clouds or skies of blue,
To that great star which rules the night,—
The star of Liberty and Right.

Lover of peace, oh set thy soul,
Thy strength, thy wealth, thy conscience whole
To win the peace thine eyes foresee,—
The triumph of Democracy.

December 19, 1917.

RIGHTEOUS WRATH

THERE are many kinds of anger, as many kinds of fire;
And some are fierce and fatal with murderous desire;
And some are mean and craven, revengeful, sullen, slow,
They hurt the man that holds them more than they
    hurt his foe.

And yet there is an anger that purifies the heart:
The anger of the better against the baser part,
Against the false and wicked, against the tyrant's sword,
Against the enemies of love, and all that hate the Lord.

O cleansing indignation, O flame of righteous wrath,
Give me a soul to feel thee and follow in thy path!
Save me from selfish virtue, arm me for fearless fight,
And give me strength to carry on, a soldier of the Right!

January, 1918.

THE PEACEFUL WARRIOR

I HAVE no joy in strife,
  Peace is my great desire;
Yet God forbid I lose my life
  Through fear to face the fire.

A peaceful man must fight
  For that which peace demands,—
Freedom and faith, honor and right,
  Defend with heart and hands.

Farewell, my friendly books;
  Farewell, ye woods and streams;
The fate that calls me forward looks
  To a duty beyond dreams.

Oh, better to be dead
  With a face turned to the sky,
Than live beneath a slavish dread
  And serve a giant lie.

Stand up, my heart, and strive
  For the things most dear to thee!
Why should we care to be alive
  Unless the world is free?

May, 1918.

FROM GLORY UNTO GLORY

AMERICAN FLAG SONG

1776

O DARK the night and dim the day
  When first our flag arose;
It fluttered bravely in the fray
  To meet o'erwhelming foes.
Our fathers saw the splendor shine,
  They dared and suffered all;
They won our freedom by the sign—
The holy sign, the radiant sign—
  Of the stars that never fall.

Chorus

  All hail to thee, Young Glory!
    Among the flags of earth
  We'll ne'er forget the story
    Of thy heroic birth.

1861

O wild the later storm that shook
  The pillars of the State,
When brother against brother took
  The final arms of fate.
But union lived and peace divine
  Enfolded brothers all;

FROM GLORY UNTO GLORY

The flag floats o'er them with the sign—
The loyal sign, the equal sign—
  Of the stars that never fall.

Chorus

All hail to thee, Old Glory!
  Of thee our heart's desire
Foretells a golden story,
  For thou hast come through fire.

1917

O fiercer than all wars before
  That raged on land or sea,
The Giant Robber's world-wide war
  For the things that shall not be!
Thy sister banners hold the line;
  To thee, dear flag, they call;
And thou hast joined them with the sign
The heavenly sign, the victor sign—
  Of the stars that never fall.

Chorus

All hail to thee, New Glory!
  We follow thee unfurled
To write the larger story
  Of Freedom for the World.

September 4, 1918.

BRITAIN, FRANCE, AMERICA

THE rough expanse of democratic sea
Which parts the lands that live by liberty
Is no division; for their hearts are one.
To fight together till their cause is won.

For land and water let us make our pact,
And seal the solemn word with valiant act
No continent is firm, no ocean pure,
Until on both the rights of man are sure.

April, 1917.

THE RED CROSS

Sign of the Love Divine
  That bends to bear the load
Of all who suffer, all who bleed,
  Along life's thorny road:

Sign of the Heart Humane,
  That through the darkest fight
Would bring to wounded friend and foe
  A ministry of light:

O dear and holy sign,
  Lead onward like a star!
The armies of the just are thine,
  And all we have and are.

October 20, 1918.
For the Red Cross Christmas Roll Call.

EASTER ROAD

1918

UNDER the cloud of world-wide war,
While earth is drenched with sorrow,
I have no heart for idle merrymaking,
Or for the fashioning of glad raiment.
I will retrace the divine footmarks,
On the Road of the first Easter

Down through the valley of utter darkness
Dripping with blood and tears;
Over the hill of the skull, the little hill of great anguish,
The ambuscade of Death.
Into the no-man's-land of Hades
Bearing despatches of hope to spirits in prison,
Mortally stricken and triumphant
Went the faithful Captain of Salvation.

Then upward, swiftly upward,—
Victory, liberty, glory,
The feet that were wounded walked in the tranquil garden,
Bathed in dew and the light of deathless dawn.

O my soul, my comrades, soldiers of freedom,
Follow the pathway of Easter, for there is no other.

EASTER ROAD

Follow it through to peace, yea, follow it fighting.
This Armageddon is not darker than Calvary.
The day will break when the Dragon is vanquished;
He that exalteth himself as God shall be cast down,
And the Lords of war shall fall,
And the long, long terror be ended,
Victory, justice, peace enduring!
They that die in this cause shall live forever,
And they that live shall never die,
They shall rejoice together in the Easter of a new world

March 31, 1918.

AMERICA'S WELCOME HOME

Oh, gallantly they fared forth in khaki and in blue,
America's crusading host of warriors bold and true;
They battled for the rights of man beside our brave Allies,
And now they're coming home to us with glory in their eyes.

Oh, it's home again, and home again, America for me!
Our hearts are turning home again and there we long to be,
In our beautiful big country beyond the ocean bars,
Where the air is full of sunlight and the flag is full of stars.

Our boys have seen the Old World as none have seen before.
They know the grisly horror of the German gods of war:
The noble faith of Britain and the hero-heart of France,
The soul of Belgium's fortitude and Italy's romance.

They bore our country's great word across the rolling sea,
"America swears brotherhood with all the just and free."
They wrote that word victorious on fields of mortal strife,
And many a valiant lad was proud to seal it with his life.

AMERICA'S WELCOME HOME

Oh, welcome home in Heaven's peace, dear spirits of the dead!
And welcome home ye living sons America hath bred!
The lords of war are beaten down, your glorious task is done;
You fought to make the whole world free, and the victory is won.

Now it's home again, and home again, our hearts are turning west,
Of all the lands beneath the sun America is best.
We're going home to our own folks, beyond the ocean bars,
Where the air is full of sunlight and the flag is full of stars.

November 11, 1918.
A sequel to "America For Me," written in 1909. Page 314.

THE SURRENDER OF THE GERMAN FLEET

Ship after ship, and every one with a high-resounding name,
From the robber-nest of Heligoland the German war-fleet came;
Not victory or death they sought, but a rendezvous of shame.

>   *Sing out, sing out,*
>   *A joyful shout,*
>   *Ye lovers of the sea!*
>   *The "Kaiser" and the "Kaiserin,"*
>   *The "König" and the "Prinz,"*
>   *The potentates of piracy,*
>   *Are coming to surrender,*
>   *And the ocean shall be free.*

They never dared the final fate of battle on the blue;
Their sea-wolves murdered merchantmen and mocked the drowning crew;
They stained the wave with martyr-blood,—but we sent our transports through!

SURRENDER OF THE GERMAN FLEET

What flags are these that dumbly droop from the gaff o'
   the mainmast tall?
The black of the Kaiser's iron cross, the red of the Em-
   pire's fall!
Come down, come down, ye pirate flags. Yea, strike
   your colors all.

The Union Jack and the Tricolor and the Starry Flag o'
   the West
Shall guard the fruit of Freedom's war and the victory
   confest,
The flags of the brave and just and free shall rule on the
   ocean's breast.

> *Sing out, sing out,*
> *A mighty shout,*
> *Ye lovers of the sea!*
> *The "Kaiser" and the "Kaiserin,"*
> *The "König" and the "Prinz,"*
> *The robber-lords of death and sin,*
> *Have come to their surrender,*
> *And the ocean shall be free!*

November 20, 1918.

GOLDEN STARS

I

It was my lot of late to travel far
Through all America's domain,
A willing, gray-haired servitor
Bearing the Fiery Cross of righteous war.
And everywhere, on mountain, vale and plain,
In crowded street and lonely cottage door,
I saw the symbol of the bright blue star.
Millions of stars! Rejoice, dear land, rejoice
That God hath made thee great enough to give
Beneath thy starry flag unfurled
A gift to all the world,—
Thy living sons that Liberty might live.

II

It seems but yesterday they sallied forth
Boys of the east, the west, the south, the north
High-hearted, keen, with laughter and with song
Fearless of lurking danger on the sea,
Eager to fight in Flanders or in France
Against the monstrous German wrong,
And sure of victory!
Brothers in soul with British and with French

412

GOLDEN STARS

They held their ground in many a bloody trench;
And when the swift word came—
Advance!
Over the top they went through waves of flame,—
Confident, reckless, irresistible,
Real Americans,—
Their rush was never stayed
Until the foe fell back, defeated and dismayed.
O land that bore them, write upon thy roll
Of battles won
To liberate the human soul,
Château Thierry and Saint Mihiel
And the fierce agony of the Argonne;
Yea, count among thy little rivers, dear
Because of friends whose feet have trodden there,
The Marne, the Meuse, and the Moselle.

III

Now the vile sword
In Potsdam forged and bathed in hell,
Is beaten down, the victory given
To the sword forged in faith and bathed in heaven
Now home again our heroes come:
Oh, welcome them with bugle and with drum,
Ring bells, blow whistles, make a joyful noise
Unto the Lord,
And welcome home our blue-star boys,

GOLDEN STARS

Whose manhood has made known
To all the world America,
Unselfish, brave and free, the Great Republic,
Who lives not to herself alone.

IV

But many a lad we hold
Dear in our heart of hearts
Is missing from the home-returning host.
Ah, say not they are lost,
For they have found and given their life
In sacrificial strife:
Their service stars have changed from blue to gold!
That sudden rapture took them far away,
Yet are they here with us to-day,
Even as the heavenly stars we cannot see
Through the bright veil of sunlight,
Shed their influence still
On our vexed life, and promise peace
From God to all men of good will.

V

What wreaths shall we entwine
For our dear boys to deck their holy shrine?
  Mountain-laurel, morning-glory,
  Goldenrod and asters blue,
  Purple loosestrife, prince's-pine,

GOLDEN STARS

Wild-azalea, meadow-rue,
Nodding-lilies, columbine,—
All the native blooms that grew
In these fresh woods and pastures new,
Wherein they loved to ramble and to play.
Bring no exotic flowers:
America was in their hearts,
And they are ours
For ever and a day.

VI

O happy warriors, forgive the tear
Falling from eyes that miss you:
Forgive the word of grief from mother-lips
That ne'er on earth shall kiss you;
Hear only what our hearts would have you hear,-
Glory and praise and gratitude and pride
From the dear country in whose cause you died.
Now you have run your race and won your prize
Old age shall never burden you, the fears
And conflicts that beset our lingering years
Shall never vex your souls in Paradise.
Immortal, young, and crowned with victory,
From life's long battle you have found release.
And He who died for all on Calvary
Has welcomed you, brave soldiers of the cross,
Into eternal Peace.

GOLDEN STARS

VII

Come, let us gird our loins and lift our load,
Companions who are left on life's rough road,
And bravely take the way that we must tread
To keep true faith with our beloved dead.
To conquer war they dared their lives to give,
To safeguard peace our hearts must learn to live
Help us, dear God, our forward faith to hold!
We want a better world than that of old.
Lead us on paths of high endeavor,
Toiling upward, climbing ever,
Ready to suffer for the right,
Until at last we gain a loftier height,
More worthy to behold
Our guiding stars, our hero-stars of gold.

Ode for the Memorial Service,
Princeton University, December 15, 1918.

IN THE BLUE HEAVEN

In the blue heaven the clouds will come and go,
Scudding before the gale, or drifting slow
As galleons becalmed in Sundown Bay:
And through the air the birds will wing their way
Soaring to far-off heights, or flapping low,
Or darting like an arrow from the bow;
And when the twilight comes the stars will show,
One after one, their tranquil bright array
          In the blue heaven.

But ye who fearless flew to meet the foe,
Eagles of freedom,—nevermore, we know,
Shall we behold you floating far away.
Yet clouds and birds and every starry ray
Will draw our heart to where your spirits glow
          In the blue Heaven.

For the American Aviators who died in the war.
March, 1919.

A SHRINE IN THE PANTHEON

FOR THE UNNAMED SOLDIERS WHO DIED IN FRANCE

Universal approval has been accorded the proposal made in the French Chamber that the ashes of an unnamed French soldier, fallen for his country, shall be removed with solemn ceremony to the Pantheon. In this way it is intended to honor by a symbolic ceremony the memory of all who lie in unmarked graves.

> HERE the great heart of France,
>   Victor in noble strife,
> Doth consecrate a Poilu's tomb
>   To those who saved her life.
>
> Brave son without a name,
>   Your country calls you home,
> To rest among her heirs of fame,
>   Beneath the Pantheon's dome!
>
> Now from the height of Heaven,
>   The souls of heroes look;
> Their names, ungraven on this stone,
>   Are written in God's book.
>
> Women of France, who mourn
>   Your dead in unmarked ground,
> Come hither! Here the man you loved
>   In the heart of France is found!

IN PRAISE OF POETS

MOTHER EARTH

Mother of all the high-strung poets and singers departed,
Mother of all the grass that weaves over their graves the glory of the field,
Mother of all the manifold forms of life, deep-bosomed, patient, impassive,
Silent brooder and nurse of lyrical joys and sorrows!
Out of thee, yea, surely out of the fertile depth below thy breast,
Issued in some strange way, thou lying motionless, voiceless,
All these songs of nature, rhythmical, passionate, yearning,
Coming in music from earth, but not unto earth returning.

Dust are the blood-red hearts that beat in time to these measures,
Thou hast taken them back to thyself, secretly, irresistibly
Drawing the crimson currents of life down, down, down
Deep into thy bosom again, as a river is lost in the sand.
But the souls of the singers have entered into the songs that revealed them,—
Passionate songs, immortal songs of joy and grief and love and longing,

IN PRAISE OF POETS

Floating from heart to heart of thy children, they echo above thee:
Do they not utter thy heart, the voices of those that love thee?

Long hadst thou lain like a queen transformed by some old enchantment
Into an alien shape, mysterious, beautiful, speechless,
Knowing not who thou wert, till the touch of thy Lord and Lover
Wakened the man-child within thee to tell thy secret.
All of thy flowers and birds and forests and flowing waters
Are but the rhythmical forms to reveal the life of the spirit;
Thou thyself, earth-mother, in mountain and meadow and ocean,
Holdest the poem of God, eternal thought and emotion.

December, 1905.

MILTON

I

Lover of beauty, walking on the height
  Of pure philosophy and tranquil song;
  Born to behold the visions that belong
To those who dwell in melody and light;
Milton, thou spirit delicate and bright!
  What drew thee down to join the Roundhead throng
  Of iron-sided warriors, rude and strong,
Fighting for freedom in a world half night?

Lover of Liberty at heart wast thou,
  Above all beauty bright, all music clear:
To thee she bared her bosom and her brow,
  Breathing her virgin promise in thine ear,
And bound thee to her with a double vow,—
  Exquisite Puritan, grave Cavalier!

II

The cause, the cause for which thy soul resigned
  Her singing robes to battle on the plain,
  Was won, O poet, and was lost again;
And lost the labour of thy lonely mind
On weary tasks of prose. What wilt thou find
  To comfort thee for all the toil and pain?
  What solace, now thy sacrifice is vain
And thou art left forsaken, poor, and blind?

IN PRAISE OF POETS

Like organ-music comes the deep reply:
  "The cause of truth looks lost, but shall be won
For God hath given to mine inward eye
  Vision of England soaring to the sun.
And granted me great peace before I die,
  In thoughts of lowly duty bravely done."

III

O bend again above thine organ-board,
  Thou blind old poet longing for repose!
  Thy Master claims thy service not with those
Who only stand and wait for His reward;
He pours the heavenly gift of song restored
  Into thy breast, and bids thee nobly close
  A noble life, with poetry that flows
In mighty music of the major chord.

Where hast thou learned this deep, majestic strain,
  Surpassing all thy youthful lyric grace,
To sing of Paradise? Ah, not in vain
  The griefs that won at Dante's side thy place,
And made thee, Milton, by thy years of pain,
  The loftiest poet of the English race!

1908.

WORDSWORTH

Wordsworth, thy music like a river rolls
  Among the mountains, and thy song is fed
    By living springs far up the watershed;
No whirling flood nor parching drought controls
The crystal current: even on the shoals
  It murmurs clear and sweet; and when its bed
  Deepens below mysterious cliffs of dread,
Thy voice of peace grows deeper in our souls.

But thou in youth hast known the breaking stress
  Of passion, and hast trod despair's dry ground
    Beneath black thoughts that wither and destroy
Ah, wanderer, led by human tenderness
  Home to the heart of Nature, thou hast found
    The hidden Fountain of Recovered Joy.

October, 1906.

KEATS

The melancholy gift Aurora gained
  From Jove, that her sad lover should not see
  The face of death, no goddess asked for thee,
My Keats! But when the scarlet blood-drop stained
Thy pillow, thou didst read the fate ordained,—
  Brief life, wild love, a flight of poesy!
  And then,—a shadow fell on Italy:
Thy star went down before its brightness waned.

Yet thou hast won the gift Tithonus missed:
  Never to feel the pain of growing old,
    Nor lose the blissful sight of beauty's truth,
But with the ardent lips Urania kissed
  To breathe thy song, and, ere thy heart grew cold,
    Become the Poet of Immortal Youth.

August, 1906.

SHELLEY

KNIGHT-ERRANT of the Never-ending Quest,
  And Minstrel of the Unfulfilled Desire;
  For ever tuning thy frail earthly lyre
To some unearthly music, and possessed
With painful passionate longing to invest
  The golden dream of Love's immortal fire
  With mortal robes of beautiful attire,
And fold perfection to thy throbbing breast!

What wonder, Shelley, that the restless wave
  Should claim thee and the leaping flame consume
    Thy drifted form on Viareggio's beach?
These were thine elements,—thy fitting grave.
  But still thy soul rides on with fiery plume,
    Thy wild song rings in ocean's yearning speech!

August, 1906.

ROBERT BROWNING

How blind the toil that burrows like the mole,
  In winding graveyard pathways underground,
  For Browning's lineage! What if men have found
Poor footmen or rich merchants on the roll
Of his forbears? Did they beget his soul?
  Nay, for he came of ancestry renowned
  Through all the world,—the poets laurel-crowned
With wreaths from which the autumn takes no toll.

The blazons on his coat-of-arms are these:
  The flaming sign of Shelley's heart on fire,
    The golden globe of Shakespeare's human stage,
    The staff and scrip of Chaucer's pilgrimage,
  The rose of Dante's deep, divine desire,
The tragic mask of wise Euripides.

November, 1906.

TENNYSON

In Lucem Transitus, October, 1892

From the misty shores of midnight, touched with splendours of the moon,
To the singing tides of heaven, and the light more clear than noon,
Passed a soul that grew to music till it was with God in tune.

Brother of the greatest poets, true to nature, true to art;
Lover of Immortal Love, uplifter of the human heart;
Who shall cheer us with high music, who shall sing, if thou depart?

Silence here—for love is silent, gazing on the lessening sail;
Silence here—for grief is voiceless when the mighty minstrels fail;
Silence here—but far beyond us, many voices crying, Hail!

"IN MEMORIAM"

THE record of a faith sublime,
    And hope, through clouds, far-off discerned
    The incense of a love that burned
Through pain and doubt defying Time:

The story of a soul at strife
    That learned at last to kiss the rod,
    And passed through sorrow up to God,
From living to a higher life:

A light that gleams across the wave
    Of darkness, down the rolling years,
    Piercing the heavy mist of tears—
A rainbow shining o'er a grave.

VICTOR HUGO
1802–1902

HEART of France for a hundred years,
  Passionate, sensitive, proud, and strong,
Quick to throb with her hopes and fears,
  Fierce to flame with her sense of wrong!
  You, who hailed with a morning song
Dream-light gilding a throne of old:
You, who turned when the dream grew cold,
Singing still, to the light that shone
Pure from Liberty's ancient throne,
    Over the human throng!
You, who dared in the dark eclipse,—
  When the pygmy heir of a giant name
  Dimmed the face of the land with shame,—
Speak the truth with indignant lips,
Call him little whom men called great,
  Scoff at him, scorn him, deny him,
Point to the blood on his robe of state,
  Fling back his bribes and defy him!

You, who fronted the waves of fate
  As you faced the sea from your island home
Exiled, yet with a soul elate,
  Sending songs o'er the rolling foam,
Bidding the heart of man to wait
    For the day when all should see

IN PRAISE OF POETS

Floods of wrath from the frowning skies
Fall on an Empire founded in lies,
   And France again be free!
You, who came in the Terrible Year
   Swiftly back to your broken land,
Now to your heart a thousand times more dear,—
   Prayed for her, sung to her, fought for her,
   Patiently, fervently wrought for her,
      Till once again,
   After the storm of fear and pain,
High in the heavens the star of France stood clear

You, who knew that a man must take
Good and ill with a steadfast soul,
Holding fast, while the billows roll
   Over his head, to the things that make
Life worth living for great and small,
    Honour and pity and truth,
    The heart and the hope of youth,
And the good God over all!
   You, to whom work was rest,
Dauntless Toiler of the Sea,
   Following ever the joyful quest
Of beauty on the shores of old Romance,
   Bard of the poor of France,
   And warrior-priest of world-wide charity!
   You who loved little children best
Of all the poets that ever sung,

VICTOR HUGO

Great heart, golden heart,
Old, and yet ever young,
    Minstrel of liberty,
Lover of all free, winged things,
    Now at last you are free,—
Your soul has its wings!
Heart of France for a hundred years,
    Floating far in the light that never fails you,
Over the turmoil of mortal hopes and fears
    Victor, forever victor, the whole world hails you!

March, 1902.

LONGFELLOW

In a great land, a new land, a land full of labour and riches and confusion,
Where there were many running to and fro, and shouting, and striving together,
In the midst of the hurry and the troubled noise, I heard the voice of one singing.

"What are you doing there, O man, singing quietly amid all this tumult?
This is the time for new inventions, mighty shoutings, and blowings of the trumpet."
But he answered, "I am only shepherding my sheep with music."

So he went along his chosen way, keeping his little flock around him;
And he paused to listen, now and then, beside the antique fountains,
Where the faces of forgotten gods were refreshed with musically falling waters;

Or he sat for a while at the blacksmith's door, and heard the cling-clang of the anvils;
Or he rested beneath old steeples full of bells, that showered their chimes upon him;
Or he walked along the border of the sea, drinking in the long roar of the billows;

LONGFELLOW

Or he sunned himself in the pine-scented shipyard, amid
    the tattoo of the mallets;
Or he leaned on the rail of the bridge, letting his thoughts
    flow with the whispering river;
He hearkened also to ancient tales, and made them
    young again with his singing.

Then a flaming arrow of death fell on his flock, and
    pierced the heart of his dearest!
Silent the music now, as the shepherd entered the
    mystical temple of sorrow:
Long he tarried in darkness there: but when he came
    out he was singing.

And I saw the faces of men and women and children
    silently turning toward him;
The youth setting out on the journey of life, and the old
    man waiting beside the last mile-stone;
The toiler sweating beneath his load; and the happy
    mother rocking her cradle;

The lonely sailor on far-off seas; and the gray-minded
    scholar in his book-room;
The mill-hand bound to a clacking machine; and the
    hunter in the forest;
And the solitary soul hiding friendless in the wilderness
    of the city;

IN PRAISE OF POETS

Many human faces, full of care and longing, were drawn
    irresistibly toward him,
By the charm of something known to every heart, yet
    very strange and lovely,
And at the sound of his singing wonderfully all their
    faces were lightened.

"Why do you listen, O you people, to this old and world-
    worn music?
This is not for you, in the splendour of a new age, in the
    democratic triumph!
Listen to the clashing cymbals, the big drums, the brazen
    trumpets of your poets."

But the people made no answer, following in their hearts
    the simpler music:
For it seemed to them, noise-weary, nothing could be
    better worth the hearing
Than the melodies which brought sweet order into life's
    confusion.

So the shepherd sang his way along, until he came unto
    a mountain:
And I know not surely whether the mountain was called
    Parnassus,
But he climbed it out of sight, and still I heard the
    voice of one singing.

January, 1907.

THOMAS BAILEY ALDRICH

I

BIRTHDAY VERSES, 1906

DEAR Aldrich, now November's mellow days
  Have brought another *Festa* round to you,
You can't refuse a loving-cup of praise
  From friends the fleeting years have bound to you

Here come your Marjorie Daw, your dear Bad Boy,
  Prudence, and Judith the Bethulian,
And many more, to wish you birthday joy,
  And sunny hours, and sky cerulean!

Your children all, they hurry to your den,
  With wreaths of honour they have won for you,
To merry-make your threescore years and ten.
  You, old? Why, life has just begun for you!

There's many a reader whom your silver songs
  And crystal stories cheer in loneliness.
What though the newer writers come in throngs?
  You're sure to keep your charm of only-ness.

IN PRAISE OF POETS

You do your work with careful, loving touch,—
    An artist to the very core of you,—
You know the magic spell of "not-too-much":
    We read,—and wish that there was more of you

And more there is: for while we love your books
    Because their subtle skill is part of you;
We love *you* better, for our friendship looks
    Behind them to the human heart of you.

II

MEMORIAL SONNET, 1908

This is the house where little Aldrich read
    The early pages of Life's wonder-book
    With boyish pleasure: in this ingle-nook
He watched the drift-wood fire of Fancy shed
Bright colour on the pictures blue and red:
    Boy-like he skipped the longer words, and took
    His happy way, with searching, dreamful look
Among the deeper things more simply said.

Then, came his turn to write: and still the flame
    Of Fancy played through all the tales he told,
And still he won the laurelled poet's fame
    With simple words wrought into rhymes of gold.
Look, here's the face to which this house is frame,-
    A man too wise to let his heart grow old!

EDMUND CLARENCE STEDMAN

(Read at His Funeral, January 21, 1908)

Oh, quick to feel the lightest touch
  Of beauty or of truth,
Rich in the thoughtfulness of age,
  The hopefulness of youth,
The courage of the gentle heart,
  The wisdom of the pure,
The strength of finely tempered souls
  To labour and endure!

The blue of springtime in your eyes
  Was never quenched by pain;
And winter brought your head the crown
  Of snow without a stain.
The poet's mind, the prince's heart,
  You kept until the end,
Nor ever faltered in your work,
  Nor ever failed a friend.

IN PRAISE OF POETS

You followed, through the quest of life,
　The light that shines above
The tumult and the toil of men,
　And shows us what to love.
Right loyal to the best you knew,
　Reality or dream,
You ran the race, you fought the fight,
　A follower of the Gleam.

We lay upon your folded hands
　The wreath of asphodel;
We speak above your peaceful face
　The tender word *Farewell!*
For well you fare, in God's good care,
　Somewhere within the blue,
And know, to-day, your dearest dreams
　Are true,—and true,—and true!

TO JAMES WHITCOMB RILEY

ON HIS "BOOK OF JOYOUS CHILDREN"

Yours is a garden of old-fashioned flowers;
    Joyous children delight to play there;
Weary men find rest in its bowers,
    Watching the lingering light of day there.

Old-time tunes and young love-laughter
    Ripple and run among the roses;
Memory's echoes, murmuring after,
    Fill the dusk when the long day closes.

Simple songs with a cadence olden—
    These you learned in the Forest of Arden
Friendly flowers with hearts all golden—
    These you borrowed from Eden's garden.

This is the reason why all men love you;
    Truth to life is the finest art:
Other poets may soar above you—
    You keep close to the human heart.

December, 1903.

RICHARD WATSON GILDER

IN MEMORIAM

Soul of a soldier in a poet's frame,
    Heart of a hero in a body frail;
    Thine was the courage clear that did not quail
Before the giant champions of shame
Who wrought dishonour to the city's name;
    And thine the vision of the Holy Grail
    Of Love, revealed through Music's lucid veil,
Filling thy life with heavenly song and flame.

Pure was the light that lit thy glowing eye,
    And strong the faith that held thy simple creed
    Ah, poet, patriot, friend, to serve our need
Thou leavest two great gifts that will not die:
Above the city's noise, thy lyric cry,—
    Amid the city's strife, thy noble deed

November, 1909.

THE VALLEY OF VAIN VERSES

The grief that is but feigning,
And weeps melodious tears
Of delicate complaining
From self-indulgent years;
The mirth that is but madness,
And has no inward gladness
Beneath its laughter straining,
To capture thoughtless ears;

The love that is but passion
Of amber-scented lust;
The doubt that is but fashion;
The faith that has no trust;
These Thamyris disperses,
In the Valley of Vain Verses
Below the Mount Parnassian,—
And they crumble into dust.

MUSIC

MUSIC

I

PRELUDE

1

Daughter of Psyche, pledge of that wild night
When, pierced with pain and bitter-sweet delight,
She knew her Love and saw her Lord depart,
Then breathed her wonder and her woe forlorn
Into a single cry, and thou wast born!
Thou flower of rapture and thou fruit of grief;
Invisible enchantress of the heart;
  Mistress of charms that bring relief
  To sorrow, and to joy impart
A heavenly tone that keeps it undefiled,—
    Thou art the child
  Of Amor, and by right divine
    A throne of love is thine,
Thou flower-folded, golden-girdled, star-crowned Queen
Whose bridal beauty mortal eyes have never seen!

2

Thou art the Angel of the pool that sleeps,
While peace and joy lie hidden in its deeps,
Waiting thy touch to make the waters roll
In healing murmurs round the weary soul.

MUSIC

Ah, when wilt thou draw near,
 Thou messenger of mercy robed in song?
 My lonely heart has listened for thee long;
 And now I seem to hear
Across the crowded market-place of life,
 Thy measured foot-fall, ringing light and clear
Above unmeaning noises and unruly strife.
  In quiet cadence, sweet and slow,
  Serenely pacing to and fro,
 Thy far-off steps are magical and dear,—
 Ah, turn this way, come close and speak to me!
From this dull bed of languor set my spirit free,
And bid me rise, and let me walk awhile with thee

II

INVOCATION

 Where wilt thou lead me first?
  In what still region
   Of thy domain,
  Whose provinces are legion,
 Wilt thou restore me to myself again,
  And quench my heart's long thirst?
 I pray thee lay thy golden girdle down,
  And put away thy starry crown:
   For one dear restful hour
   Assume a state more mild.
Clad only in thy blossom-broidered gown

448

MUSIC

That breathes familiar scent of many a flower,
Take the low path that leads through pastures green
    And though thou art a Queen,
Be Rosamund awhile, and in thy bower,
By tranquil love and simple joy beguiled,
Sing to my soul, as mother to her child.

III

PLAY SONG

  O lead me by the hand,
    And let my heart have rest,
And bring me back to childhood land,
To find again the long-lost band
    Of playmates blithe and blest.

  Some quaint, old-fashioned air,
    That all the children knew,
Shall run before us everywhere,
Like a little maid with flying hair,
    To guide the merry crew.

  Along the garden ways
    We chase the light-foot tune,
And in and out the flowery maze,
With eager haste and fond delays,
    In pleasant paths of June.

MUSIC

    For us the fields are new,
    For us the woods are rife
With fairy secrets, deep and true,
And heaven is but a tent of blue
      Above the game of life.

    The world is far away:
    The fever and the fret,
And all that makes the heart grow gray,
Is out of sight and far away,
Dear Music, while I hear thee play
That olden, golden roundelay,
      "Remember and forget!"

IV

SLEEP SONG

    Forget, forget!
  The tide of life is turning;
  The waves of light ebb slowly down the west
Along the edge of dark some stars are burning
To guide thy spirit safely to an isle of rest.
    A little rocking on the tranquil deep
      Of song, to soothe thy yearning,
    A little slumber and a little sleep,
      And so, forget, forget!

MUSIC

    Forget, forget,—
  The day was long in pleasure;
Its echoes die away across the hill;
Now let thy heart beat time to their slow measure,
That swells, and sinks, and faints, and falls, till all is still.
    Then, like a weary child that loves to keep
      Locked in its arms some treasure,
    Thy soul in calm content shall fall asleep,
      And so forget, forget.

    Forget, forget,—
  And if thou hast been weeping,
Let go the thoughts that bind thee to thy grief:
Lie still, and watch the singing angels, reaping
The golden harvest of thy sorrow, sheaf by sheaf;
    Or count thy joys like flocks of snow-white sheep
      That one by one come creeping
    Into the quiet fold, until thou sleep,
      And so forget, forget!

    Forget, forget,—
  Thou art a child and knowest
So little of thy life! But music tells
The secret of the world through which thou goest
To work with morning song, to rest with evening bells:
    Life is in tune with harmony so deep
      That when the notes are lowest
    Thou still canst lay thee down in peace and sleep,
      For God will not forget.

MUSIC

V

HUNTING SONG

Out of the garden of playtime, out of the bower of rest,
Fain would I follow at daytime, music that calls to a quest.
    Hark, how the galloping measure
    Quickens the pulses of pleasure;
    Gaily saluting the morn
With the long, clear note of the hunting-horn,
    Echoing up from the valley,
    Over the mountain side,—
    Rally, you hunters, rally,
    Rally, and ride!

Drink of the magical potion music has mixed with her wine,
Full of the madness of motion, joyful, exultant, divine!
    Leave all your troubles behind you,
    Ride where they never can find you,
    Into the gladness of morn,
With the long, clear note of the hunting-horn,
    Swiftly o'er hillock and hollow,
    Sweeping along with the wind,—
    Follow, you hunters, follow,
    Follow and find!

What will you reach with your riding? What is the charm of the chase?
Just the delight and the striding swing of the jubilant pace.

MUSIC

    Danger is sweet when you front her,—
    In at the death, every hunter!
    Now on the breeze the mort is borne
In the long, clear note of the hunting-horn,
        Winding merrily, over and over,—
            Come, come, come!
        Home again, Ranger! home again, Rover!
        Turn again, home!

VI

DANCE-MUSIC

1

Now let the sleep-tune blend with the play-tune
Weaving the mystical spell of the dance;
Lighten the deep tune, soften the gay tune,
Mingle a tempo that turns in a trance.
Half of it sighing, half of it smiling,
Smoothly it swings, with a triplicate beat;
Calling, replying, yearning, beguiling,
Wooing the heart and bewitching the feet.
      Every drop of blood
      Rises with the flood,
   Rocking on the waves of the strain;
      Youth and beauty glide
      Turning with the tide—
     Music making one out of twain,

MUSIC

Bearing them away, and away, and away,
    Like a tone and its terce—
Till the chord dissolves, and the dancers stay,
    And reverse.

Violins leading, take up the measure,
Turn with the tune again,—clarinets clear
Answer their pleading,—harps full of pleasure
Sprinkle their silver like light on the mere.
    Semiquaver notes,
    Merry little motes,
    Tangled in the haze
    Of the lamp's golden rays,
    Quiver everywhere
      In the air,
      Like a spray,—
Till the fuller stream of the might of the tune
Gliding like a dream in the light of the moon,
Bears them all away, and away, and away,
    Floating in the trance of the dance.

2

    Then begins a measure stately,
        Languid, slow, serene;
    All the dancers move sedately,
    Stepping leisurely and straitly,
        With a courtly mien;

MUSIC

Crossing hands and changing places,
    Bowing low between,
While the minuet inlaces
Waving arms and woven paces,—
    Glittering damaskeen.
Where is she whose form is folden
    In its royal sheen?
From our longing eyes withholden
By her mystic girdle golden,
    Beauty sought but never seen,
Music walks the maze, a queen.

VII

WAR-MUSIC

Break off! Dance no more!
    Danger is at the door.
    Music is in arms.
    To signal war's alarms.

Hark, a sudden trumpet calling
    Over the hill!
Why are you calling, trumpet, calling?
    What is your will?

Men, men, men!
Men who are ready to fight
For their country's life, and the right

MUSIC

Of a liberty-loving land to be
   Free, free, free!
Free from a tyrant's chain,
Free from dishonor's stain,
Free to guard and maintain
All that her fathers fought for,
All that her sons have wrought for,
   Resolute, brave, and free!

   Call again, trumpet, call again,
      Call up the men!

Do you hear the storm of cheers
Mingled with the women's tears
And the tramp, tramp, tramp of marching feet?
   Do you hear the throbbing drum
   As the hosts of battle come
Keeping time, time, time to its beat?
   O Music give a song
   To make their spirit strong
For the fury of the tempest they must meet.

   The hoarse roar
   Of the monster guns;
   And the sharp bark
   Of the lesser guns;
   The whine of the shells,
   The rifles' clatter

MUSIC

Where the bullets patter,
The rattle, rattle, rattle
Of the mitrailleuse in battle,
And the yells
Of the men who charge through hells
Where the poison gas descends,
And the bursting shrapnel rends
Limb from limb
In the dim
Chaos and clamor of the strife
Where no man thinks of his life
But only of fighting through,
Blindly fighting through, through!

'Tis done
At last!
The victory won,
The dissonance of warfare past!

O Music mourn the dead
Whose loyal blood was shed,
And sound the taps for every hero slain;
Then lead into the song
That made their spirit strong,
And tell the world they did not die in vain

Thank God we can see, in the glory of morn
The invincible flag that our fathers defended

MUSIC

And our hearts can repeat what the heroes have sworn
  That war shall not end till the war-lust is ended.
Then the bloodthirsty sword shall no longer be lord
Of the nations oppressed by the conqueror's horde,
  But the banners of Liberty proudly shall wave
  O'er the *world* of the free and the lands of the brave

May, 1916.

VIII

THE SYMPHONY

Music, they do thee wrong who say thine art
  Is only to enchant the sense.
For every timid motion of the heart,
  And every passion too intense
To bear the chain of the imperfect word,
  And every tremulous longing, stirred
By spirit winds that come we know not whence
    And go we know not where,
    And every inarticulate prayer
Beating about the depths of pain or bliss,
  Like some bewildered bird
That seeks its nest but knows not where it is,
And every dream that haunts, with dim delight,
The drowsy hour between the day and night,
The wakeful hour between the night and day,—
    Imprisoned, waits for thee,
    Impatient, yearns for thee,

MUSIC

The queen who comes to set the captive free!
Thou lendest wings to grief to fly away,
And wings to joy to reach a heavenly height;
And every dumb desire that storms within the breast
Thou leadest forth to sob or sing itself to rest.

All these are thine, and therefore love is thine.
    For love is joy and grief,
And trembling doubt, and certain-sure belief,
And fear, and hope, and longing unexpressed,
In pain most human, and in rapture brief
        Almost divine.
Love would possess, yet deepens when denied;
And love would give, yet hungers to receive;
Love like a prince his triumph would achieve;
And like a miser in the dark his joys would hide.
    Love is most bold,
He leads his dreams like armèd men in line;
Yet when the siege is set, and he must speak,
    Calling the fortress to resign
Its treasure, valiant love grows weak,
And hardly dares his purpose to unfold.
Less with his faltering lips than with his eyes
    He claims the longed-for prize:
Love fain would tell it all, yet leaves the best untold.
But thou shalt speak for love. Yea, thou shalt teach
    The mystery of measured tone,
      The Pentecostal speech

MUSIC

That every listener heareth as his own.
For on thy head the cloven tongues of fire,—
Diminished chords that quiver with desire,
And major chords that glow with perfect peace,—
    Have fallen from above;
    And thou canst give release
In music to the burdened heart of love.

Sound with the 'cellos' pleading, passionate strain
The yearning theme, and let the flute reply
In placid melody, while violins complain,
    And sob, and sigh,
    With muted string;
  Then let the oboe half-reluctant sing
Of bliss that trembles on the verge of pain,
  While 'cellos plead and plead again,
With throbbing notes delayed, that would impart
To every urgent tone the beating of the heart.
  So runs the andante, making plain
The hopes and fears of love without a word.
Then comes the adagio, with a yielding theme
Through which the violas flow soft as in a dream
    While horns and mild bassoons are heard
    In tender tune, that seems to float
      Like an enchanted boat
    Upon the downward-gliding stream,
    Toward the allegro's wide, bright sea
    Of dancing, glittering, blending tone,

MUSIC

Where every instrument is sounding free,
And harps like wedding-chimes are rung, and trumpets
    blown
    Around the barque of love
    That rides, with smiling skies above,
        A royal galley, many-oared,
Into the happy harbour of the perfect chord.

IX

IRIS

    Light to the eye and Music to the ear,—
These are the builders of the bridge that springs
From earth's dim shore of half-remembered things
    To reach the heavenly sphere
Where nothing silent is and nothing dark.
    So when I see the rainbow's arc
Spanning the showery sky, far-off I hear
    Music, and every colour sings:
And while the symphony builds up its round
Full sweep of architectural harmony
Above the tide of Time, far, far away I see
A bow of colour in the bow of sound.
    Red as the dawn the trumpet rings;
    Blue as the sky, the choir of strings
Darkens in double-bass to ocean's hue,
Rises in violins to noon-tide's blue,
With threads of quivering light shot through and through;

MUSIC

    Green as the mantle that the summer flings
Around the world, the pastoral reeds in tune
Embroider melodies of May and June.
        Purer than gold,
          Yea, thrice-refinèd gold,
And richer than the treasures of the mine,
    Floods of the human voice divine
Along the arch in choral song are rolled.
        So bends the bow complete:
          And radiant rapture flows
Across the bridge, so full, so strong, so sweet,
    That the uplifted spirit hardly knows
        Whether the Music-Light that glows
  Within the arch of tones and colours seven,
Is sunset-peace of earth or sunrise-joy of Heaven.

X

SEA AND SHORE

    Music, I yield to thee
      As swimmer to the sea,
I give my spirit to the flood of song!
      Bear me upon thy breast
      In rapture and at rest,
Bathe me in pure delight and make me strong;
    From strife and struggle bring release,
And draw the waves of passion into tides of peace

MUSIC

    Remembered songs most dear
    In living songs I hear,
While blending voices gently swing and sway,
    In melodies of love,
    Whose mighty currents move
With singing near and singing far away;
    Sweet in the glow of morning light,
And sweeter still across the starlit gulf of night.

    Music, in thee we float,
    And lose the lonely note
Of self in thy celestial-ordered strain,
    Until at last we find
    The life to love resigned
In harmony of joy restored again;
    And songs that cheered our mortal days
Break on the shore of light in endless hymns of praise

December, 1901—May, 1903—May, 1916.

MASTER OF MUSIC

(In memory of Theodore Thomas, 1905)

GLORY of architect, glory of painter, and sculptor, and bard,
  Living forever in temple and picture and statue and song,—
Look how the world with the lights that they lit is illumined and starred;
  Brief was the flame of their life, but the lamps of their art burn long!

Where is the Master of Music, and how has he vanished away?
  Where is the work that he wrought with his wonderful art in the air?
Gone,—it is gone like the glow on the cloud at the close of the day!
  The Master has finished his work and the glory of music is—where?

MASTER OF MUSIC

Once, at the wave of his wand, all the billows of musical sound
    Followed his will, as the sea was ruled by the prophet of old:
Now that his hand is relaxed, and his rod has dropped to the ground,
    Silent and dark are the shores where the marvellous harmonies rolled!

Nay, but not silent the hearts that were filled by that life-giving sea;
    Deeper and purer forever the tides of their being will roll,
Grateful and joyful, O Master, because they have listened to thee;
    The glory of music endures in the depths of the human soul.

THE PIPES O' PAN

GREAT Nature had a million words,
In tongues of trees and songs of birds
But none to breathe the heart of man
Till Music filled the pipes o' Pan.
1909.

TO A YOUNG GIRL SINGING

Oh, what do you know of the song, my dear,
  And how have you made it your own?
You have caught the turn of the melody clear,
    And you give it again with a golden tone,
    Till the wonder-word and the wedded note
    Are flowing out of your beautiful throat
    With a liquid charm for every ear:
    And they talk of your art,—but for you alone
    The song is a thing, unheard, unknown;
    You only have learned it by rote.

But when you have lived for awhile, my dear,
  I think you will learn it anew!
For a joy will come, or a grief, or a fear,
    That will alter the look of the world for you;
    And the lyric you learned as a bit of art,
    Will wake to life as a wonderful part
    Of the love you feel so deep and true;
    And the thrill of a laugh or the throb of a tear
    Will come with your song to all who hear;
    For then you will know it by heart.

April, 1911.

THE OLD FLUTE

The time will come when I no more can play
This polished flute: the stops will not obey
My gnarled fingers; and the air it weaves
In modulations, like a vine with leaves
Climbing around the tower of song, will die
In rustling autumn rhythms, confused and dry.
My shortened breath no more will freely fill
This magic reed with melody at will;
My stiffened lips will try and try in vain
To wake the liquid, leaping, dancing strain;
The heavy notes will falter, wheeze, and faint,
Or mock my ear with shrillness of complaint.

Then let me hang this faithful friend of mine
Upon the trunk of some old, sacred pine,
And sit beneath the green protecting boughs
To hear the viewless wind, that sings and soughs
Above me, play its wild, aerial lute,
And draw a ghost of music from my flute!

So will I thank the gods; and most of all
The Delian Apollo, whom men call
The mighty master of immortal sound,—
Lord of the billows in their chanting round,
Lord of the winds that fill the wood with sighs,

THE OLD FLUTE

Lord of the echoes and their sweet replies,
Lord of the little people of the air
That sprinkle drops of music everywhere,
Lord of the sea of melody that laves
The universe with never silent waves,—
Him will I thank that this brief breath of mine
Has caught one cadence of the song divine;
And these frail fingers learned to rise and fall
In time with that great tune which throbs thro' all
And these poor lips have lent a lilt of joy
To songless men whom weary tasks employ!
My life has had its music, and my heart
In harmony has borne a little part,
And now I come with quiet, grateful breast
To Death's dim hall of silence and of rest.

Freely rendered from the French of Auguste Angellier, 1911.

THE FIRST BIRD O' SPRING

TO OLIVE WHEELER

WINTER on Mount Shasta,
April down below;
Golden hours of glowing sun,
Sudden showers of snow!
Under leafless thickets
Early wild-flowers cling;
But, oh, my dear, I'm fain to hear
The first bird o' Spring!

Alders are in tassel,
Maples are in bud;
Waters of the blue McCloud
Shout in joyful flood;
Through the giant pine-trees
Flutters many a wing;
But, oh, my dear, I long to hear
The first bird o' Spring!

THE FIRST BIRD O' SPRING

Candle-light and fire-light
Mingle at "the Bend;"
'Neath the roof of Bo-hai-pan
Light and shadow blend.
Sweeter than a wood-thrush
A maid begins to sing;
And, oh, my dear, I'm glad to hear
The first bird o' Spring!

The Bend, California, April 29, 1913.

THE HOUSE OF RIMMON

A DRAMA IN FOUR ACTS

DRAMATIS PERSONÆ

BENHADAD:	King of Damascus.
REZON:	High Priest of the House of Rimmon
SABALLIDIN:	A Noble.
HAZAEL } IZDUBHAR } RAKHAZ	Courtiers.
SHUMAKIM:	The King's Fool.
ELISHA:	Prophet of Israel.
NAAMAN:	Captain of the Armies of Damascus.
RUAHMAH:	A Captive Maid of Israel.
TSARPI:	Wife to Naaman.
KHAMMA } NUBTA	Attendants of Tsarpi.

Soldiers, Servants, Citizens, etc., etc.

SCENE: *Damascus and the Mountains of Samaria.*

TIME: 850 *B. C.*

ACT I

Scene I

Night, in the garden of NAAMAN *at Damascus. At the left the palace, with softly gleaming lights and music coming from the open latticed windows. The garden is full of oleanders, roses, pomegranates, abundance of crimson flowers; the air is heavy with their fragrance: a fountain at the right is plashing gently: behind it is an arbour covered with vines. Near the centre of the garden stands a small, hideous image of the god Rimmon. Beyond the arbour rises the lofty square tower of the House of Rimmon, which casts a shadow from the moon across the garden. The background is a wide, hilly landscape, with the snow-clad summit of Mount Hermon in the distance. Enter by the palace door, the lady* TSARPI, *robed in red and gold, and followed by her maids,* KHAMMA *and* NUBTA. *She remains on the terrace: they go down into the garden, looking about, and returning to her.*

KHAMMA:

There's no one here; the garden is asleep.

NUBTA:

The flowers are nodding, all the birds abed,—
Nothing awake except the watchful stars!

KHAMMA:

The stars are sentinels discreet and mute:
How many things they know and never tell!

TSARPI: [*Impatiently.*]

> Unlike the stars, how many things you tell
> And do not know! When comes your master home?

NUBTA:

> Lady, his armour-bearer brought us word,—
> At moonset, not before.

TSARPI:

> He haunts the camp
> And leaves me much alone; yet I can pass
> The time of absence not unhappily,
> If I but know the time of his return.
> An hour of moonlight yet! Khamma, my mirror!
> These curls are ill arranged, this veil too low,—
> So,—that is better, careless maids! Withdraw,—
> But bring me word if Naaman appears!

KHAMMA:

> Mistress, have no concern; for when we hear
> The clatter of his horse along the street,
> We'll run this way and lead your dancers down
> With song and laughter,—you shall know in time.

> [*Exeunt* KHAMMA *and* NUBTA *laughing*, TSARPI
> *descends the steps.*]

TSARPI:

> My guest is late; but he will surely come!
> The man who burns to drain the cup of love,
> The priest whose greed of glory never fails,
> Both, both have need of me, and he will come.
> And I,—what do I need? Why everything

That helps my beauty to a higher throne;
All that a priest can promise, all a man
Can give, and all a god bestow, I need:
This may a woman win, and this will I.

> [*Enter* REZON *quietly from the shadow of the trees. He stands behind* TSARPI *and listens, smiling, to her last words. Then he drops his mantle of leopard-skin, and lifts his high priest's rod of bronze, shaped at one end like a star.*]

REZON:

Tsarpi!

TSARPI: [*Bowing low before him.*]

The mistress of the house of Naaman
Salutes the master of the House of Rimmon.

REZON:

Rimmon receives you with his star of peace,
For you were once a handmaid of his altar.

> [*He lowers the star-point of the rod, which glows for a moment with rosy light above her head.*]

And now the keeper of his temple asks
The welcome of the woman for the man.

TSARPI: [*Giving him her hand, but holding off his embrace.*]

No more,—till I have heard what brings you here
By night, within the garden of the one
Who scorns you most and fears you least in all
Damascus.

REZON:

Trust me, I repay his scorn

With double hatred,—Naaman, the man
Who stands against the nobles and the priests,
This powerful fool, this impious devotee
Of liberty, who loves the people more
Than he reveres the city's ancient god:
This frigid husband who sets you below
His dream of duty to a horde of slaves:
This man I hate, and I will humble him.

TSARPI:

I think I hate him too. He stands apart
From me, ev'n while he holds me in his arms,
By something that I cannot understand.
He swears he loves his wife next to his honour!
Next? That's too low! I will be first or nothing.

REZON:

With me you are the first, the absolute!
When you and I have triumphed you shall reign;
And you and I will bring this hero down.

TSARPI:

But how? For he is strong.

REZON:

By this, the hand
Of Tsarpi; and by this, the rod of Rimmon.

TSARPI:

Your plan?

REZON:

You know the host of Nineveh
Is marching now against us. Envoys come

ACT I, SC. I] THE HOUSE OF RIMMON

To bid us yield before a hopeless war.
Our king is weak: the nobles, being rich,
Would purchase peace to make them richer still:
Only the people and the soldiers, led
By Naaman, would fight for liberty.
Blind fools! To-day the envoys came to me,
And talked with me in secret. Promises,
Great promises! For every noble house
That urges peace, a noble recompense:
The King, submissive, kept in royal state
And splendour: most of all, honour and wealth
Shall crown the House of Rimmon, and his priest,—
Yea, and his priestess! For we two will rise
Upon the city's fall. The common folk
Shall suffer; Naaman shall sink with them
In wreck; but I shall rise, and you shall rise
Above me! You shall climb, through incense-smoke
And days of pomp, and nights of revelry,
Unto the topmost room in Rimmon's tower,
The secret, lofty room, the couch of bliss,
And the divine embraces of the god.
TSARPI: [*Throwing out her arms in exultation.*]
All, all I wish! What must I do for this?
REZON:
Turn Naaman away from thoughts of war.
TSARPI:
But if I fail? His will is proof against
The lure of kisses and the wile of tears.

REZON:

>   Where woman fails, woman and priest succeed.
>   Before the King decides, he must consult
>   The oracle of Rimmon. This my hands
>   Prepare,—and you shall read the signs prepared
>   In words of fear to melt the brazen heart
>   Of Naaman.

TSARPI:

>   But if it flame instead?

REZON:

>   I know a way to quench that flame. The cup,
>   The parting cup your hand shall give to him!
>   What if the curse of Rimmon should infect
>   That sacred wine with poison, secretly
>   To work within his veins, week after week
>   Corrupting all the currents of his blood,
>   Dimming his eyes, wasting his flesh? What then?
>   Would he prevail in war? Would he come back
>   To glory, or to shame? What think you?

TSARPI:

>   I?—
>   I do not think; I only do my part.
>   But can the gods bless this?

REZON:

>   The gods can bless
>   Whatever they decree; their will makes right;
>   And this is for the glory of the House

ACT I, SC. I] THE HOUSE OF RIMMON

Of Rimmon,—and for thee, my queen. Come, come!
The night grows dark: we'll perfect our alliance.
> [REZON *draws her with him, embracing her, through the shadows of the garden. RUAHMAH, who has been sleeping in the arbour, has been awakened during the dialogue, and has been dimly visible in her white dress, behind the vines. She parts them and comes out, pushing back her long, dark hair from her temples.*]

RUAHMAH:

What have I heard? O God, what shame is this
Plotted beneath Thy pure and silent stars!
Was it for this that I was brought away
A captive from the hills of Israel
To serve the heathen in a land of lies?
Ah, treacherous, shameful priest! Ah, shameless wife
Of one too noble to suspect thy guilt!
The very greatness of his generous heart
Betrays him to their hands. What can I do!
Nothing,—a slave,—hated and mocked by all
My fellow-slaves! O bitter prison-life!
I smother in this black, betraying air
Of lust and luxury; I faint beneath
The shadow of this House of Rimmon. God
Have mercy! Lead me out to Israel.
To Israel!
> [*Music and laughter heard within the palace. The doors fly open and a flood of men and women,*

dancers, players, flushed with wine, dishevelled, pour down the steps, KHAMMA and NUBTA with them. They crown the image with roses and dance around it. RUAHMAH is discovered crouching beside the arbour. They drag her out beside the image.]

NUBTA:
                Look! Here's the Hebrew maid,—
She's homesick; let us comfort her!

KHAMMA: [*They put their arms around her.*]
Yes, dancing is the cure for homesickness.
We'll make her dance.

RUAHMAH: [*She slips away.*]
                I pray you, let me go!
I cannot dance, I do not know your measures.

KHAMMA:
Then sing for us,—a song of Israel!

RUAHMAH:
How can I sing the songs of Israel
In this strange country? O my heart would break!

A SERVANT:
A stubborn and unfriendly maid! We'll whip her.
    [*They circle around her, striking her with rose-branches; she sinks to her knees, covering her face with her bare arms, which bleed.*]

NUBTA:
Look, look! She kneels to Rimmon, she is tamed.

ACT I, SC. I] THE HOUSE OF RIMMON

RUAHMAH: [*Springing up and lifting her arms.*]
Nay, not to this dumb idol, but to Him
Who made Orion and the seven stars!

ALL:
She raves,—she mocks at Rimmon! Punish her!
The fountain! Wash her blasphemy away!

> [*They push her toward the fountain, laughing and shouting. In the open door of the palace NAAMAN appears, dressed in blue and silver, bareheaded and unarmed. He comes to the top of the steps and stands for a moment, astonished and angry.*]

NAAMAN:
Silence! What drunken rout is this? Begone,
Ye barking dogs and mewing cats! Out, all!
Poor child, what have they done to thee?

> [*Exeunt all except RUAHMAH, who stands with her face covered by her hands. NAAMAN comes to her, laying his hand on her shoulder.*]

RUAHMAH: [*Looking up in his face.*]
                              Nothing,
My lord and master! They have harmed me not.

NAAMAN: [*Touching her arm.*]
Dost call this nothing?

RUAHMAH:
                    Since my lord is come!

NAAMAN:
I do not know thy face,—who art thou, child?

483

RUAHMAH:
   The handmaid of thy wife.
NAAMAN:
                              Whence comest thou?
   Thy voice is like thy mistress, but thy looks
   Have something foreign. Tell thy name, thy land.
RUAHMAH:
   Ruahmah is my name, a captive maid,
   The daughter of a prince in Israel,
   Where once, in olden days, I saw my lord
   Ride through our highlands, when Samaria
   Was allied with Damascus to defeat
   Our common foe.
NAAMAN:
                   And thou rememberest this?
RUAHMAH:
   As clear as yesterday! Master, I saw
   Thee riding on a snow-white horse beside
   Our king; and all we joyful little maids
   Strewed boughs of palm along the victors' way,
   For you had driven out the enemy,
   Broken; and both our lands were friends and free.
NAAMAN: [*Sadly.*]
   Well, they are past, those noble days! The days
   When nations would imperil all to keep
   Their liberties, are only memories now.
   The common cause is lost,—and thou art brought,
   The captive of some mercenary raid,

ACT I, SC. I] **THE HOUSE OF RIMMON**

    Some skirmish of a gold-begotten war,
    To serve within my house. Dost thou fare well?

RUAHMAH:
    Master, thou seest.

NAAMAN:
                   Yes, I see! My child,
    Why do they hate thee so?

RUAHMAH:
                     I do not know,
    Unless because I will not bow to Rimmon.

NAAMAN:
    Thou needest not. I fear he is a god
    Who pities not his people, will not save.
    My heart is sick with doubt of him. But thou
    Shalt hold thy faith,—I care not what it is,—
    Worship thy god; but keep thy spirit free.
        [*He takes the amulet from his neck and gives it to
            her.*]
    Here, take this chain and wear it with my seal,
    None shall molest the maid who carries this.
    Thou hast found favour in thy master's eyes;
    Hast thou no other gift to ask of me?

RUAHMAH: [*Earnestly.*]
    My lord, I do entreat thee not to go
    To-morrow to the council. Seek the King
    And speak with him in secret; but avoid
    The audience-hall.

NAAMAN:

                       Why, what is this? Thy wits
Are wandering. My honour is engaged
To speak for war, to lead in war against
The Assyrian Bull and save Damascus.

RUAHMAH: [*With confused earnestness.*]
   Then, lord, if thou must go, I pray thee speak,—
   I know not how,—but so that all must hear.
   With magic of unanswerable words
   Persuade thy foes. Yet watch,—beware,—

NAAMAN:

                              Of what?

RUAHMAH: [*Turning aside.*]
   I am entangled in my speech,—no light,—
   How shall I tell him? He will not believe.
   O my dear lord, thine enemies are they
   Of thine own house. I pray thee to beware,—
   Beware,—of Rimmon!

NAAMAN:

                         Child, thy words are wild:
Thy troubles have bewildered all thy brain.
Go, now, and fret no more; but sleep, and dream
Of Israel! For thou shalt see thy home
Among the hills again.

RUAHMAH:

                     Master, good-night.
And may thy slumber be as sweet and deep
As if thou camped at snowy Hermon's foot,

Amid the music of his waterfalls.
There friendly oak-trees bend their boughs above
The weary head, pillowed on earth's kind breast,
And unpolluted breezes lightly breathe
A song of sleep among the murmuring leaves.
There the big stars draw nearer, and the sun
Looks forth serene, undimmed by city's mirk
Or smoke of idol-temples, to behold
The waking wonder of the wide-spread world.
There life renews itself with every morn
In purest joy of living. May the Lord
Deliver thee, dear master, from the nets
Laid for thy feet, and lead thee out along
The open path, beneath the open sky!

[*Exit* RUAHMAH: NAAMAN *stands looking after her.*]

SCENE II

TIME: *The following morning*

The audience-hall in BENHADAD's *palace. The sides of the hall are lined with lofty columns: the back opens toward the city, with descending steps: the House of Rimmon with its high tower is seen in the background. The throne is at the right in front: opposite is the royal door of entrance, guarded by four tall sentinels. Enter at the rear between the columns,* RAKHAZ, SABALLIDIN, HAZAEL, IZDUBHAR.

IZDUBHAR: [*An excited old man.*]

The city is all in a turmoil. It boils like a pot of

lentils. The people are foaming and bubbling round and round like beans in the pottage.

HAZAEL: [*A lean, crafty man.*]

Fear is a hot fire.

RAKHAZ: [*A fat, pompous man.*]

Well may they fear, for the Assyrians are not three days distant. They are blazing along like a waterspout to chop Damascus down like a pitcher of spilt milk.

SABALLIDIN: [*Young and frank.*]

Cannot Naaman drive them back?

RAKHAZ: [*Puffing and blowing.*]

Ho! Naaman? Where have you been living? Naaman is a broken reed whose claws have been cut. Build no hopes on that foundation, for it will run away and leave you all adrift in the conflagration.

SABALLIDIN:

He clatters like a windmill. What would he say, Hazael?

HAZAEL:

Naaman can do nothing without the command of the King; and the King fears to order the army to march without the approval of the gods. The High Priest is against it. The House of Rimmon is for peace with Asshur.

RAKHAZ:

Yes, and all the nobles are for peace. We are the

ACT I, SC. II] THE HOUSE OF RIMMON

    men whose wisdom lights the rudder that upholds the chariot of state. Would we be rich if we were not wise? Do we not know better than the rabble what medicine will silence this fire that threatens to drown us?

IZDUBHAR:

    But if the Assyrians come, we shall all perish; they will despoil us all.

HAZAEL:

    Not us, my lord, only the common people. The envoys have offered favourable terms to the priests, and the nobles, and the King. No palace, no temple, shall be plundered. Only the shops, and the markets, and the houses of the multitude shall be given up to the Bull. He will eat his supper from the pot of lentils, not from our golden plate.

RAKHAZ:

    Yes, and all who speak for peace in the council shall be enriched; our heads shall be crowned with seats of honour in the procession of the Assyrian king. He needs wise counsellors to help him guide the ship of empire onto the solid rock of prosperity. You must be with us, my lords Izdubhar and Saballidin, and let the stars of your wisdom roar loudly for peace.

IZDUBHAR:

    He talks like a tablet read upside down,—a wild ass

489

braying in the wilderness. Yet there is policy in his words.

SABALLIDIN:

I know not. Can a kingdom live without a people or an army? If we let the Bull in to sup on the lentils, will he not make his breakfast in our vineyards?

[*Enter other courtiers following* SHUMAKIM, *a humpbacked jester, in blue, green and red, a wreath of poppies around his neck and a flagon in his hand. He walks unsteadily, and stutters in his speech.*]

HAZAEL:

Here is Shumakim, the King's fool, with his legs full of last night's wine.

SHUMAKIM: [*Balancing himself in front of them and chuckling.*]

Wrong, my lords, very wrong! This is not last night's wine, but a draught the King's physician gave me this morning for a cure. It sobers me amazingly! I know you all, my lords: any fool would know you. You, master, are a statesman; and you are a politician; and you are a patriot.

RAKHAZ:

Am I a statesman? I felt something of the kind about me. But what is a statesman?

SHUMAKIM:

A politician that is stuffed with big words; a fat

man in a mask; one that plays a solemn tune on a sackbut full o' wind.

HAZEL:

And what is a politician?

SHUMAKIM:

A statesman that has dropped his mask and cracked his sackbut. Men trust him for what he is, and he never deceives them, because he always lies.

IZDUBHAR:

Why do you call me a patriot?

SHUMAKIM:

Because you know what is good for you; you love your country as you love your pelf. You feel for the common people,—as the wolf feels for the sheep.

SABALLIDIN:

And what am I?

SHUMAKIM:

A fool, master, just a plain fool; and there is hope of thee for that reason. Embrace me, brother, and taste this; but not too much,—it will intoxicate thee with sobriety.

[*The hall has been slowly filling with courtiers and soldiers; a crowd of people begin to come up the steps at the rear, where they are halted by a chain guarded by servants of the palace. A bell tolls; the royal door is thrown open; the aged King totters across the hall and takes his seat on*

*the throne with the four tall sentinels standing
behind him. All bow down shading their eyes
with their hands.*]

BENHADAD:

The hour of royal audience is come.
I'll hear the envoys. Are my counsellors
At hand? Where are the priests of Rimmon's house?

[*Gongs sound.* REZON *comes in from the side,
followed by a procession of priests in black and
yellow. The courtiers bow; the King rises;*
REZON *takes his stand on the steps of the throne
at the left of the King.*]

BENHADAD:

Where is my faithful servant Naaman,
The captain of my host?

[*Trumpets sound from the city. The crowd on the
steps divide; the chain is lowered;* NAAMAN
*enters, followed by six soldiers. He is dressed
in chain-mail with a silver helmet and a cloak of
blue. He uncovers, and kneels on the steps of
the throne at the King's right.*]

NAAMAN:

My lord the King,
The bearer of thy sword is here.

BENHADAD: [*Giving* NAAMAN *his hand, and sitting down.*]

Welcome,
My strong right arm that never me failed yet!
I am in doubt,—but stay thou close to me

THE HOUSE OF RIMMON

While I decide this cause. Where are the envoys?
Let them appear and give their message.

> [*Enter the Assyrian envoys; one in white and the other in red; both with the golden Bull's head embroidered on their robes. They come from the right, rear, bow slightly before the throne, and take the centre of the hall.*]

WHITE ENVOY: [*Stepping forward.*]

Greeting from Shalmaneser, Asshur's son,
Who rules the world from Nineveh,
Unto Benhadad, monarch in Damascus!
The conquering Bull has led his army forth;
The south has fallen before him, and the west
His feet have trodden; Hamath is laid waste;
He pauses at your gate, invincible,—
To offer peace. The princes of your court,
The priests of Rimmon's house, and you, the King,
If you pay homage to your Overlord,
Shall rest secure, and flourish as our friends.
Assyria sends to you this gilded yoke;
Receive it as the sign of proffered peace.

> [*He lays a yoke on the steps of the throne.*]

BENHADAD:

What of the city? Said your king no word
Of our Damascus, and the many folk
That do inhabit her and make her great?
What of the soldiers who have fought for us?

THE HOUSE OF RIMMON [ACT I, SC. II

WHITE ENVOY:
Of these my royal master did not speak.
BENHADAD:
Strange silence! Must we give them up to him?
Is this the price at which he offers us
The yoke of peace? What if we do refuse?
RED ENVOY: [*Stepping forward.*]
Then ruthless war! War to the uttermost.
No quarter, no compassion, no escape!
The Bull will gore and trample in his fury
Nobles and priests and king,—none shall be spared!
Before the throne we lay our second gift;
This bloody horn, the symbol of red war.
   [*He lays a long bull's horn, stained with blood, on
      the steps of the throne.*]
WHITE ENVOY:
Our message is delivered. We return
Unto our master. He will wait three days
To know your royal choice between his gifts.
Keep which you will and send the other back.
The red bull's horn your youngest page may bring;
But with the yoke, best send your mightiest army!
   [*The* ENVOYS *retire, amid confused murmurs of
      the people, the King silent, his head, sunken on
      his breast.*]
BENHADAD:
Proud words, a bitter message, hard to endure!
We are not now that force which feared no foe:

ACT I, SC. II] THE HOUSE OF RIMMON

    Our old allies have left us. Can we face the Bull
Alone, and beat him back? Give me your counsel.
    [*Many speak at once, confusedly.*]
    What babblement is this? Were ye born at Babel?
Give me clear words and reasonable speech.
RAKHAZ: [*Pompously.*]
    O King, I am a reasonable man!
And there be some who call me very wise
And prudent; but of this I will not speak,
For I am also modest. Let me plead,
Persuade, and reason you to choose for peace.
This golden yoke may be a bitter draught,
But better far to fold it in our arms,
Than risk our cargoes in the savage horn
Of war. Shall we imperil all our wealth,
Our valuable lives? Nobles are few,
Rich men are rare, and wise men rarer still;
The precious jewels on the tree of life,
Wherein the common people are but bricks
And clay and rubble. Let the city go,
But save the corner-stones that float the ship!
Have I not spoken well?
BENHADAD: [*Shaking his head.*]

                              Excellent well!
Most eloquent! But misty in the meaning.
HAZAEL: [*With cold decision.*]
    Then let me speak, O King, in plainer words!
The days of independent states are past:

The tide of empire sweeps across the earth;
Assyria rides it with resistless power
And thunders on to subjugate the world.
Oppose her, and we fight with Destiny;
Submit to her demands, and we shall ride
With her to victory. Therefore accept
The golden yoke, Assyria's gift of peace.

NAAMAN: [*Starting forward eagerly.*]

There is no peace beneath a conqueror's yoke!
For every state that barters liberty
To win imperial favour, shall be drained
Of her best blood, henceforth, in endless wars
To make the empire greater. Here's the choice,
My King, we fight to keep our country free,
Or else we fight forevermore to help
Assyria bind the world as we are bound.
I am a soldier, and I know the hell
Of war! But I will gladly ride through hell
To save Damascus. Master, bid me ride!
Ten thousand chariots wait for your command;
And twenty thousand horsemen strain the leash
Of patience till you let them go; a throng
Of spearmen, archers, swordsmen, like the sea
Chafing against a dike, roar for the onset!
O master, let me launch your mighty host
Against the Bull,—we'll bring him to his knees!

   [*Cries of "war!" from the soldiers and the people;
       "peace!" from the courtiers and the priests.*

THE HOUSE OF RIMMON

The King rises, turning toward NAAMAN, *and seems about to speak.* REZON *lifts his rod.*]

REZON:
 Shall not the gods decide when mortals doubt?
 Rimmon is master of the city's fate;
 We read his will, by our most ancient-faith,
 In omens and in signs of mystery.
 Must we not hearken to his high commands?
BENHADAD: [*Sinking back on the throne, submissively.*]
 I am the faithful son of Rimmon's House.
 Consult the oracle. But who shall read?
REZON:
 Tsarpi, the wife of Naaman, who served
 Within the temple in her maiden years,
 Shall be the mouth-piece of the mighty god,
 To-day's high-priestess. Bring the sacrifice!
   [*Gongs and cymbals sound: enter priests carrying an altar on which a lamb is bound. The altar is placed in the centre of the hall.* TSARPI *follows the priests, covered with a long transparent veil of black, sown with gold stars;* RUAHMAH, *in white, bears her train.* TSARPI *stands before the altar, facing it, and lifts her right hand holding a knife.* RUAHMAH *steps back, near the throne, her hands crossed on her breast, her head bowed. The priests close in around* TSARPI *and the altar. The knife is seen to strike downward. Gongs and cymbals sound: cries of "Rimmon.*

hear us!" *The circle of priests opens, and* TSARPI *turns slowly to face the King.*]

TSARPI: [*Monotonously.*]
Black is the blood of the victim,
Rimmon is unfavourable,
Asratu is unfavourable;
They will not war against Asshur,
They will make a league with the God of Nineveh.
Evil is in store for Damascus,
A strong enemy will lay waste the land.
Therefore make peace with the Bull;
Hearken to the voice of Rimmon.

[*She turns again to the altar, and the priests close in around her.* REZON *lifts his rod toward the tower of the temple. A flash of lightning followed by thunder; smoke rises from the altar; all except* NAAMAN *and* RUAHMAH *cover their faces. The circle of priests opens again, and* TSARPI *comes forward slowly, chanting.*]

CHANT:

Hear the words of Rimmon! Thus your Maker speaketh:
I, the god of thunder, riding on the whirlwind,
I, the god of lightning leaping from the storm-cloud,
I will smite with vengeance him who dares defy me!
He who leads Damascus into war with Asshur,
Conquering or conquered, bears my curse upon him.

Surely shall my arrow strike his heart in secret,
Burn his flesh with fever, turn his blood to poison,
Brand him with corruption, drive him into darkness;
He shall surely perish by the doom of Rimmon.

> [*All are terrified and look toward* NAAMAN, *shuddering.* RUAHMAH *alone seems not to heed the curse, but stands with her eyes fixed on* NAAMAN.]

RUAHMAH:

Be not afraid! There is a greater God
Shall cover thee with His almighty wings:
Beneath his shield and buckler shalt thou trust.

BENHADAD:

Repent, my son, thou must not brave this curse.

NAAMAN:

My King, there is no curse as terrible
As that which lights a bosom-fire for him
Who gives away his honour, to prolong
A craven life whose every breath is shame!
If I betray the men who follow me,
The city that has put her trust in me,
What king can shield me from my own deep scorn
What god release me from that self-made hell?
The tender mercies of Assyria
I know; and they are cruel as creeping tigers.
Give up Damascus, and her streets will run
Rivers of innocent blood; the city's heart,
That mighty, labouring heart, wounded and crushed
Beneath the brutal hooves of the wild Bull,

Will cry against her captain, sitting safe
Among the nobles, in some pleasant place.
I shall be safe,—safe from the threatened wrath
Of unknown gods, but damned forever by
The men I know,—that is the curse I fear.

BENHADAD:
Speak not so high, my son. Must we not bow
Our heads before the sovereignties of heaven?
The unseen rulers are Divine.

NAAMAN:
      O King,
I am unlearned in the lore of priests;
Yet well I know that there are hidden powers
About us, working mortal weal and woe
Beyond the force of mortals to control.
And if these powers appear in love and truth,
I think they must be gods, and worship them.
But if their secret will is manifest
In blind decrees of sheer omnipotence,
That punish where no fault is found, and smite
The poor with undeserved calamity,
And pierce the undefended in the dark
With arrows of injustice, and foredoom
The innocent to burn in endless pain,
I will not call this fierce almightiness
Divine. Though I must bear, with every man,
The burden of my life ordained, I'll keep
My soul unterrified, and tread the path

Of truth and honour with a steady heart!
Have ye not heard, my lords? The oracle
Proclaims to me, to me alone, the doom
Of vengeance if I lead the army out.
"Conquered or conquering!" I grip that chance!
Damascus free, her foes all beaten back,
The people saved from slavery, the King
Upheld in honour on his ancient throne,—
O what's the cost of this? I'll gladly pay
Whatever gods there be, whatever price
They ask for this one victory. Give me
This gilded sign of shame to carry back;
I'll shake it in the face of Asshur's king,
And break it on his teeth.

BENHADAD: [*Rising.*]

Then go, my never-beaten captain, go!
And may the powers that hear thy solemn vow
Forgive thy rashness for Damascus' sake,
Prosper thy fighting, and remit thy pledge.

REZON: [*Standing beside the altar.*]

The pledge, O King, this man must seal his pledge
At Rimmon's altar. He must take the cup
Of soldier-sacrament, and bind himself
By thrice-performed libation to abide
The fate he has invoked.

NAAMAN: [*Slowly.*]

           And so I will.

[*He comes down the steps, toward the altar, where*

Rezon is filling the cup which Tsarpi holds.
Ruahmah throws herself before Naaman, clasping his knees.]

RUAHMAH: [*Passionately and wildly.*]

  My lord, I do beseech you, stay! There's death
  Within that cup. It is an offering
  To devils. See, the wine blazes like fire,
  It flows like blood, it is a cursed cup,
  Fulfilled of treachery and hate.
  Dear master, noble master, touch it not!

NAAMAN:

  Poor maid, thy brain is still distraught. Fear not,
  But let me go! Here, treat her tenderly!
    [*Gives her into the hands of* SABALLIDIN.]
  Can harm befall me from the wife who bears
  My name? I take the cup of fate from her.
  I greet the unknown powers; [*Pours libation.*]
  I will perform my vow; [*Again.*]
  I will abide my fate; [*Again.*]
  I pledge my life to keep Damascus free.
    [*He drains the cup, and lets it fall.*]

  CURTAIN.

ACT II

TIME: *A week later*

The fore-court of the House of Rimmon. At the back the broad steps and double doors of the shrine; above them the tower of the god, its summit invisible. Enter various groups of citizens, talking, laughing, shouting: RAKHAZ, HAZAEL, SHUMAKIM *and others.*

FIRST CITIZEN:

Great news, glorious news, the Assyrians are beaten!

SECOND CITIZEN:

Naaman is returning, crowned with victory. Glory to our noble captain!

THIRD CITIZEN:

No, he is killed. I had it from one of the camp-followers who saw him fall at the head of the battle. They are bringing his body to bury it with honour. O sorrowful victory!

RAKHAZ:

Peace, my good fellows, you are ignorant, you have not been rightly informed, I will misinform you. The accounts of Naaman's death are overdrawn. He was killed, but his life has been preserved. One of his wounds was mortal, but the other three were curable, and by these the physicians have saved him.

SHUMAKIM: [*Balancing himself before* RAKHAZ *in pretended admiration.*]

    O wonderful! Most admirable logic! One mortal, and three curable, therefore he must recover as it were, by three to one. Rakhaz, do you know that you are a marvelous man?

RAKHAZ:

    Yes, I know it, but I make no boast of my knowledge.

SHUMAKIM:

    Too modest, for in knowing this you know more than any other in Damascus!

    [*Enter, from the right,* SABALLIDIN *in armour: from the left,* TSARPI *with her attendants, among whom is* RUAHMAH.]

HAZAEL:

    Here is Saballidin, we'll question him;
    He was enflamed by Naaman's wild words,
    And rode with him to battle. Give us news,
    Of your great captain! Is he safe and well?
    When will he come? Or will he come at all?

    [*All gather around him listening eagerly.*]

SABALLIDIN:

    He comes but now, returning from the field
    Where he hath gained a crown of deathless fame!
    Three times he led the charge; three times he fell
    Wounded, and the Assyrians beat us back.
    Yet every wound was but a spur to urge
    His valour onward. In the last attack

THE HOUSE OF RIMMON

>He rode before us as the crested wave
>That leads the flood; and lo, our enemies
>Were broken like a dam of river-reeds.
>The flying King encircled by his guard
>Was lodged like driftwood on a little hill.
>Then Naaman, who led our foremost band
>Of whirlwind riders, hammered through the hedge
>Of spearmen, brandishing the golden yoke.
>"Take back this gift," he cried; and shattered it
>On Shalmaneser's helmet. So the fight
>Dissolved in universal rout; the King,
>His chariots and his horsemen fled away;
>Our captain stood the master of the field,
>And saviour of Damascus! Now he brings,
>First to the King, report of this great triumph.
>
>[*Shouts of joy and applause.*]

RUAHMAH: [*Coming close to* SABALLIDIN.]

>But what of him who won it? Fares he well?
>My mistress would receive some word of him.

SABALLIDIN:

>Hath she not heard?

RUAHMAH:

>But one brief message came
>A letter saying, "We have fought and conquered,'
>No word of his own person. Fares he well?

SABALLIDIN:

>Alas, most ill! For he is like a man
>Consumed by some strange sickness: wasted, wan,—

His eyes are dimmed so that he scarce can see;
His ears are dulled; his fearless face is pale
As one who walks to meet a certain doom
Yet will not flinch. It is most pitiful,—
But you shall see.

RUAHMAH:
>Yea, we shall see a man
Who dared to face the wrath of evil powers
Unknown, and hazard all to save his country.
[*Enter* BENHADAD *with courtiers*.]

BENHADAD:
Where is my faithful servant Naaman,
The captain of my host?

SABALLIDIN:
>My lord, he comes.
[*Trumpet sounds. Enter company of soldiers in armour. Then four soldiers bearing captured standards of Asshur.* NAAMAN *follows, very pale, armour dinted and stained; he is blind, and guides himself by cords from the standards on each side, but walks firmly. The doors of the temple open slightly, and* REZON *appears at the top of the steps.* NAAMAN *lets the cords fall, and gropes his way for a few paces.*]

NAAMAN: [*Kneeling.*]
>Where is my King?
Master, the bearer of thy sword returns.
The golden yoke thou gavest me I broke
On him who sent it. Asshur's Bull hath fled

Dehorned. The standards of his host are thine!
Damascus is all thine, at peace, and free!
BENHADAD: [*Holding out his arms.*]
Thou art a mighty man of valour! Come,
And let me fold thy courage to my heart.
REZON: [*Lifting his rod.*]
Forbear, O King! Stand back from him, all men!
By the great name of Rimmon I proclaim
This man a leper! See, upon his brow,
This little mark, the death-white seal of doom!
That tiny spot will spread, eating his flesh,
Gnawing his fingers bone from bone, until
The impious heart that dared defy the gods
Dissolves in the slow death which now begins.
Unclean! unclean! Henceforward he is dead:
No human hand shall touch him, and no home
Of men shall give him shelter. He shall walk
Only with corpses of the selfsame death
Down the long path to a forgotten tomb.
Avoid, depart, I do adjure you all,
Leave him to god,—the leper Naaman!

> [*All shrink back horrified.* REZON *retires into the temple; the crowd melts away, wailing;* TSARPI *is among the first to go, followed by her attendants, except* RUAHMAH, *who crouches, with her face covered, not far from* NAAMAN.]

BENHADAD: [*Lingering and turning back.*]
Alas, my son! O Naaman, my son!
Why did I let thee go? I must obey.

Who can resist the gods? Yet none shall take
Thy glorious title, captain of my host!
I will provide for thee, and thou shalt dwell
With guards of honour in a house of mine
Always. Damascus never shall forget
What thou hast done! O miserable words
Of crowned impotence! O mockery of power
Given to kings who cannot even defend
Their dearest from the secret wrath of heaven!
O Naaman, my son, my son! [*Exit.*]

NAAMAN: [*Slowly passing his hand over his eyes, and looking up.*]

          Am I alone
With thee, inexorable one, whose pride
Offended takes this horrible revenge?
I must submit my mortal flesh to thee,
Almighty, but I will not call thee god!
Yet thou hast found the way to wound my soul
Most deeply through the flesh; and I must find
The way to let my wounded soul escape!

    [*Drawing his sword.*]

Come, my last friend, thou art more merciful
Than Rimmon. Why should I endure the doom
He sends me? Irretrievably cut off
From all dear intercourse of human love,
From all the tender touch of human hands,
From all brave comradeship with brother-men,
With eyes that see no faces through this dark,

ACT II] THE HOUSE OF RIMMON

With ears that hear all voices far away,
Why should I cling to misery, and grope
My long, long way from pain to pain, alone?

RUAHMAH: [*At his feet.*]

Nay, not alone, dear lord, for I am here;
And I will never leave thee, nor forsake thee!

NAAMAN:

What voice is that? The silence of my tomb
Is broken by a ray of music,—whose?

RUAHMAH: [*Rising.*]

The one who loves thee best in all the world.

NAAMAN:

Why that should be,—O dare I dream it true?
Tsarpi, my wife? Have I misjudged thy heart
As cold and proud? How nobly thou forgivest
Thou com'st to hold me from the last disgrace,-
The coward's flight into the dark. Go back
Unstained, my sword! Life is endurable
While there is one alive on earth who loves us.

RUAHMAH:

My lord,—my lord,—O listen! You have erred
You do mistake me now,—this dream—

NAAMAN:

Ah, wake me not! For I can conquer death
Dreaming this dream. Let me at last believe,
Though gods are cruel, a woman can be kind.
Grant me but this! For see,—I ask so little,—

Only to know that thou art faithful,
That thou art near me, though I touch thee not,—
O this will hold me up, though it be given
From pity more than love.

RUAHMAH: [*Trembling, and speaking slowly.*]

                            Not so, my lord!
My pity is a stream; my pride of thee
Is like the sea that doth engulf the stream;
My love for thee is like the sovereign moon
That rules the sea. The tides that fill my soul
Flow unto thee and follow after thee;
And where thou goest I will go; and where
Thou diest I will die,—in the same hour.
    [*She lays her hand on his arm. He draws back.*]

NAAMAN:

O touch me not! Thou shalt not share my doom.

RUAHMAH:

Entreat me not to go. I will obey
In all but this; but rob me not of this,—
The only boon that makes life worth the living,—
To walk beside thee day by day, and keep
Thy foot from stumbling; to prepare thy food
When thou art hungry, music for thy rest,
And cheerful words to comfort thy black hour;
And so to lead thee ever on, and on,
Through darkness, till we find the door of hope.

NAAMAN:

What word is that? The leper has no hope.

RUAHMAH:
> Dear lord, the mark upon thy brow is yet
> No broader than my little finger-nail.
> Thy force is not abated, and thy step
> Is firm. Wilt thou surrender to the enemy
> Before thy strength is touched? Why, let me put
> A drop of courage from my breast in thine!
> There is a hope for thee. The captive maid
> Of Israel who dwelt within thy house
> Knew of a god very compassionate,
> Long-suffering, slow to anger, one who heals
> The sick, hath pity on the fatherless,
> And saves the poor and him who has no helper.
> His prophet dwells nigh to Samaria;
> And I have heard that he hath brought the dead
> To life again. We'll go to him. The King,
> If I beseech him, will appoint a guard
> Of thine own soldiers and Saballidin,
> Thy friend, to convoy us upon our journey.
> He'll give us royal letters to the King
> Of Israel to make our welcome sure;
> And we will take the open road, beneath
> The open sky, to-morrow, and go on
> Together till we find the door of hope.
> Come, come with me!
>   [*She grasps his hand.*]

NAAMAN: [*Drawing back.*]
> Thou must not touch me!

RUAHMAH: [*Unclasping her girdle and putting the end in his hand.*]

                        Take my girdle, then!

NAAMAN: [*Kissing the clasp of the girdle.*]
    I do begin to think there is a God,
Since love on earth can work such miracles!

CURTAIN

ACT III

TIME: *A month later: dawn*

SCENE I

NAAMAN's *tent, on high ground among the mountains near Samaria: the city below. In the distance, a wide and splendid landscape.* SABALLIDIN *and soldiers on guard below the tent. Enter* RUAHMAH *in hunter's dress, with a lute slung from her shoulder.*

RUAHMAH:

Peace and good health to you, Saballidin.
Good morrow to you all.   How fares my lord?

SABALLIDIN:

The curtains of his tent are folded still:
They have not moved since we returned, last night,
And told him what befell us in the city.

RUAHMAH:

Told him! Why did you make report to him
And not to me? Am I not captain here,
Intrusted by the King's command with care
Of Naaman until he is restored?
'Tis mine to know the first of good or ill
In this adventure: mine to shield his heart
From every arrow of adversity.
What have you told him? Speak!

513

SABALLIDIN:

                       Lady, we feared
To bring our news to you. For when the King
Of Israel had read our monarch's letter,
He rent his clothes, and cried, "Am I a god,
To kill and make alive, that I should heal
A leper? Ye have come with false pretence,
Damascus seeks a quarrel with me. Go!"
But when we told our lord, he closed his tent,
And there remains enfolded in his grief.
I trust he sleeps; 'twere kind to let him sleep!
For now he doth forget his misery,
And all the burden of his hopeless woe
Is lifted from him by the gentle hand
Of slumber. Oh, to those bereft of hope
Sleep is the only blessing left,—the last
Asylum of the weary, the one sign
Of pity from impenetrable heaven.
Waking is strife; sleep is the truce of God!
Ah, lady, wake him not. The day will be
Full long for him to suffer, and for us
To turn our disappointed faces home
On the long road by which we must return.

RUAHMAH:

Return! Who gave you that command? Not I!
The King made me the leader of this quest,
And bound you all to follow me, because
He knew I never would return without

THE HOUSE OF RIMMON

> The thing for which he sent us. I'll go on
> Day after day, unto the uttermost parts
> Of earth, if need be, and beyond the gates
> Of morning, till I find that which I seek,—
> New life for Naaman. Are ye ashamed
> To have a woman lead you? Then go back
> And tell the King, "This huntress went too far
> For us to follow: she pursues the trail
> Of hope alone, refusing to forsake
> The quarry: we grew weary of the chase;
> And so we left her and retraced our steps,
> Like faithless hounds, to sleep beside the fire."
> Did Naaman forsake his soldiers thus
> When you went forth to hunt the Assyrian Bull?
> Your manly courage is less durable
> Than woman's love, it seems. Go, if you will,—
> Who bids me now farewell?

SOLDIERS:
> Not I, not I!

SABALLIDIN:
> Lady, lead on, we'll follow you forever!

RUAHMAH:
> Why, now you speak like men! Brought you no word
> Out of Samaria, except that cry
> Of impotence and fear from Israel's King?

SABALLIDIN:
> I do remember while he spoke with us

A rustic messenger came in, and cried
"Elisha saith, bring Naaman to me
At Dothan, he shall surely know there is
A God in Israel."

RUAHMAH:
                    What said the King?

SABALLIDIN:
He only shouted "Go!" more wildly yet,
And rent his clothes again, as if he were
Half-maddened by a coward's fear, and thought
Only of how he might be rid of us.
What comfort could there be for him, what hope
For us, in the rude prophet's misty word?

RUAHMAH:
It is the very word for which I prayed!
My trust was not in princes; for the crown,
The sceptre, and the purple robe are not
Significant of vital power. The man
Who saves his brother-men is he who lives
His life with Nature, takes deep hold on truth,
And trusts in God. A prophet's word is more
Than all the kings on earth can speak. How far
Is Dothan?

SOLDIER:
                Lady, 'tis but three hours' ride
Along the valley southward.

RUAHMAH:
                    Near! so near?

[ACT III, SC. I] THE HOUSE OF RIMMON

I had not thought to end my task so soon!
Prepare yourselves with speed to take the road.
I will awake my lord.
  [*Exeunt all but* SABALLIDIN *and* RUAHMAH. *She goes toward the tent.*]

SABALLIDIN:
      Ruahmah, stay! [*She turns back.*]
I've been your servant in this doubtful quest,
Obedient, faithful, loyal to your will,—
What have I earned by this?

RUAHMAH:
      The gratitude
Of him we both desire to serve: your friend,—
My master and my lord.

SABALLIDIN:
      No more than this?

RUAHMAH:
Yes, if you will, take all the thanks my hands
Can hold, my lips can speak.

SABALLIDIN:
      I would have more.

RUAHMAH:
My friend, there's nothing more to give to you.
My service to my lord is absolute.
There's not a drop of blood within my veins
But quickens at the very thought of him;
And not a dream of mine but he doth stand
Within its heart and make it bright. No man

To me is other than his friend or foe.
You are his friend, and I believe you true!

SABALLIDIN:
  I have been true to him,—now, I am true
  To you.

RUAHMAH:
              Why, then, be doubly true to him.
  O let us match our loyalties, and strive
  Between us who shall win the higher crown!
  Men boast them of a friendship stronger far
  Than love of woman. Prove it! I'll not boast,
  But I'll contend with you on equal terms
  In this brave race: and if you win the prize
  I'll hold you next to him: and if I win
  He'll hold you next to me; and either way
  We'll not be far apart. Do you accept
  My challenge?

SABALLIDIN:
              Yes! For you enforce my heart
  By honour to resign its great desire,
  And love itself to offer sacrifice
  Of all disloyal dreams on its own altar.
  Yet love remains; therefore I pray you, think
  How surely you must lose in our contention.
  For I am known to Naaman: but you
  He blindly takes for Tsarpi. 'Tis to her
  He gives his gratitude: the praise you win
  Endears her name.

[ACT III, SC. 1] **THE HOUSE OF RIMMON**

RUAHMAH:

              Her name? Why, what is that?
A name is but an empty shell, a mask
That does not change the features of the face
Beneath it. Can a name rejoice, or weep,
Or hope? Can it be moved by tenderness
To daily services of love, or feel the warmth
Of dear companionship? How many things
We call by names that have no meaning! Kings
That cannot rule; and gods that are not good;
And wives that do not love! It matters not
What syllables he utters when he calls,
'Tis I who come,—'tis I who minister
Unto my lord, and mine the living heart
That feels the comfort of his confidence,
The thrill of gladness when he speaks to me,—
I do not hear the name!

SABALLIDIN:

                    And yet, be sure
There's danger in this error,—and no gain!

RUAHMAH:

I seek no gain: I only tread the path
Marked for me daily by the hand of love.
And if his blindness spared my lord one pang
Of sorrow in his black, forsaken hour,—
And if this error makes his burdened heart
More quiet, and his shadowed way less dark,
Whom do I rob? Not her who chose to stay

At ease in Rimmon's House! Surely not him!
Only myself! And that enriches me.
Why trouble we the master? Let it go,—
To-morrow he must know the truth,—and then
He shall dispose of me e'en as he will!

SABALLIDIN:

To-morrow?

RUAHMAH:

              Yes, for I will tarry here,
While you conduct him to Elisha's house
To find the promised healing. I forebode
A sudden danger from the craven King
Of Israel, or else a secret ambush
From those who hate us in Damascus. Go,
But leave me twenty men: this mountain-pass
Protects the road behind you. Make my lord
Obey the prophet's word, whatever he commands,
And come again in peace. Farewell!

   [*Exit* SABALLIDIN. RUAHMAH *goes toward the
      tent, then pauses and turns back. She takes her
      lute and sings.*]

SONG

*Above the edge of dark appear the lances of the sun;
Along the mountain-ridges clear his rosy heralds run;
   The vapours down the valley go
   Like broken armies, dark and low.
   Look up, my heart, from every hill*

ACT III, SC. I] THE HOUSE OF RIMMON

In folds of rose and daffodil
The sunrise banners flow.

O fly away on silent wing, ye boding owls of night!
O welcome little birds that sing the coming-in of light!
For new, and new, and ever-new,
The golden bud within the blue;
And every morning seems to say:
"There's something happy on the way,
"And God sends love to you!"

NAAMAN: [*Appearing at the entrance of his tent.*]
O let me ever wake to music! For the soul
Returns most gently then, and finds its way
By the soft, winding clue of melody,
Out of the dusky labyrinth of sleep,
Into the light. My body feels the sun
Though I behold naught that his rays reveal.
Come, thou who art my daydawn and my sight,
Sweet eyes, come close, and make the sunrise mine!

RUAHMAH: [*Coming near.*]
A fairer day, dear lord, was never born
In Paradise! The sapphire cup of heaven
Is filled with golden wine: the earth, adorned
With jewel-drops of dew, unveils her face
A joyful bride, in welcome to her king.
And look! He leaps upon the Eastern hills
All ruddy fire, and claims her with a kiss.

Yonder the snowy peaks of Hermon float
Unmoving as a wind-dropt cloud. The gulf
Of Jordan, filled with violet haze, conceals
The river's winding trail with wreaths of mist.
Below us, marble-crowned Samaria thrones
Upon her emerald hill amid the Vale
Of Barley, while the plains to northward change
Their colour like the shimmering necks of doves.
The lark springs up, with morning on her wings,
To climb her singing stairway in the blue,
And all the fields are sprinkled with her joy!

NAAMAN:

Thy voice is magical: thy words are visions!
I must content myself with them, for now
My only hope is lost: Samaria's King
Rejects our monarch's message,—hast thou heard?
"Am I a god that I should cure a leper?"
He sends me home unhealed, with angry words,
Back to Damascus and the lingering death.

RUAHMAH:

What matter where he sends? No god is he
To slay or make alive. Elisha bids
You come to him at Dothan, there to learn
There is a God in Israel.

NAAMAN:

                         I fear
That I am grown mistrustful of all gods;
Their secret counsels are implacable.

RUAHMAH:
> Fear not! There's One who rules in righteousness
> High over all.

NAAMAN:
> What knowest thou of Him?

RUAHMAH:
> Oh, I have heard,—the maid of Israel,—
> Rememberest thou? She often said her God
> Was merciful and kind, and slow to wrath,
> And plenteous in forgiveness, pitying us
> Like as a father pitieth his children.

NAAMAN:
> If there were such a God, I'd worship Him
> Forever!

RUAHMAH:
> Then make haste to hear the word
> His prophet promises to speak to thee!
> Obey it, my dear lord, and thou shalt find
> Healing and peace. The light shall fill thine eyes.
> Thou wilt not need my leading any more,—
> Nor me,—for thou wilt see me, all unveiled,—
> I tremble at the thought.

NAAMAN:
> Why, what is this?
> Why shouldst thou tremble? Art thou not mine own?

RUAHMAH: [*Turning to him and speaking in broken words.*]
> I am,—thy handmaid,—all and only thine,—

THE HOUSE OF RIMMON [ACT III, SC. I

The very pulses of my heart are thine!
Feel how they throb to comfort thee to-day—
To-day! Because it is thy time of trouble.
> [*She takes his hand and puts it to her forehead and her lips, but before she can lay it upon her heart, he draws away from her.*]

NAAMAN:
Thou art too dear to injure with a kiss,—
How should I take a gift may bankrupt thee,
Or drain the fragrant chalice of thy love
With lips that may be fatal? Tempt me not
To sweet dishonour; strengthen me to wait
Until thy prophecy is all fulfilled,
And I can claim thee with a joyful heart.

RUAHMAH: [*Turning away.*]
Thou wilt not need me then,—and I shall be
No more than the faint echo of a song
Heard half asleep. We shall go back to where
We stood before this journey.

NAAMAN:
                        Never again!
For thou art changed by some deep miracle.
The flower of womanhood hath bloomed in thee,—
Art thou not changed?

RUAHMAH:
                Yea, I am changed,—and changed
Again,—bewildered,—till there's nothing clear
To me but this: I am the instrument

In an Almighty hand to rescue thee
From death. This will I do,—and afterward—
[*A trumpet is blown without.*]
Hearken, the trumpet sounds, the chariot waits.
Away, dear lord, follow the road to light!

Scene II*

The house of Elisha, upon a terraced hillside. A low stone cottage with vine-trellises and flowers; a flight of steps, at the foot of which is Naaman's *chariot. He is standing in it;* Saballidin *beside it. Two soldiers come down the steps.*

First Soldier:
  We have delivered my lord's greeting and his message.

Second Soldier:
  Yes, and near lost our noses in the doing of it! For the servant slammed the door in our faces. A most unmannerly reception!

First Soldier:
  But I take that as a good omen. It is a mark of holy men to keep ill-conditioned servants. Look, the door opens, the prophet is coming.

Second Soldier:
  No, by my head, it is that notable mark of his mas-

* Note that this scene is not intended to be put upon the stage, the effect of the action upon the drama being given at the beginning of Act IV.

ter's holiness, that same lantern-jawed lout of a servant.

[GEHAZI *loiters down the steps and comes to* NAAMAN *with a slight obeisance.*]

GEHAZI:

My master, the prophet of Israel, sends word to Naaman the Syrian,—are you he?—"Go wash in Jordan seven times and be healed."

[GEHAZI *turns and goes slowly up the steps.*]

NAAMAN:

What insolence is this? Am I a man
To be put off with surly messengers?
Has not Damascus rivers more renowned
Than this rude muddy Jordan? Crystal streams,
Abana! Pharpar! flowing smoothly through
A paradise of roses? Might I not
Have bathed in them and been restored at ease?
Come up, Saballidin, and guide me home!

SABALLIDIN:

Bethink thee, master, shall we lose our quest
Because a servant is uncouth? The road
That seeks the mountain leads us through the vale.
The prophet's word is friendly after all;
For had it been some mighty task he set,
Thou wouldst perform it. How much rather then
This easy one? Hast thou not promised her
Who waits for thy return? Wilt thou go back
To her unhealed?

ACT III, SC. II] **THE HOUSE OF RIMMON**

NAAMAN:
                        No! not for all my pride!
I'll make myself most humble for her sake,
And stoop to anything that gives me hope
Of having her. Make haste, Saballidin,
Bring me to Jordan. I will cast myself
Into that river's turbulent embrace
A hundred times, until I save my life
Or lose it!
> [*Exeunt. The light fades: musical interlude. The light increases again with ruddy sunset shining on the door of* ELISHA's *house. The prophet appears and looks off, shading his eyes with his hand as he descends the steps. Trumpet blows,—*NAAMAN's *call;—sound of horses galloping and men shouting.* NAAMAN *enters joyously, followed by* SABALLIDIN *and soldiers, with gifts.*]

NAAMAN:

Behold a man delivered from the grave
By thee! I rose from Jordan's waves restored
To youth and vigour, as the eagle mounts
Upon the sunbeam and renews his strength!
O mighty prophet deign to take from me
These gifts too poor to speak my gratitude;
Silver and gold and jewels, damask robes,—

ELISHA: [*Interrupting.*]

As thy soul liveth I will not receive

A gift from thee, my son! Give all to Him
Whose mercy hath redeemed thee from thy plague.

NAAMAN:

He is the only God! I worship Him!
Grant me a portion of the blessed soil
Of this most favoured land where I have found
His mercy; in Damascus will I build
An altar to His name, and praise Him there
Morning and night. There is no other God
In all the world.

ELISHA:

     Thou needst not
This load of earth to build a shrine for Him;
Yet take it if thou wilt. But be assured
God's altar is in every loyal heart,
And every flame of love that kindles there
Ascends to Him and brightens with His praise.
There is no other God! But evil Powers
Make war against Him in the darkened world;
And many temples have been built to them.

NAAMAN:

I know them well! Yet when my master goes
To worship in the House of Rimmon, I
Must enter with him; for he trusts me, leans
Upon my hand; and when he bows himself
I cannot help but make obeisance too,—
But not to Rimmon! To my country's King

ACT III, SC. II] **THE HOUSE OF RIMMON**

I'll bow in love and honour. Will the Lord
Pardon thy servant in this thing?

ELISHA:

My son,
Peace has been granted thee. 'Tis thine to find
The only way to keep it. Go in peace.

NAAMAN:

Thou hast not answered me,—may I bow down?

ELISHA:

The answer must be thine. The heart that knows
The perfect peace of gratitude and love,
Walks in the light and needs no other rule.
When next thou comest into Rimmon's House,
Thy heart will tell thee how to go in peace.

CURTAIN

ACT IV

Scene I

The interior of NAAMAN's *tent, at night.* RUAHMAH *alone, sleeping on the ground. A vision appears to her through the curtains of the tent:* ELISHA *standing on the hillside at Dothan:* NAAMAN, *restored to sight, comes in and kneels before him.* ELISHA *blesses him, and he goes out rejoicing. The vision of the prophet turns to* RUAHMAH *and lifts his hand in warning.*

ELISHA:
    Daughter of Israel, what dost thou here?
    Thy prayer is granted. Naaman is healed:
    Mar not true service with a selfish thought.
    Nothing remains for thee to do, except
    Give thanks, and go whither the Lord commands.
    Obey,—obey! Ere Naaman returns
    Thou must depart to thine own house in Shechem.
      [*The vision vanishes.*]

RUAHMAH: [*Waking and rising slowly.*]
    A dream, a dream, a messenger of God!
    O dear and dreadful vision, art thou true?
    Then am I glad with all my broken heart.
    Nothing remains,—nothing remains but this,—
    Give thanks, obey, depart,—and so I do.

ACT IV, SC, I] **THE HOUSE OF RIMMON**

>Farewell, my master's sword! Farewell to you,
>My amulet! I lay you on the hilt
>His hand shall clasp again: bid him farewell
>For me, since I must look upon his face
>No more for ever!—Hark, what sound was that?
>>[*Enter soldier hurriedly.*]

SOLDIER:
>Mistress, an armèd troop, footmen and horse,
>Mounting the hill!

RUAHMAH:
>>My lord returns in triumph.

SOLDIER:
>Not so, for these are enemies; they march
>In haste and silence, answering not our cries.

RUAHMAH:
>Our enemies? Then hold your ground,—on guard!
>Fight! fight! Defend the pass, and drive them down.
>>[*Exit soldier.* RUAHMAH *draws* NAAMAN'S *sword
>>from the scabbard and hurries out of the tent.
>>Confused noise of fighting outside. Three or
>>four soldiers are driven in by a troop of men in
>>disguise.* RUAHMAH *follows: she is beaten to
>>her knees, and her sword is broken.*]

REZON: [*Throwing aside the cloth which covers his face.*]
>Hold her! So, tiger-maid, we've found your lair
>And trapped you. Where is Naaman,
>Your master?

RUAHMAH: [*Rising, her arms held by two of* REZON's *followers.*]
>He is far beyond your reach.

REZON:
>Brave captain! He has saved himself, the leper,
>And left you here?

RUAHMAH:
>The leper is no more.

REZON:
>What mean you?

RUAHMAH:
>He has gone to meet his God.

REZON:
>Dead? Dead? Behold how Rimmon's wrath is swift!
>Damascus shall be mine; I'll terrify
>The King with this, and make my terms. But no!
>False maid, you sweet-faced harlot, you have lied
>To save him,—speak.

RUAHMAH:
>I am not what you say,
>Nor have I lied, nor will I ever speak
>A word to you, vile servant of a traitor-god.

REZON:
>Break off this little flute of blasphemy,
>This ivory neck,—twist it, I say!
>Give her a swift despatch after her leper!
>But stay,—if he still lives he'll follow her,
>And so we may ensnare him. Harm her not!

Bind her! Away with her to Rimmon's House!
Is all this carrion dead? There's one that moves,—
A spear,—fasten him down! All quiet now?
Then back to our Damascus! Rimmon's face
Shall be made bright with sacrifice.

> [*Exeunt, forcing* RUAHMAH *with them. Musical interlude. A wounded soldier crawls from a dark corner of the tent and finds the chain with* NAAMAN'S *seal, which has fallen to the ground in the struggle.*]

WOUNDED SOLDIER:

The signet of my lord, her amulet!
Lost, lost! Ah, noble lady,—let me die
With this upon my breast.

> [*The tent is dark. Enter* NAAMAN *and his company in haste, with torches.*]

NAAMAN:

                      What bloody work
Is here? God, let me live to punish him
Who wrought this horror! Treacherously slain
At night, by unknown hands, my brave companions:
Tsarpi, my best beloved, light of my soul,
Put out in darkness! O my broken lamp
Of life, where art thou? Nay, I cannot find her.

WOUNDED SOLDIER: [*Raising himself on his arm.*]

Master!

NAAMAN: [*Kneels beside him.*]

                One living? Quick, a torch this way!

Lift up his head,—so,—carefully!
Courage, my friend, your captain is beside you.
Call back your soul and make report to him.

WOUNDED SOLDIER:
Hail, captain! O my captain,—here!

NAAMAN:
Be patient,—rest in peace,—the fight is done.
Nothing remains but render your account.

WOUNDED SOLDIER:
They fell upon us suddenly,—we fought
Our fiercest,—every man,—our lady fought
Fiercer than all. They beat us down,—she's gone.
Rezon has carried her away a captive. See,—
Her amulet,—I die for you, my captain.

NAAMAN: [*He gently lays the dead soldier on the ground, and rises.*]
Farewell. This last report was brave; but strange
Beyond my thought! How came the High Priest here?
And what is this? my chain, my seal! But this
Has never been in Tsarpi's hand. I gave
This signet to a captive maid one night,—
A maid of Israel. How long ago?
Ruahmah was her name,—almost forgotten!
So long ago,—how comes this token here?
What is this mystery, Saballidin?

SABALLIDIN:
Ruahmah is her name who brought you hither.

NAAMAN:
  Where then is Tsarpi?
SABALLIDIN:
                    In Damascus.
  She left you when the curse of Rimmon fell,—
  Took refuge in his House,—and there she waits
  Her lord's return,—Rezon's return.
NAAMAN:
                              'Tis false!
SABALLIDIN:
  The falsehood is in her. She hath been friend
  With Rezon in his priestly plot to win
  Assyria's favour,—friend to his design
  To sell his country to enrich his temple,—
  And friend to him in more,—I will not name it
NAAMAN:
  Nor will I credit it. Impossible!
SABALLIDIN:
  Did she not plead with you against the war,
  Counsel surrender, seek to break your will?
NAAMAN:
  She did not love my work, a soldier's task.
  She never seemed to be at one with me
  Until I was a leper.
SABALLIDIN:
                    From whose hand
  Did you receive the sacred cup?
NAAMAN:
                              From hers.

SABALLIDIN:
>And from that hour the curse began to work.

NAAMAN:
>But did she not have pity when she saw
>Me smitten? Did she not beseech the King
>For letters and a guard to make this journey?
>Has she not been the fountain of my hope,
>My comforter and my most faithful guide
>In this adventure of the dark? All this
>Is proof of perfect love that would have shared
>A leper's doom rather than give me up.
>Can I doubt her who dared to love like this?

SABALLIDIN:
>O master, doubt her not,—but know her name;
>Ruahmah! It was she alone who wrought
>This wondrous work of love. She won the King
>To furnish forth this company. She led
>Our march, kept us in heart, fought off despair,
>Watched over you as if you were her child,
>Prepared your food, your cup, with her own hands,
>Sang you asleep at night, awake at dawn,—

NAAMAN: [*Interrupting.*]
>Enough! I do remember every hour
>Of that sweet comradeship! And now her voice
>Wakens the echoes in my lonely breast.
>Shall I not see her, thank her, speak her name?
>Ruahmah! Let me live till I have looked
>Into her eyes and called her my Ruahmah!

ACT IV, SC. II] **THE HOUSE OF RIMMON**

[*To his soldiers.*]
Away! away! I burn to take the road
That leads me back to Rimmon's House,—
But not to bow,—by God, never to bow!

Scene II

Time: *Three days later*

Inner court of the House of Rimmon; a temple with huge pillars at each side. In the right foreground the seat of the King; at the left, of equal height, the seat of the High Priest. In the background a broad flight of steps, rising to a curtain of cloudy gray, embroidered with two gigantic hands holding thunderbolts. The temple is in half darkness at first. Enter Khamma *and* Nubta, *robed as Kharimati, or religious dancers, in gowns of black gauze with yellow embroideries and mantles.*

Khamma:

All is ready for the rites of worship; our lady will play a great part in them. She has put on her Tyrian robes, and all her ornaments.

Nubta:

That is a sure sign of a religious purpose. She is most devout, our lady Tsarpi!

Khamma:

A favourite of Rimmon, too! The High Priest has assured her of it. He is a great man,—next to the King, now that Naaman is gone.

NUBTA:

> But if Naaman should come back, healed of the leprosy?

KHAMMA:

> How can he come back? The Hebrew slave that went away with him, when they caught her, said that he was dead. The High Priest has shut her up in the prison of the temple, accusing her of her master's death.

NUBTA:

> Yet I think he does not believe it, for I heard him telling our mistress what to do if Naaman should return.

KHAMMA:

> What, then?

NUBTA:

> She will claim him as her husband. Was she not wedded to him before the god? That is a sacred bond. Only the High Priest can loose it. She will keep her hold on Naaman for the sake of the House of Rimmon. A wife knows her husband's secrets, she can tell——
>
> [*Enter* SHUMAKIM, *with his flagon, walking unsteadily.*]

KHAMMA:

> Hush! here comes the fool Shumakim. He is never sober.

SHUMAKIM: [*Laughing.*]

> Are there two of you? I see two, but that is no proof. I think there is only one, but beautiful enough for two. What were you talking to yourself about, fairest one!

KHAMMA:

> About the lady Tsarpi, fool, and what she would do if her husband returned.

SHUMAKIM:

> Fie! fie! That is no talk for an innocent fool to hear. Has she a husband?

NUBTA:

> You know very well that she is the wife of Lord Naaman.

SHUMAKIM:

> I remember that she used to wear his name and his jewels. But I thought he had exchanged her,— for a leprosy.

KHAMMA:

> You must have heard that he went away to Samaria to look for healing. Some say that he died on the journey; but others say he has been cured, and is on his way home to his wife.

SHUMAKIM:

> It may be, for this is a mad world, and men never know when they are well off,—except us fools. But he must come soon if he would find his wife as he parted from her,—or the city where he left

it. The Assyrians have returned with a greater army, and this time they will make an end of us. There is no Naaman now, and the Bull will devour Damascus like a bunch of leeks, flowers and all,— flowers and all, my double-budded fair one! Are you not afraid?

NUBTA:

We belong to the House of Rimmon. He will protect us.

SHUMAKIM:

What? The mighty one who hides behind the curtain there, and tells his secrets to Rezon? No doubt he will take care of you, and of himself. Whatever game is played, the gods never lose. But for the protection of the common people and the rest of us fools, I would rather have Naaman at the head of an army than all the sacred images between here and Babylon.

KHAMMA:

You are a wicked old man. You mock the god. He will punish you.

SHUMAKIM: [*Bitterly.*]

How can he punish me? Has he not already made me a fool? Hark, here comes my brother the High Priest, and my brother the King. Rimmon made us all; but nobody knows who made Rimmon, except the High Priest; and he will never tell.

Gongs and cymbals sound. Enter REZON *with priests, and*

*the King with courtiers. They take their seats. A throng
of Khali and Kharimati come in,* TSARPI *presiding; a
sacred dance is performed with torches, burning incense,
and chanting, in which* TSARPI *leads.*]

CHANT

*Hail, mighty Rimmon, ruler of the whirl-storm,
Hail, shaker of mountains, breaker-down of forests,
Hail, thou who roarest terribly in the darkness,
Hail, thou whose arrows flame across the heavens!
Hail, great destroyer, lord of flood and tempest,
In thine anger almighty, in thy wrath eternal,
Thou who delightest in ruin, maker of desolations,
Immeru, Addu, Berku, Rimmon!
See we tremble before thee, low we bow at thine altar,
Have mercy upon us, be favourable unto us,
Save us from our enemy, accept our sacrifice,
Barku, Immeru, Addu, Rimmon!*

[*Silence follows, all bowing down.*]

REZON:

O King, last night the counsel from above
Was given in answer to our divination.
Ambassadors must go forthwith to crave
Assyria's pardon, and a second offer
Of the same terms of peace we did reject
Not long ago.

BENHADAD:

Dishonour! Yet I see

No other way! Assyria will refuse,
Or make still harder terms. Disaster, shame
For this gray head, and ruin for Damascus!

REZON:
Yet may we trust Rimmon will favour us,
If we adhere devoutly to his worship.
He will incline his brother-god, the Bull,
To spare us, if we supplicate him now
With costly gifts. Therefore I have prepared
A sacrifice: Rimmon shall be well pleased
With the red blood that bathes his knees to-night!

BENHADAD:
My mind is dark with doubt,—I do forebode
Some horror! Let me go,—I am an old man,—
If Naaman my captain were alive!
But he is dead,—the glory is departed!

[*He rises, trembling, to leave the throne. Trumpet sounds,—*NAAMAN'S *call;—enter* NAAMAN, *followed by soldiers; he kneels at the foot of the throne.*]

BENHADAD: [*Half-whispering.*]
Art thou a ghost escaped from Allatu?
How didst thou pass the seven doors of death?
O noble ghost I am afraid of thee,
And yet I love thee,—let me hear thy voice!

NAAMAN:
No ghost, my King, but one who lives to serve
Thee and Damascus with his heart and sword

As in the former days. The only God
Has healed my leprosy: my life is clean
To offer to my country and my King.
BENHADAD: [*Starting toward him.*]
O welcome to thy King! Thrice welcome!
REZON: [*Leaving his seat and coming toward NAAMAN.*]
Stay!
The leper must appear before the priest,
The only one who can pronounce him clean.
[NAAMAN *turns; they stand looking each other in the face.*]
Yea,—thou art cleansed: Rimmon hath pardoned thee,—
In answer to the daily prayers of her
Whom he restores to thine embrace,—thy wife.
[TSARPI *comes slowly toward* NAAMAN.]
NAAMAN:
From him who rules this House will I receive
Nothing! I seek no pardon from his priest,
No wife of mine among his votaries!
TSARPI: [*Holding out her hands.*]
Am I not yours? Will you renounce our vows?
NAAMAN:
The vows were empty,—never made you mine
In aught but name. A wife is one who shares
Her husband's thought, incorporates his heart
With hers by love, and crowns him with her trust.
She is God's remedy for loneliness,

And God's reward for all the toil of life.
This you have never been to me,—and so
I give you back again to Rimmon's House
Where you belong. Claim what you will of mine,—
Not me! I do renounce you,—or release you,—
According to the law. If you demand
A further cause than what I have declared,
I will unfold it fully to the King.

REZON: [*Interposing hurriedly.*]

No need of that! This duteous lady yields
To your caprice as she has ever done:
She stands a monument of loyalty
And woman's meekness.

NAAMAN:

      Let her stand for that!
Adorn your temple with her piety!
But you in turn restore to me the treasure
You stole at midnight from my tent.

REZON:

What treasure! I have stolen none from you.

NAAMAN:

The very jewel of my soul,—Ruahmah!
My King, the captive maid of Israel,
To whom thou didst commit my broken life
With letters to Samaria,—my light,
My guide, my saviour in this pilgrimage,—
Dost thou remember?

ACT IV, SC. II] **THE HOUSE OF RIMMON**

BENHADAD:
                          I recall the maid,—
But dimly,—for my mind is old and weary,
She was a fearless maid, I trusted her
And gave thee to her charge. Where is she now?

NAAMAN:
This robber fell upon my camp by night,—
While I was with Elisha at the Jordan,—
Slaughtered my soldiers, carried off the maid,
And holds her somewhere in imprisonment.
O give this jewel back to me, my King,
And I will serve thee with a grateful heart
For ever. I will fight for thee, and lead
Thine armies on to glorious victory
Over all foes! Thou shalt no longer fear
The host of Asshur, for thy throne shall stand
Encompassed with a wall of dauntless hearts,
And founded on a mighty people's love,
And guarded by the God of righteousness.

BENHADAD:
I feel the flame of courage at thy breath
Leap up among the ashes of despair.
Thou hast returned to save us! Thou shalt have
The maid; and thou shalt lead my host again!
Priest, I command you give her back to him.

REZON:
O master, I obey thy word as thou
Hast ever been obedient to the voice

Of Rimmon. Let thy fiery captain wait
Until the sacrifice has been performed,
And he shall have the jewel that he claims.
Must we not first placate the city's god
With due allegiance, keep the ancient faith,
And pay our homage to the Lord of Wrath?

BENHADAD: [*Sinking back upon his throne in fear.*]
I am the faithful son of Rimmon's House,—
And lo, these many years I worship him!
My thoughts are troubled,—I am very old,
But still a King! O Naaman, be patient!
Priest, let the sacrifice be offered.

> [*The High Priest lifts his rod. Gongs and cymbals sound. The curtain is rolled back, disclosing the image of Rimmon; a gigantic and hideous idol, with a cruel human face, four horns, the mane of a lion, and huge paws stretched in front of him enclosing a low altar of black stone.* RUAHMAH *stands on the altar, chained, her arms are bare and folded on her breast. The people prostrate themselves in silence, with signs of astonishment and horror.*]

REZON:
Behold the sacrifice! Bow down, bow down!

NAAMAN: [*Stabbing him.*]
Bow thou, black priest! Down,—down to hell!
Ruahmah! do not die! I come to thee.

> [NAAMAN *rushes toward her, attacked by the priests, crying "Sacrilege! Kill him!" But the sol-*

[ACT IV, SC. II] **THE HOUSE OF RIMMON**

>*diers stand on the steps and beat them back. He springs upon the altar and clasps her by the hand. Tumult and confusion. The King rises and speaks with a loud voice, silence follows.*]

BENHADAD:

Peace, peace! The King commands all weapons down!
O Naaman, what wouldst thou do? Beware
Lest thou provoke the anger of a god.

NAAMAN:

There is no God but one, the Merciful,
Who gave this perfect woman to my soul
That I might learn through her to worship Him,
And know the meaning of immortal Love.

BENHADAD: [*Agitated.*]

Yet she is consecrated, bound, and doomed
To sacrificial death; but thou art sworn
To live and lead my host,—Hast thou not sworn?

NAAMAN:

Only if thou wilt keep thy word to me!
Break with this idol of iniquity
Whose shadow makes a darkness in the land;
Give her to me who gave me back to thee;
And I will lead thine army to renown
And plant thy banners on the hill of triumph.
But if she dies, I die with her, defying Rimmon.

>[*Cries of "Spare them! Release her! Give us back our Captain!" and "Sacrilege! Let them die!" Then silence, all turning toward the King.*]

THE HOUSE OF RIMMON [ACT IV, SC. II

BENHADAD:
>   Is this the choice? Must we destroy the bond
>   Of ancient faith, or slay the city's living hope!
>   I am an old, old man,—and yet the King!
>   Must I decide?—O let me ponder it!
>   [*His head sinks upon his breast. All stand eagerly looking at him.*]

NAAMAN:
>   Ruahmah, my Ruahmah! I have come
>   To thee at last! And art thou satisfied?

RUAHMAH: [*Looking into his face.*]
>   Belovéd, my belovéd, I am glad
>   Of all, and glad for ever, come what may.
>   Nothing can harm me,—since my lord is come!

APPENDIX
CARMINA FESTIVA

APPENDIX

GEMINAE FESTIVA

THE LITTLE–NECK CLAM

A modern verse-sequence, showing how a native American subject, strictly realistic, may be treated in various manners adapted to the requirements of different magazines, thus combining Art-for-Art's-Sake with Writing-for-the-Market. Read at the First Dinner of the American Periodical Publishers' Association, in Washington, April, 1904.

I

THE ANTI-TRUST CLAM

For *McClure's Magazine*

The clam that once, on Jersey's banks,
Was like the man who dug it, free,
Now slave-like thro' the market clanks
In chains of corporate tyranny.

The Standard Fish-Trust of New York
Holds every clam-bank in control;
And like base Beef and menial Pork,
The free-born Clam has lost its soul.

No more the bivalve treads the sands
In freedom's rapture, free from guilt:
It follows now the harsh commands
Of Morgiman and Rockabilt.

Rise, freemen, rise! Your wrath is just!
Call on the Sherman Act to dam
The floods of this devouring Trust,
And liberate the fettered Clam.

CARMINA FESTIVA

II

THE WHITMANIAC CLAM
For the *Bookman*

Not Dante when he wandered by the river Arno,
Not Burns who plowed the banks and braes of bonnie
  Ayr,
Not even Shakspere on the shores of Avon,—ah, no!
Not one of those great bards did taste true Poet's Fare.

But Whitman, loafing in Long Island and New Jersey,
Found there the sustenance of mighty ode and psalm,
And while his rude emotions swam around in verse, he
Fed chiefly on the wild, impassioned, sea-born clam.

Thus in his work we feel the waves' bewildering motion,
And winds from mighty mud-flats, weird and wild:
His clam-filled bosom answered to the voice of ocean,
And rose and fell responsively with every tide.

THE LITTLE–NECK CLAM

III

Il Mercatore Italiano Della Clamma

For the *Century Magazine*

"Clam O! Fres' Clam!" How strange it sounds and sweet,
The Dago's cry along the New York street!
"Dago" we call him, like the thoughtless crowd;
And yet this humble man may well be proud
To hail from Petrarch's land, Boccaccio's home,—
Firenze, Gubbio, Venezia, Rome,—
From fair Italia, whose enchanted soil
Transforms the lowly cotton-seed to olive-oil.

To me his chant, with alien accent sung,
Brings back an echo of great Virgil's tongue:
It seems to cry against the city's woe,
In liquid Latin syllables,—*Clamo!*
As thro' the crowded street his cart he jams
And cries aloud, ah, think of more than clams!
Receive his secret plaint with pity warm,
And grant Italia's plea for Tenement-House Reform!

CARMINA FESTIVA

IV

THE SOCIAL CLAM

For the *Smart Set*

Fair Phyllis is another's bride:
Therefore I like to sit beside
Her at a very smart set dinner,
And whisper love, and try to win her.

The little-necks,—in number six,—
That from their pearly shells she picks
And swallows whole,—ah, is it selfish
To wish my heart among those shell-fish?

"But Phyllis is another's wife;
And if she should absorb thy life
'T would leave thy bosom vacant."—Well,
I'd keep at least the empty shell!

V

THE RECREANT CLAM

For the *Outlook*

Low dost thou lie amid the languid ooze,
Because thy slothful spirit doth refuse
The bliss of battle and the strain of strife.
Rise, craven clam, and lead the strenuous life!

A FAIRY TALE

For the Mark Twain Dinner, December 5, 1905

SOME three-score years and ten ago
A prince was born at Florida, Mo.;
And though he came *incognito*,
With just the usual yells of woe,
The watchful fairies seemed to know
    Precisely what the row meant;
For when he was but five days old,
(December fifth as I've been told,)
They pattered through the midnight cold
And came around his crib, to hold
    A Council of Endowment."

"I give him Wit," the eldest said,
And stooped above the little bed,
To touch his forehead round and red.
"Within this bald, unfurnished head,
"Where wild luxuriant locks shall spread
    "And wave in years hereafter,
"I kindle now the lively spark,
"That still shall flash by day and dark,
"And everywhere he goes shall mark
    "His way with light and laughter.

CARMINA FESTIVA

The fairies laughed to think of it
That such a rosy, wrinkled bit
Of flesh should be endowed with Wit!
But something serious seemed to hit
The mind of one, as if a fit
     Of fear had come upon her.
"I give him Truth," she quickly cried,
"That laughter may not lead aside
"To paths where scorn and falsehood hide,—
     "I give him Truth and Honour!"

"I give him Love," exclaimed the third;
And as she breathed the mystic word,
I know not if the baby heard,
But softly in his dream he stirred,
And twittered like a little bird,
     And stretched his hands above him.
The fairy's gift was sealed and signed
With kisses twain the deed to bind:
"A heart of love to human-kind,
     "And human-kind to love him!"

A FAIRY TALE

"Now stay your giving!" cried the Queen.
"These gifts are passing rich I ween;
"And if reporters should be mean
"Enough to spy upon this scene,
"'Twould make all other babies green
    "With envy at the rumour.
"Yet since I love this child, forsooth,
"I'll mix your gifts, Wit, Love and Truth,
"With spirits of Immortal Youth,
    "And call the mixture Humour!"

The fairies vanished with their glittering train;
But here's the Prince with all their gifts,—*Mark Twain*

THE BALLAD OF THE SOLEMN ASS

Recited at the Century Club, New York: Twelfth Night. 1906

Come all ye good Centurions and wise men of the times,
You've made a Poet Laureate, now you must hear his rhymes.
Extend your ears and I'll respond by shortening up my tale:—
Man cannot live by verse alone, he must have cakes and ale.

So while you wait for better things and muse on schnapps and salad,
I'll try my Pegasus his wings and sing a little ballad:
A legend of your ancestors, the Wise Men of the East,
Who brought among their baggage train a quaint and curious beast.

Their horses were both swift and strong, and we should think it lucky
If we could buy, by telephone, such horses from Kentucky;
Their dromedaries paced along, magnificent and large,
Their camels were as stately as if painted by La Farge.

But this amazing little ass was never satisfied,
He made more trouble every day than all the rest beside:

THE BALLAD OF THE SOLEMN ASS

His ears were long, his legs were short, his eyes were bleared and dim,
But nothing in the wide, wide world was good enough for him.

He did not like the way they went, but lifted up his voice
And said that any other way would be a better choice.
He braced his feet and stood his ground, and made the wise men wait,
While with his heels at all around he did recalcitrate.

It mattered not how fair the land through which the road might run,
He found new causes for complaint with every Morning Sun:
And when the shades of twilight fell and all the world grew nappy,
They tied him to his Evening Post, but still he was not happy.

He thought his load was far too large, he thought his food was bad,
He thought the Star a poor affair, he thought the Wise Men mad:
He did not like to hear them laugh,—'twas childish to be jolly;
And if perchance they sang a hymn,—'twas sentimental folly!

CARMINA FESTIVA

So day by day this little beast performed his level best
To make their life, in work and play, a burden to the rest:
And when they laid them down at night, he would not
    let them sleep,
But criticized the Universe with hee-haws loud and deep.

One evening, as the Wise Men sat before their fire-lit
    tent,
And ate and drank and talked and sang, in grateful
    merriment,
The solemn donkey butted in, in his most solemn way,
And broke the happy meeting up with a portentous bray.

"Now by my head," Balthazar said (his real name was
    Choate),
"We've had about enough of this! I'll put it to the
    vote.
"I move the donkey be dismissed; let's turn him out to
    grass,
"And travel on our cheerful way, without the solemn ass."

The vote was aye! and with a whack the Wise Men
    drove him out;
But still he wanders up and down, and all the world
    about;
You'll know him by his long, sad face and supercilious
    ways,
And likewise by his morning kicks and by his evening
    brays.

THE BALLAD OF THE SOLEMN ASS

But while we sit at Eagle Roost and make our Twelfth Night cheer,
Full well we know the solemn ass will not disturb us here:
For pleasure rules the roost to-night, by order of the King,
And every one must play his part, and laugh, and likewise sing.

The road of life is long, we know, and often hard to find,
And yet there's many a pleasant turn for men of cheerful mind:
We've done our day's work honestly, we've earned the right to rest,
We'll take a cup of friendship now and spice it with a jest.

A silent health to absent friends, their memories are bright!
A hearty health to all who keep the feast with us to-night!
A health to dear Centuria, oh, may she long abide!
A health, a health to all the world,—and the solemn ass, *outside!*

A BALLAD OF SANTA CLAUS

For the St. Nicholas Society of New York

AMONG the earliest saints of old, before the first Hegira,
I find the one whose name we hold, St. Nicholas of Myra:
The best-beloved name, I guess, in sacred nomenclature,—
The patron-saint of helpfulness, and friendship, and good-nature.

A bishop and a preacher too, a famous theologian,
He stood against the Arian crew and fought them like a Trojan:
But when a poor man told his need and begged an alms in trouble,
He never asked about his creed, but quickly gave him double.

Three pretty maidens, so they say, were longing to be married;
But they were paupers, lack-a-day, and so the suitors tarried.
St. Nicholas gave each maid a purse of golden ducats chinking,
And then, for better or for worse, they wedded quick as winking.

A BALLAD OF SANTA CLAUS

Once, as he sailed, a storm arose; wild waves the ship surrounded;
The sailors wept and tore their clothes, and shrieked "We'll all be drownded!"
St. Nicholas never turned a hair; serenely shone his halo;
He simply said a little prayer, and all the billows lay low.

The wicked keeper of an inn had three small urchins taken,
And cut them up in a pickle-bin, and salted them for bacon.
St. Nicholas came and picked them out, and put their limbs together,—
They lived, they leaped, they gave a shout, "St. Nicholas forever!"

And thus it came to pass, you know, that maids without a nickel,
And sailor-lads when tempest blow, and children in a pickle,
And every man that's fatherly, and every kindly matron,
In choosing saints would all agree to call St. Nicholas patron.

CARMINA FESTIVA

He comes again at Christmas-time and stirs us up to giving;
He rings the merry bells that chime good-will to all the living;
He blesses every friendly deed and every free donation;
He sows the secret, golden seed of love through all creation.

Our fathers drank to Santa Claus, the sixth of each December,
And still we keep his feast because his virtues we remember.
Among the saintly ranks he stood, with smiling human features,
And said, "*Be good! But not too good to love your fellow-creatures!*"

December 6, 1907.

ARS AGRICOLARIS

An Ode for the "Farmer's Dinner," University Club, New York
January 23, 1913

ALL hail, ye famous Farmers!
Ye vegetable-charmers,
Who know the art of making barren earth
Smile with prolific mirth
And bring forth twins or triplets at a birth!
Ye scientific fetilizers of the soil,
And horny-handed sons of toil!
To-night from all your arduous cares released,
With manly brows no longer sweat-impearled,
Ye hold your annual feast,
And like the Concord farmers long ago,
Ye meet above the "Bridge" below,
And draw the cork heard round the world!

What memories are yours! What tales
Of triumph have your tongues rehearsed,
Telling how ye have won your first
Potatoes from the stubborn mead,
(Almost as many as ye sowed for seed!)
And how the luscious cabbages and kails
Have bloomed before you in their bed
At seven dollars a head!
And how your onions took a prize

CARMINA FESTIVA

For bringing tears into the eyes
Of a hard-hearted cook! And how ye slew
The Dragon Cut-worm at a stroke!
    And how ye broke,
Routed, and put to flight the horrid crew
Of vile potato-bugs and Hessian flies!
    And how ye did not quail
Before th' invading armies of San José Scale,
    But met them bravely with your little pail
    Of poison, which ye put upon each tail
O' the dreadful beasts and made their courage fail!
    And how ye did acquit yourselves like men
    In fields of agricultural strife, and then,
    Like generous warriors, sat you down at ease
    And gently to your gardener said, "Let us have
        Pease!"

But *were* there Pease? Ah, no, dear Farmers, no!
The course of Nature is not ordered so.
    For when we want a vegetable most,
        She holds it back;
        And when we boast
    To our week-endly friends
    Of what we'll give them on our farm, alack,
Those things the old dam, Nature, never sends.

ARS AGRICOLARIS

O Pease in bottles, Sparrow-grass in jars,
How often have ye saved from scars
Of shame, and deep embarrassment,
The disingenuous farmer-gent,
    To whom some wondering guest has cried,
    "How *do* you raise such Pease and Sparrow-grass?
    Whereat the farmer-gent has not denied
    The compliment, but smiling has replied,
    "To raise such things you must have lots of glass.

From wiles like these, true Farmers, hold aloof;
Accept no praise unless you have the proof.
If niggard Nature should withhold the green
And sugary Pea, welcome the humble Bean.
Even the easy Radish, and the Beet,
If grown by your own toil are extra sweet.
Let malefactors of great wealth and banker-felons
Rejoice in foreign artichokes, imported melons;
But you, my Farmers, at your frugal board
Spread forth the fare your Sabine Farms afford.
Say to Mæcenas, when he is your guest,
"No peaches! try this turnip, 'tis my best."
Thus shall ye learn from labors in the field
What honesty a farmer's life may yield,
And like G. Washington in early youth,
Though cherries fail, produce a crop of truth

CARMINA FESTIVA

But think me not too strict, O followers of the plough
Some place for fiction in your lives I would allow.
In January when the world is drear,
And bills come in, and no results appear,
    And snow-storms veil the skies,
    And ice the streamlet clogs,
Then may you warm your heart with pleasant lies
And revel in the seedsmen's catalogues!
What visions and what dreams are these
    Of cauliflower obese,—
Of giant celery, taller than a mast,—
    Of strawberries
Like red pincushions, round and vast,—
    Of succulent and spicy gumbo,—
    Of cantaloupes, as big as Jumbo,—
    Of high-strung beans without the strings,—
And of a host of other wild, romantic things!

    Why, then, should Doctor Starr declare
That modern habits mental force impair?
    And why should H. Marquand complain
That jokes as good as his will never come again?
    And why should Bridges wear a gloomy mien
About the lack of fiction for his Magazine?
    The seedsman's catalogue is all we need
        To stir our dull imaginations
          To new creations,
        And lead us, by the hand
        Of Hope, into a fairy-land.

ARS AGRICOLARIS

So dream, my friendly Farmers, as you will;
And let your fancy all your garners fill
With wondrous crops; but always recollect
That Nature gives us less than we expect.
Scorn not the city where you earn the wealth
That, spent upon your farms, renews your health;
And tell your wife, whene'er the bills have shocked her
"A country-place is cheaper than a doctor."
May roses bloom for you, and may you find
Your richest harvest in a tranquil mind.

ANGLER'S FIRESIDE SONG

Oh, the angler's path is a very merry way,
   And his road through the world is bright;
For he lives with the laughing stream all day,
   And he lies by the fire at night.

> Sing hey nonny, ho nonny
> And likewise well-a-day!
> The angler's life is a very jolly life
> And that's what the anglers say!

Oh, the angler plays for the pleasure of the game
   And his creel may be full or light,
But the tale that he tells will be just the same
   When he lies by the fire at night.

> Sing hey nonny, ho nonny
> And likewise well-a-day!
> We love the fire and the music of the lyre,
> And that's what the anglers say!

To the San Francisco Fly-Casting Club, April, 1913.

HOW SPRING COMES TO SHASTA JIM

I NEVER seen no "red gods"; I dunno wot's a "lure";
But if it's sumpin' takin', then Spring has got it sure;
An' it doesn't need no Kiplins, ner yet no London Jacks,
To make up guff about it, w'ile settin' in their shacks.

It's sumpin' very simple 'at happens in the Spring,
But it changes all the lookin's of every blessed thing;
The buddin' woods look bigger, the mounting twice as high,
But the house looks kindo smaller, tho I couldn't tell ye why.

It's cur'ous wot a show-down the month of April makes,
Between the reely livin', an' the things 'at's only fakes!
Machines an' barns an' buildin's, they never give no sign;
But the livin' things look lively w'en Spring is on the line.

She doesn't come too suddin, ner she doesn't come too slow;
Her gaits is some cayprishus, an' the next ye never know,—
A single-foot o' sunshine, a buck o' snow er hail,—
But don't be disapp'inted, fer Spring ain't goin' ter fail.

CARMINA FESTIVA

She's loopin' down the hillside,—the driffs is fadin' out.
She's runnin' down the river,—d'ye see them risin' trout?
She's loafin' down the canyon,—the squaw-bed's growin' blue,
An' the teeny Johnny-jump-ups is jest a-peekin' thru.

A thousan' miles o' pine-trees, with Douglas firs between,
Is waitin' fer her fingers to freshen up their green;
With little tips o' brightness the firs 'ill sparkle thick,
An' every yaller pine-tree, a giant candle-stick!

The underbrush is risin' an' spreadin' all around,
Jest like a mist o' greenness 'at hangs above the ground;
A million manzanitas 'ill soon be full o' pink;
So saddle up, my sonny,—it's time to ride, I think!

We'll ford er swim the river, becos there ain't no bridge;
We'll foot the gulches careful, an' lope along the ridge;
We'll take the trail to Nowhere, an' travel till we tire,
An' camp beneath a pine-tree, an' sleep beside the fire.

We'll see the blue-quail chickens, an' hear 'em pipin' clear;
An' p'raps we'll sight a brown-bear, er else a bunch o' deer;
But nary a heathen goddess or god 'ill meet our eyes;
For why? There isn't any! They're jest a pack o' lies!

HOW SPRING COMES TO SHASTA JIM

Oh, wot's the use o' "red gods," an' "Pan," an' all that
    stuff?
The natcheral facts o' Springtime is wonderful enuff!
An' if there's Someone made 'em, I guess He understood,
To be alive in Springtime would make a man feel good.

California, 1913.

A BUNCH OF TROUT-FLIES

For Archie Rutledge

HERE's a half-a-dozen flies,
Just about the proper size
For the trout of Dickey's Run,—
Luck go with them every one!

Dainty little feathered beauties,
Listen now, and learn your duties:
Not to tangle in the box;
Not to catch on logs or rocks,
Boughs that wave or weeds that float
Nor in the angler's "pants" or coat!
Not to lure the glutton frog
From his banquet in the bog;
Nor the lazy chub to fool,
Splashing idly round the pool;
Nor the sullen hornèd pout
From the mud to hustle out!

A BUNCH OF TROUT-FLIES

None of this vulgarian crew,
Dainty flies, is game for you.
Darting swiftly through the air
Guided by the angler's care,
Light upon the flowing stream
Like a wingèd fairy dream;
Float upon the water dancing,
Through the lights and shadows glancing
Till the rippling current brings you,
And with quiet motion swings you,
Where a speckled beauty lies
Watching you with hungry eyes.

Here's your game and here's your prize!
Hover near him, lure him, tease him,
Do your very best to please him,
Dancing on the water foamy,
Like the frail and fair Salome,
Till the monarch yields at last;
Rises, and you have him fast!
Then remember well your duty,—
Do not lose, but land, your booty;
For the finest fish of all is
Salvelinus Fontinalis.

CARMINA FESTIVA

So, you plumed illusions, go,
Let my comrade Archie know
Every day he goes a-fishing
I'll be with him in well-wishing.
Most of all when lunch is laid
In the dappled orchard shade,
With Will, Corinne, and Dixie too,
Sitting as we used to do
Round the white cloth on the grass
While the lazy hours pass,
And the brook's contented tune
Lulls the sleepy afternoon,—
Then's the time my heart will be
With that pleasant company!

June 17, 1913.

INDEX OF FIRST LINES

	PAGE
A deeper crimson in the rose,	255
A fir-tree standeth lonely	197
A flawless cup: how delicate and fine	269
A little fir grew in the midst of the wood	147
A mocking question! Britain's answer came	371
A silent world,—yet full of vital joy	101
A silken curtain veils the skies,	46
A tear that trembles for a little while	4
Across a thousand miles of sea, a hundred leagues of land,	187
Afterthought of summer's bloom!	35
Ah, who will tell me, in these leaden days,	47
All along the Brazos River,	337
All day long in the city's canyon-street,	352
All hail, ye famous Farmers!	565
All night long, by a distant bell	251
All the trees are sleeping, all the winds are still,	244
Among the earliest saints of old, before the first Hegira,	562
At dawn in silence moves the mighty stream,	6
At sunset, when the rosy light was dying	13
Children of the elemental mother,	299
"Clam O! Fres' Clam!" How strange it sounds and sweet,	553
Come all ye good Centurions and wise men of the times,	558
Come, give me back my life again, you heavy-handed Death!	120
Come home, my love, come home!	209
Could every time-worn heart but see Thee once again,	230
Count not the cost of honour to the dead!	311
Daughter of Psyche, pledge of that wild night	447
Dear Aldrich, now November's mellow days	437
Dear to my heart are the ancestral dwellings of America,	289
Deeds not Words: I say so too!	276
Deep in the heart of the forest the lily of Yorrow is growing;	27
"Do you give thanks for this?—or that?" No, God be thanked	224
Do you remember, father,—	24
Does the snow fall at sea?	16

INDEX OF FIRST LINES

	PAGE
Ere thou sleepest gently lay	239
Fair Phyllis is another's bride:	554
Fair Roslin Chapel, how divine	17
Far richer than a thornless rose	280
Flowers rejoice when night is done,	9
For that thy face is fair I love thee not;	172
Four things a man must learn to do	277
From the misty shores of midnight, touched with splendours of the moon,	429
Furl your sail, my little boatie;	218
Give us a name to fill the mind	385
Glory of architect, glory of painter, and sculptor, and bard,	464
God said, "I am tired of kings,"—	376
Great Nature had a million words,	466
Hear a word that Jesus spake	83
Heart of France for a hundred years,	431
Her eyes are like the evening air,	186
Here's a half-a-dozen flies,	574
Here the great heart of France,	418
Home, for my heart still calls me;	397
Honour the brave who sleep	157
Hours fly,	259
How blind the toil that burrows like the mole,	428
"How can I tell," Sir Edmund said,	158
How long is the night, brother,	185
How long the echoes love to play	3
I count that friendship little worth	223
I envy every flower that blows	179
I have no joy in strife,	401
I love thine inland seas,	288
I never seen no "red gods"; I dunno wot's a "lure";	571
I never thought again to hear	395
I put my heart to school	45
I read within a poet's book	217
I think of thee when golden sunbeams glimmer	196
I would not even ask my heart to say	287
If all the skies were sunshine,	12
If I have erred in showing all my heart,	192
If Might made Right, life were a wild-beasts' cage;	377

INDEX OF FIRST LINES

	PAGE
If on the closèd curtain of my sight	242
In a great land, a new land, a land full of labour and riches and confusion,	434
In mirth he mocks the other birds at noon,	269
In robes of Tyrian blue the King was drest,	142
In the blue heaven the clouds will come and go,	417
In the pleasant time of Pentecost,	369
Into the dust of the making of man	316
In warlike pomp, with banners flowing,	14
It pleased the Lord of Angels (praise His name!)	125
It's little I can tell	173
It was my lot of late to travel far	412
"Joy is a Duty,"—so with golden lore	274
Joyful, joyful, we adore Thee,	232
Just to give up, and trust	231
Knight-Errant of the Never-ending Quest,	427
Let me but do my work from day to day,	166
Let me but feel thy look's embrace,	177
"Lights out" along the land,	374
Like a long arrow through the dark the train is darting,	180
Limber-limbed, lazy god, stretched on the rock,	270
Lord Jesus, Thou hast known	220
Long ago Apollo called to Aristæus, youngest of the shepherds,	129
Long had I loved this "Attic shape," the brede	268
Long, long ago I heard a little song,	249
Long, long, long the trail	55
Lover of beauty, walking on the height	423
Low dost thou lie amid the languid ooze,	554
March on, my soul, nor like a laggard stay!	234
Mother of all the high-strung poets and singers departed,	421
Not Dante when he wandered by the river Arno,	552
Not to the swift, the race:	169
Now in the oak the sap of life is welling,	51
O dark the night and dim the day	402
O garden isle, beloved by Sun and Sea,	308
O Lord our God, Thy mighty hand	364
O mighty river! strong, eternal Will,	277

INDEX OF FIRST LINES

	PAGE
O Mother mountains! billowing far to the snow-lands,	59
O Music hast thou only heard	378
O who will walk a mile with me	165
O wonderful! How liquid clear	57
O youngest of the giant brood	304
Oh, gallantly they fared forth in khaki and in blue,	408
Oh, quick to feel the lightest touch	439
Oh, the angler's path is a very merry way,	570
Oh, was I born too soon, my dear, or were you born too late,	175
Oh, what do you know of the song, my dear,	467
Oh, why are you shining so bright, big Sun,	188
Once, only once, I saw it clear,—	189
One sail in sight upon the lonely sea,	292
Only a little shrivelled seed,	224
Peace without Justice is a low estate,—	377
Read here, O friend unknown,	278
Remember, when the timid light	194
Saints are God's flowers, fragrant souls	226
Self is the only prison that can ever bind the soul;	275
Ship after ship, and every one with a high-resounding name,	410
Sign of the Love Divine	405
Some three-score years and ten ago	555
Soul of a soldier in a poet's frame,	442
Stand back, ye messengers of mercy! Stand	306
Stand fast, Great Britain!	372
The British bard who looked on Eton's walls,	330
The clam that once, on Jersey's banks,	551
The cornerstone in Truth is laid,	261
The cradle I have made for thee	198
The day returns by which we date our years:	253
The fire of love was burning, yet so low	243
The gabled roofs of old Malines	381
The glory of ships is an old, old song,	388
The grief that is but feigning,	443
The heavenly hills of Holland,—	67
The laggard winter ebbed so slow	69
The land was broken in despair,	309
The melancholy gift Aurora gained	426
The moonbeams over Arno's vale in silver flood were pouring,	29

INDEX OF FIRST LINES

	PAGE
The mountains that inclose the vale	170
The nymphs a shepherd took	270
The other night I had a dream, most clear	137
The record of a faith sublime,	430
The river of dreams runs quietly down	210
The roar of the city is low,	301
The rough expanse of democratic sea	404
The shadow by my finger cast	263
The tide flows in to the harbour,—	58
The time will come when I no more can play	468
The winds of war-news change and veer;	399
The worlds in which we live at heart are one,	274
There are many kinds of anger, as many kinds of fire;	400
There are many kinds of love, as many kinds of light,	276
There are songs for the morning and songs for the night,	53
There is a bird I know so well,	31
They tell me thou art rich, my country: gold	387
This is the soldier brave enough to tell	313
This is the window's message,	260
Thou warden of the western gate, above Manhattan Bay,	393
Thou who hast made thy dwelling fair	71
"Through many a land your journey ran,	182
'Tis fine to see the Old World, and travel up and down	314
To thee, plain hero of a rugged race,	312
Two dwellings, Peace, are thine.	235
Two hundred years of blessing I record	263
"Two things," the wise man said, "fill me with awe:	266
'Twas far away and long ago,	174
Under the cloud of world-wide war,	406
Waking from tender sleep,	248
We men that go down for a livin' in ships to the sea,—	151
We met on Nature's stage,	268
What hast thou done, O womanhood of France,	384
What is Fortune, what is Fame?	279
What makes the lingering Night so cling to thee?	61
What shall I give for thee,	229
What time the rose of dawn is laid across the lips of night,	37
When down the stair at morning	178
When May bedecks the naked trees	33
When Stävoren town was in its prime	159
When the frosty kiss of Autumn in the dark	246

INDEX OF FIRST LINES

	PAGE
When tulips bloom in Union Square,	21
When to the garden of untroubled thought	171
Where's your kingdom, little king?	41
Who knows how many thousand years ago	281
Who seeks for heaven alone to save his soul,	275
Who watched the worn-out Winter die?	10
Winter on Mount Shasta,	470
With eager heart and will on fire,	225
With memories old and wishes new	264
With two bright eyes, my star, my love,	271
Wordsworth, thy music like a river rolls	425
Ye gods of battle, lords of fear,	362
Yes, it was like you to forget,	183
You dare to say with perjured lips,	391
You only promised me a single hour:	193
Yours is a garden of old-fashioned flowers;	441

www.ingramcontent.com/pod-product-compliance
Lightning Source LLC
Chambersburg PA
CBHW011449180426
43194CB00055B/2834